Emma Micheletti

DOMENICO GHIRLANDAIO

SCALA/RIVERSIDE

CONTENTS

Editing: Karin Stephan
Translation: Anthony Brierley
Layout: Fried Rosenstock
Photographs: SCALA (M. Falsini, M. Sarri) except no. 88 (Thyssen-Bornemisza Collection, Lugano)
Produced by SCALA
Printed in Italy by: Amilcare Pizzi S.p.A. - arti grafiche Cinisello Balsamo (Milano), 1994

1. Nativity
detail with the artist's self-portrait (left)
Florence, Santa Trinita

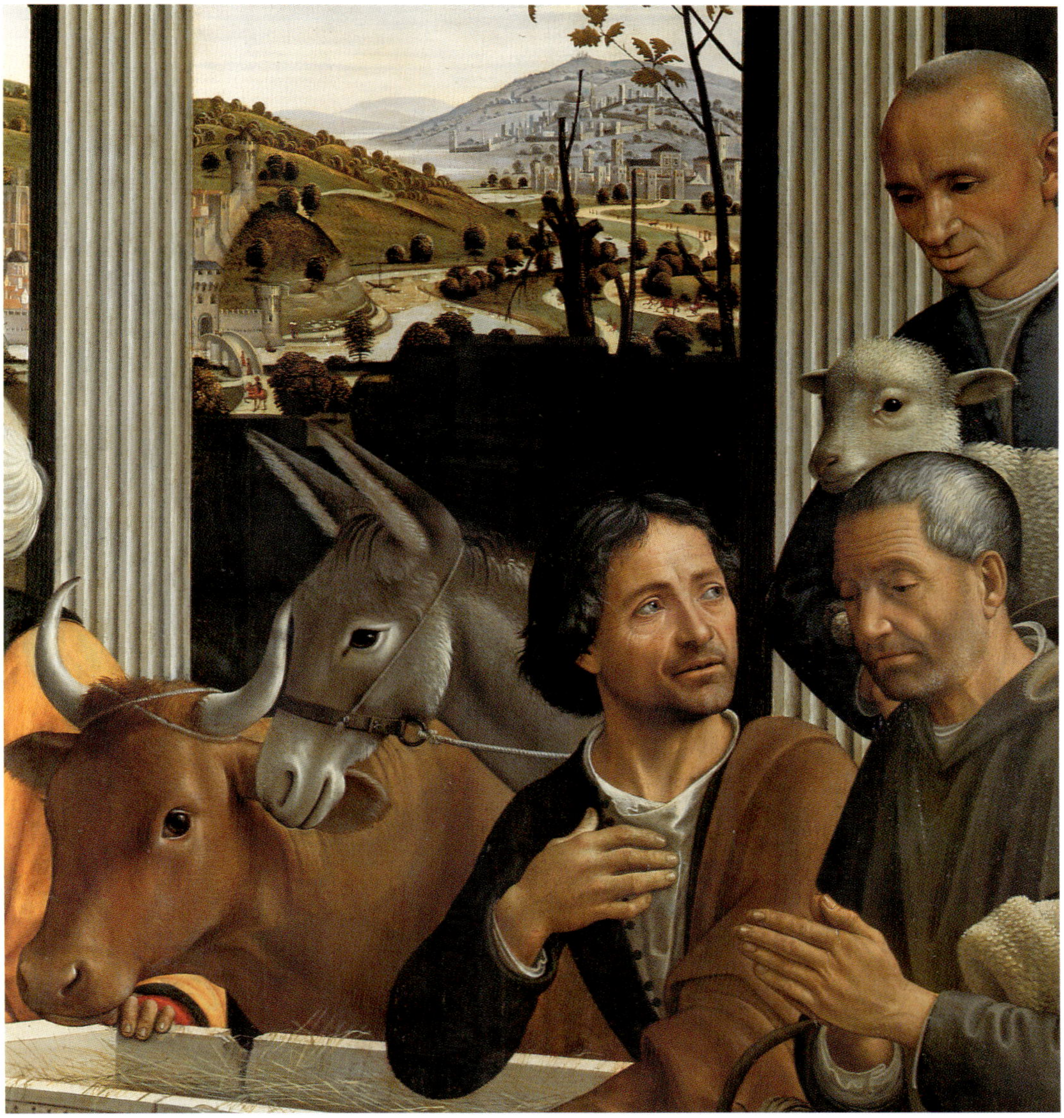

1

Domenico Ghirlandaio

Domenico Bigordi, better known as Ghirlandaio, was born in Florence in 1449, the first of the five children of the goldsmith Tommaso. He lived and worked almost exclusively in his native town. Around 1475 he frescoed the "Stories of St Fina" in the Collegiata of San Gimignano, and in 1481 and 1482 the Vatican Library in Rome and two stories of Christ in the Sistine Chapel.

His most well-known and celebrated works are the cycle of frescoes executed around 1480 in the Sassetti Chapel at Santa Trinita with the "Stories of St Francis", and between 1486 and 1490 the "Stories of the Virgin and St John the Baptist" in the Cappella del Coro of Santa Maria Novella commissioned by Giovanni Tornabuoni. He also executed numerous paintings on wood. Among the most important are the *Nativity* for the Sassetti Chapel (1485); the *Coronation* for Narni Cathedral (1486); the *Adoration of the Magi*, now in the Uffizi (1487); the *Adoration of the Magi* for the Spedale degli Innocenti (1488); and the *Portrait of Giovanna Tornabuoni*, now in the Thyssen Collection in Lugano (1488). The *Altarpiece* in Rimini, painted for Carlo Malatesta in the same years, and the *Visitation* executed for the Tornabuoni family, now in the Louvre (1491), are also his. The last works on wood show clear signs of the presence of different assistants, Ghirlandaio's direct contribution being increasingly less identifiable.

Two of his brothers, David and Benedetto, were themselves painters and assistants. His sister by a second marriage, Alessandra, married the painter Bastiano Mainardi of San Gimignano; he too was a part of the Ghirlandaio enterprise.

Domenico's first marriage was to the young Costanza di Bartolommeo Nucci, by whom Ridolfo was born (1483), the only one of his nine children to become a painter of reputable talent. The precise year in which Domenico married Antonia di Ser Paolo Paoli is not known.

Ghirlandaio died in 1494. Of his death Vasari writes: "... when they were about to do some very considerable works at Pisa and Siena Domenico fell sick of a fever, which carried him off in five days... He lived forty-four years, and was mourned deeply by his brothers David and Benedetto and his son Ridolfo. They buried him in Santa Maria Novella".

And the register of the deceased members of the San Paolo fraternity records: "Domenico di Tommaso di Churrado Bighordi, painter, called Ghirlandaio, died on the morning of Saturday 11th January 1494... He was buried on Saturday evening in Santa Maria Novella between midnight and one o'clock... It was an enormous loss and there was much grief, for he was a man of worth in every respect".

Domenico Ghirlandaio was loved therefore for his goodness, as well as "... for the excellence, size and multitude of his works...".

Early Works

"Domenico di Tommaso del Ghirlandaio, who for the excellence, size and multitude of his works deserves to be considered one of the best masters of his age, was meant by Nature to be a painter, and despite the opposition of his guardian, a thing which frequently spoils the best fruits of our great minds by diverting them from the things for which they are best fitted, he followed his natural bent and won great honour at his art for himself and his house, enriching and charming his age". Thus Giorgio Vasari begins his Life of Ghirlandaio, which although somewhat excessively eulogistic towards an evidently much-loved artist, remains one of the most valid and complete historical biographies of the painter.

Ghirlandaio's contemporaries, of just a little earlier, were artists like Verrocchio and Pollaiolo who belonged to the so-called third generation of the Renaissance, active in Florence after the 1450s. With them there was also the young Botticelli. For these masters the question of perspective had become less important; it was an issue that had been absorbed and superceded, and the focal point of their interest was now concentrated on dynamic problems of masses and the movement of lines in tension. The isolation of figures, conceived as plastic masses held in a perfect balance of volumes within an immobile space, now gave way to a continuous dynamic interplay of moving forms, in the developing of increasing tensions, even if these materialized according to a musical metre in spaces that were increasingly pervaded with vivid and intense atmosphere. What were once almost aphoristic phrases now became a more flexible dialogue shot through with agile expressions. In Florence the great lesson of Piero della Francesca was yielding to the more dynamic and restless vitality of Andrea del Castagno. Donatello was also still present, though at a distance, and it must not be forgotten that Verrocchio and Pollaiolo were painters as well as sculptors.

Also active at this time was Alesso Baldovinetti, an artist unjustly neglected by former critics, but later reappraised on the basis of certain qualities that made him a clever interpreter of his predecessors, even Piero della Francesca and Domenico Veneziano with whom he worked on the lost frescoes of Sant'Egidio. He was also open, before others, to the innovations of Flemish art which, thanks to the paintings of Memling, Van der Weyden and above all Van der Goes, were arriving in Florence through the commissions of the Baroncelli and Portinari families, agents of the Medici Bank in Bruges. Thus the great art of the north arrived alongside the Renaissance achievements of Florence and Venice. Flemish art had no interest in a superficial illustration of objects, but was profoundly attentive to every detail. With this in mind, Alesso Baldovinetti turned the landscape into a broad space, making it not just a background to, or comment on, the images but a protagonist in itself.

Baldovinetti was almost certainly Ghirlandaio's first teacher, after the latter had left the workshop of his goldsmith father to dedicate himself completely to painting. Vasari mentions "... Alesso Baldovinetti, Domenico's master in painting and mosaic", and Francesco Baldovinetti confirms it in his memoirs of the 16th century: "... and that del grillandaia... who was such a perfect master was his disciple".

Undoubtedly, Domenico also learnt from the paintings of Benozzo Gozzoli and Filippo Lippi, acquiring a taste for narration from the former, and certain vivid modes of expression and soft colours from the latter. As regards colour, the teaching of Angelico was significant and is evident in certain mother-of-pearl complexions and many delicate tones.

Ghirlandaio died young, at the age of forty-four. His artistic career was therefore intense. He began work in country churches in the immediate vicinity of Florence, at Cercina and Brozzi, and devoted himself fully to painting in San Gimignano. His guardians were the Vespucci, the most important family in his neighbourhood, whose most illustrious member was Amerigo, the great explorer.

His art was certainly popular among his Florentine contemporaries who saw their city and its most

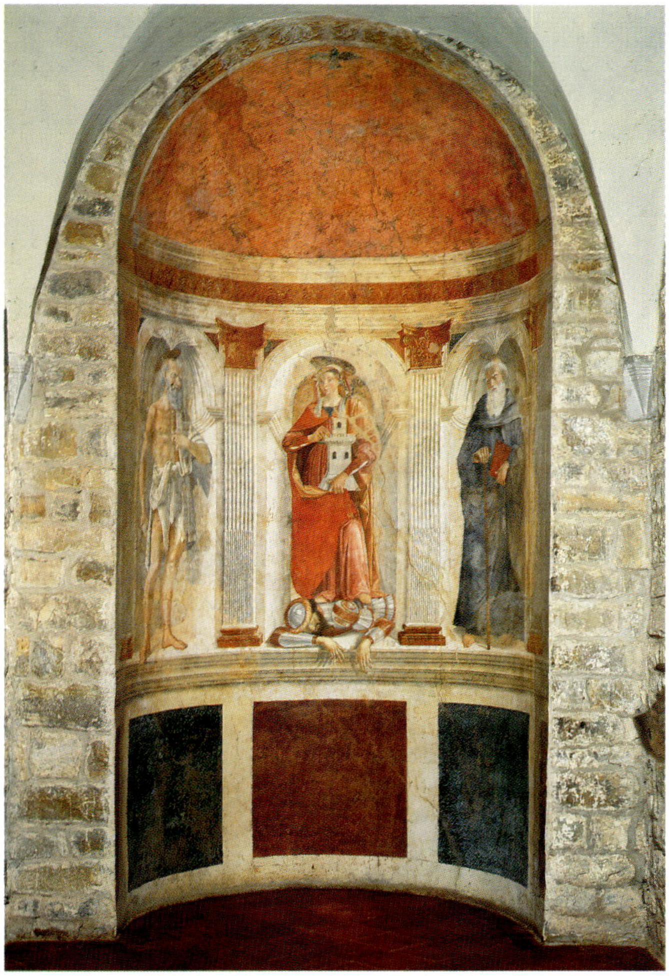 2

2. *The fresco of Cercina*
Cercina (Florence), parish church of Sant'Andrea

celebrated inhabitants, and perhaps even those who were known then but are now unidentifiable, come to life in his sacred stories. He painted a great amount and would have painted even more according to Vasari, who recounts that Domenico, in a moment of enthusiasm and also of regret, tells his brother David, "leave me to work while you make provision, because, now that I have begun to master my art, I feel sorry that I am not employed to paint the entire circuit of the walls of Florence".

The first work by Domenico Ghirlandaio that we
2 know of is the fresco decoration of the parish church
3-5 at Cercina. Saints Jerome, Barbara and Anthony Abbot are portrayed within a false noble architecture with niches divided by fluted pilaster strips and Corinthian capitals. Traces of Baldovinetti are faintly discernible here, perhaps above all in the delicate outlines which in a continuous flowing enclose the somewhat slight forms; these are complemented by soft colours that recall Domenico Veneziano.

Already in these very early works and especially in
4 the St Jerome, there is also a fleeting reminiscence of Andrea del Castagno, although by now the overall effect may be seen as the acquired and completely mature style of Ghirlandaio. There is a warmth and softness in the rather elongated figures, a harmonious, almost singable, spreading of vivid colours, a slow fluidity in the line that gives a mere hint of movement to the images, these being almost trapped in a faint, deliberate torpor. There is no dramatic force in the St Jerome either. These saints began a series of figures that by Ghirlandaio's hand would soon narrate sacred events: the stories of St Fina, St Francesco and others, half-chronicle and half-fairytale. We do not know the exact date of these frescoes, but we can be almost certain that the ones in the church of Ognissanti, depict-
6 ing the *Pietà* and the *Madonna of Mercy protecting the Vespucci family*, were executed immediately after. "His first paintings were in the Chapel of the Vespucci at Ognissanti, representing a dead Christ and some saints, and a Misericordia over an arch, containing a portrait of Amerigo Vespucci, who navigated the Indies..." (Vasari). The date of the chapel's construction is 1472. We can date the frescoes immediately after-
7-10 ward, not so very long before those of St Fina of 1475. In these Ognissanti frescoes the inspiration of Baldovinetti is marginal; more obvious are certain elements acquired from Andrea del Castagno and some clear, vivid colours that are reminiscent of Domenico Veneziano. Most interesting, however, is the artistic personality of Ghirlandaio himself, so well defined at this early age, and that attentive observation of man in every physical and interior detail that made him such an able portraitist. "(He) succeeded in becoming so facile that many relate that even while he was with the goldsmith he would draw everyone who passed the shop, making extraordinary likenesses, a story which is largely borne out by the number of excellent portraits which he produced". Here is the old man, probably the head of the family, seen from behind, kneeling, solidly built, his lean face with its hard features softened by the whiteness of his fine hair. The older woman in a cloak stands out in a contrast of lights and colours. Serenely clear, on the other hand, is the younger woman, with her hair gathered into plaits and her ample forehead shaved back according to the Florentine fashion of the time. The expression on the face of the boy, thought to be Amerigo Vespucci, is intense; his face, with its full lips and large clear eyes, is still chubby, pinkish and childlike. Domenico's attention seems to have lingered on the figures, perhaps in prayer, right there in Ognissanti, his brush faithfully reproducing and individualizing the features of each of them.

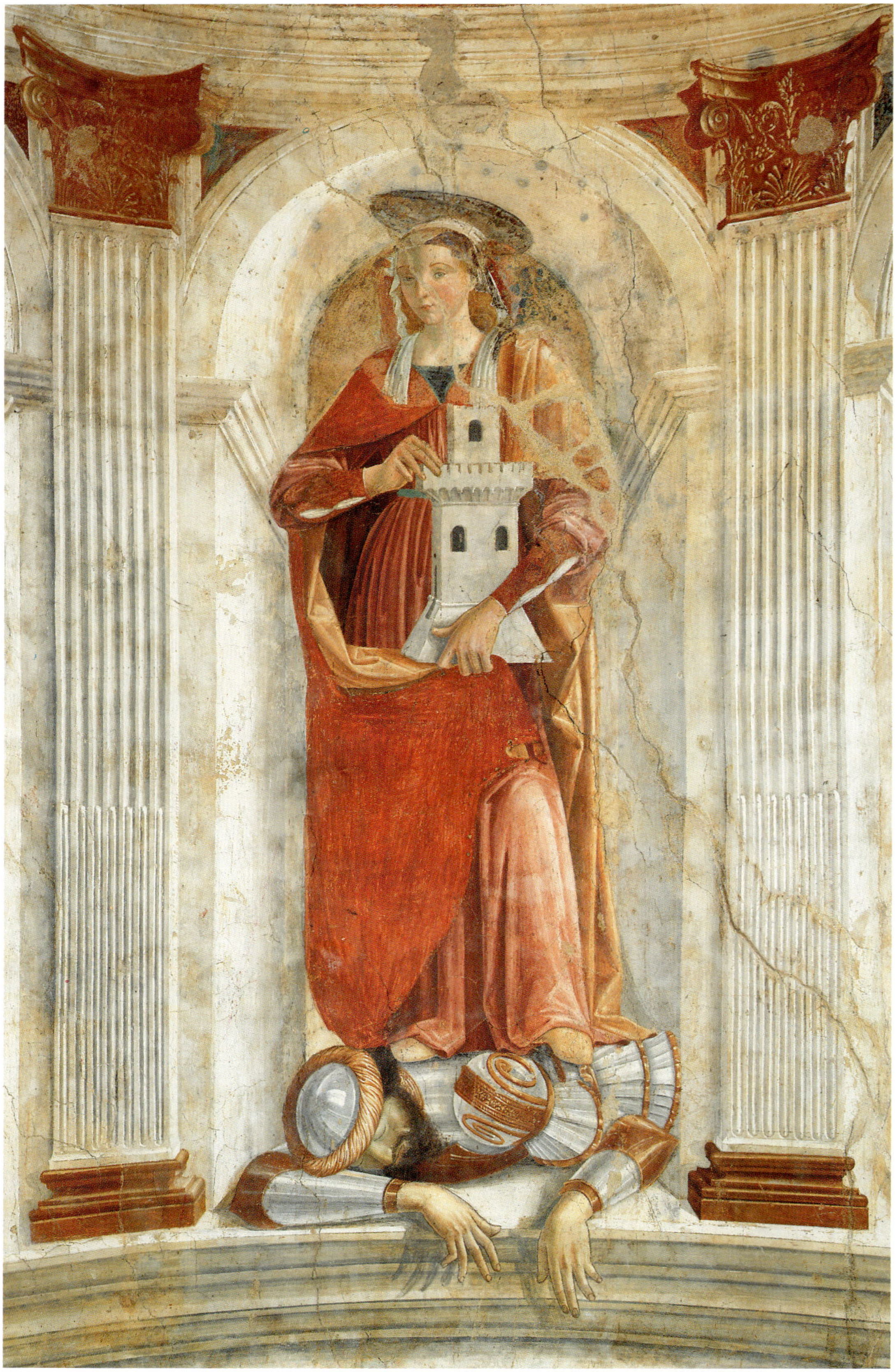

3

3-5. Saints Barbara, Jerome and Anthony Abbot
Cercina (Florence), parish church of Sant'Andrea

6. Madonna of Mercy
Florence, church of Ognissanti

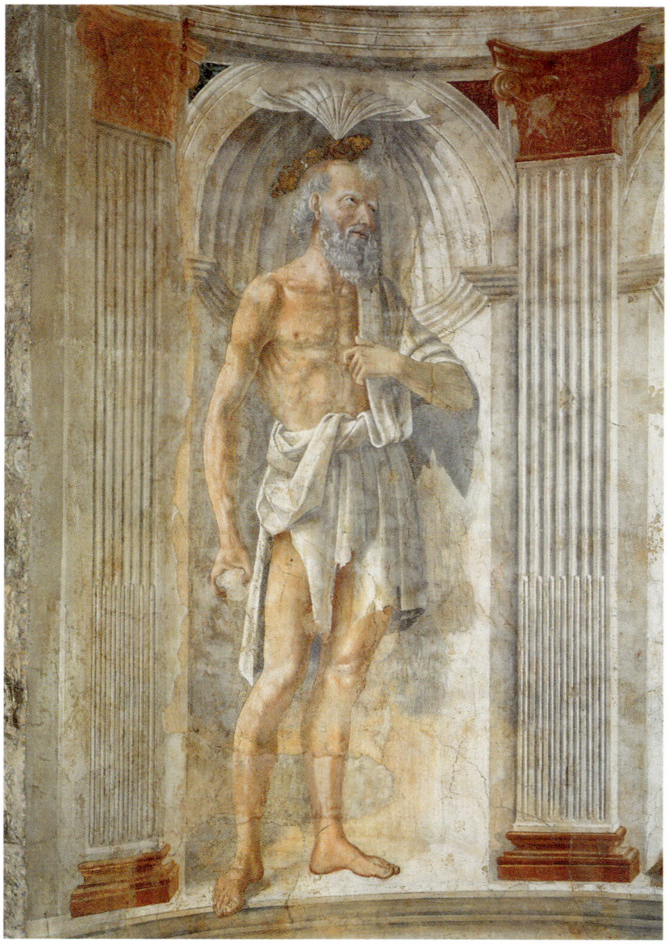

4

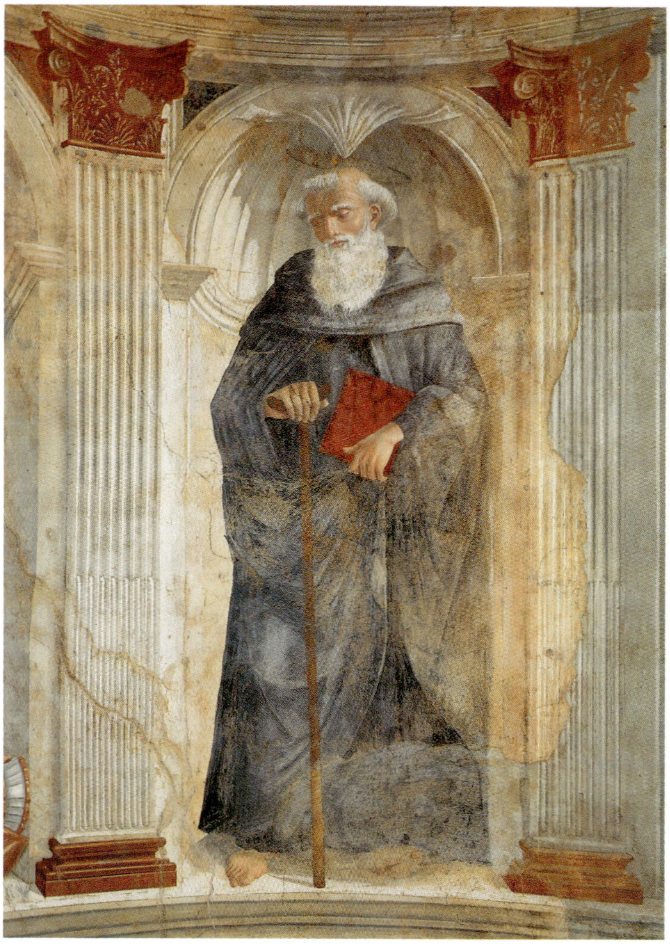

5

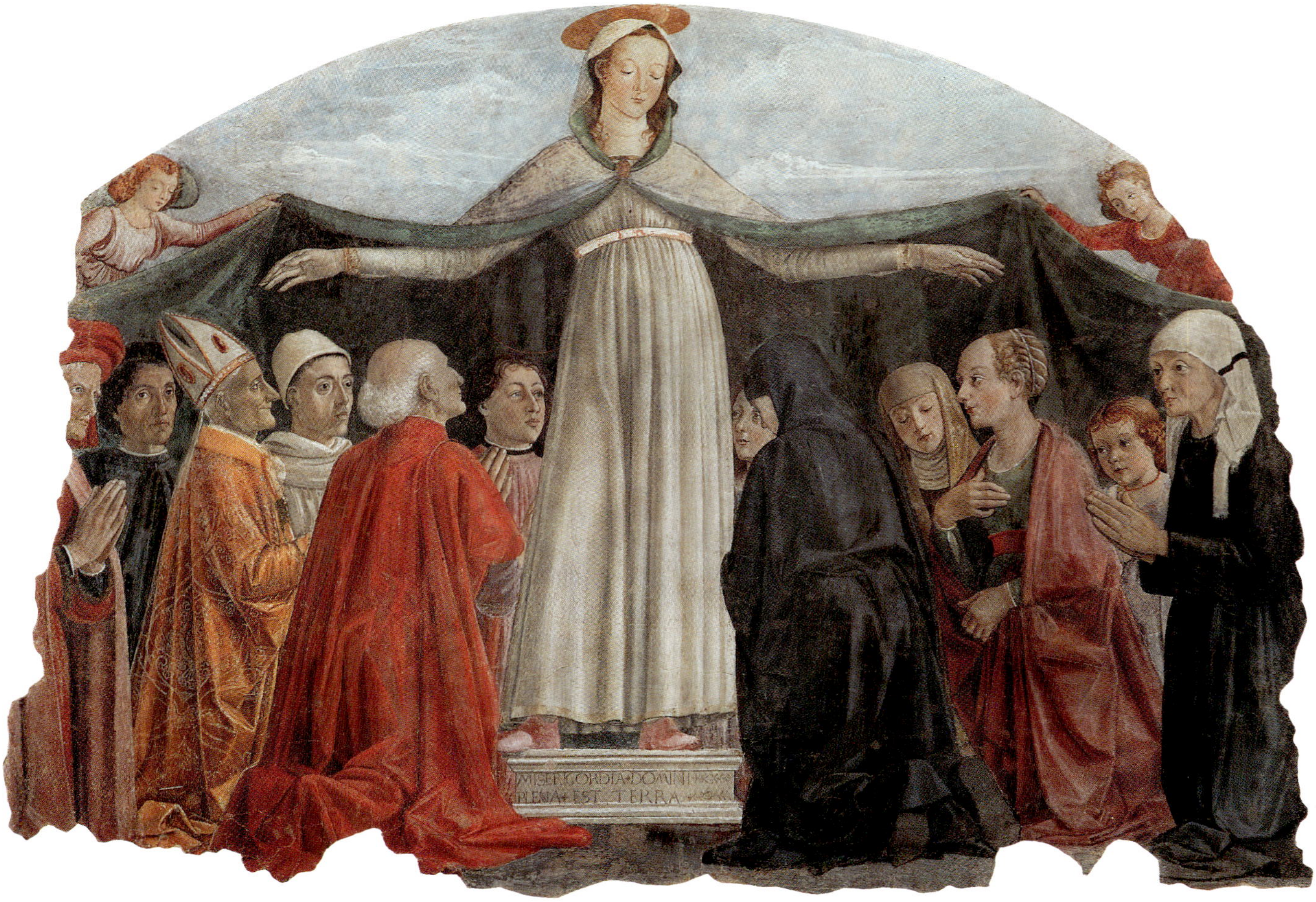

6

7

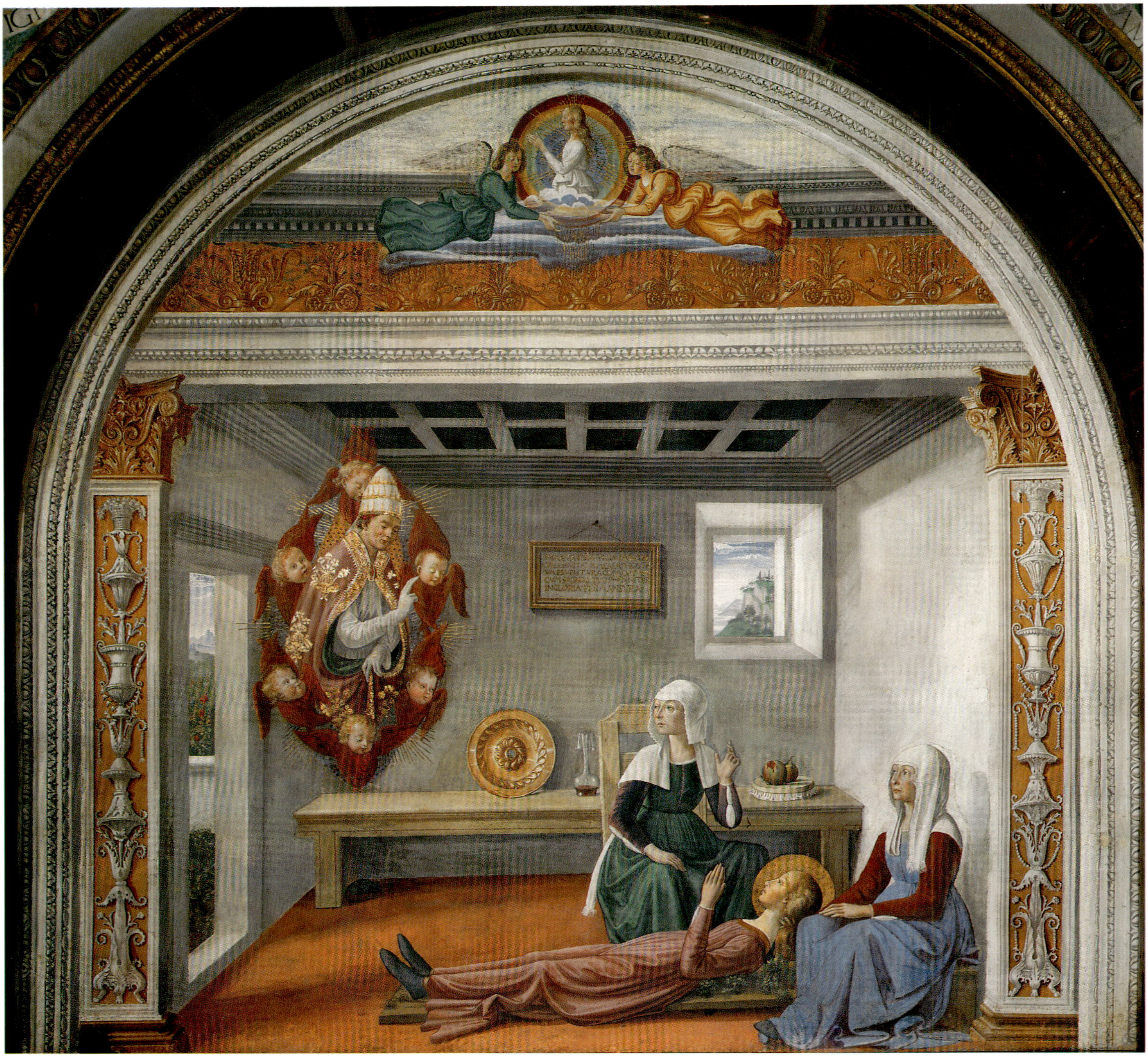

The Stories of St Fina at San Gimignano

Ghirlandaio (who had already begun working in the Vatican Library on frescoes which are referred to in documents dated 1475) then left Florence briefly for San Gimignano where in the collegiate church he painted the "Stories of St Fina", the young saint who lived her short, sick life lying serenely on a board, and smiled at the announcement of her imminent death made by St Gregory the Great. For Fina death was life, the life of the soul. She died on January 12th, and every year since that remote time, in that month, violets bloom in San Gimignano; large, distinctive, heavily-scented violets. The entire story of St Fina is poetry, and as poetry, with poetry, the now mature Domenico Ghirlandaio depicted it. The year in which the frescoes in "... the beautiful chapel of St Fina" were executed can be fixed almost with certainty at 1475 or shortly after. The inscription on the tomb of the saint evidently alludes to the cycle: *Miracula quaeris? / Perlege quae paries vivaque signa docent / MCCCCLXXV* [Are you looking for miracles? Observe those that the vivid images on these walls illustrate / 1475]. In this MCCCCLXXV Ghirlandaio had

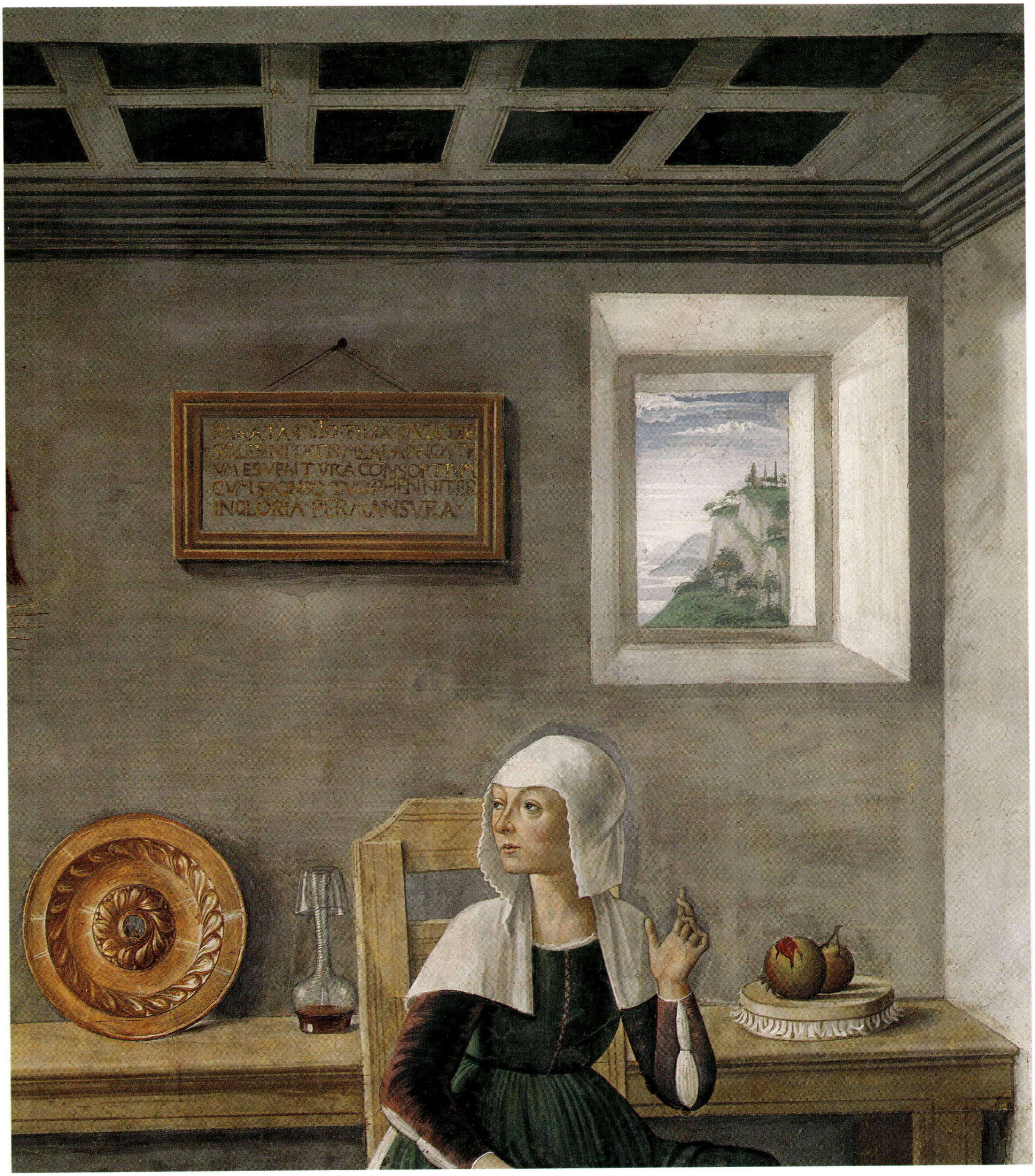

8

7, 8. Announcement of Death to the Saint
San Gimignano, Collegiate church

9
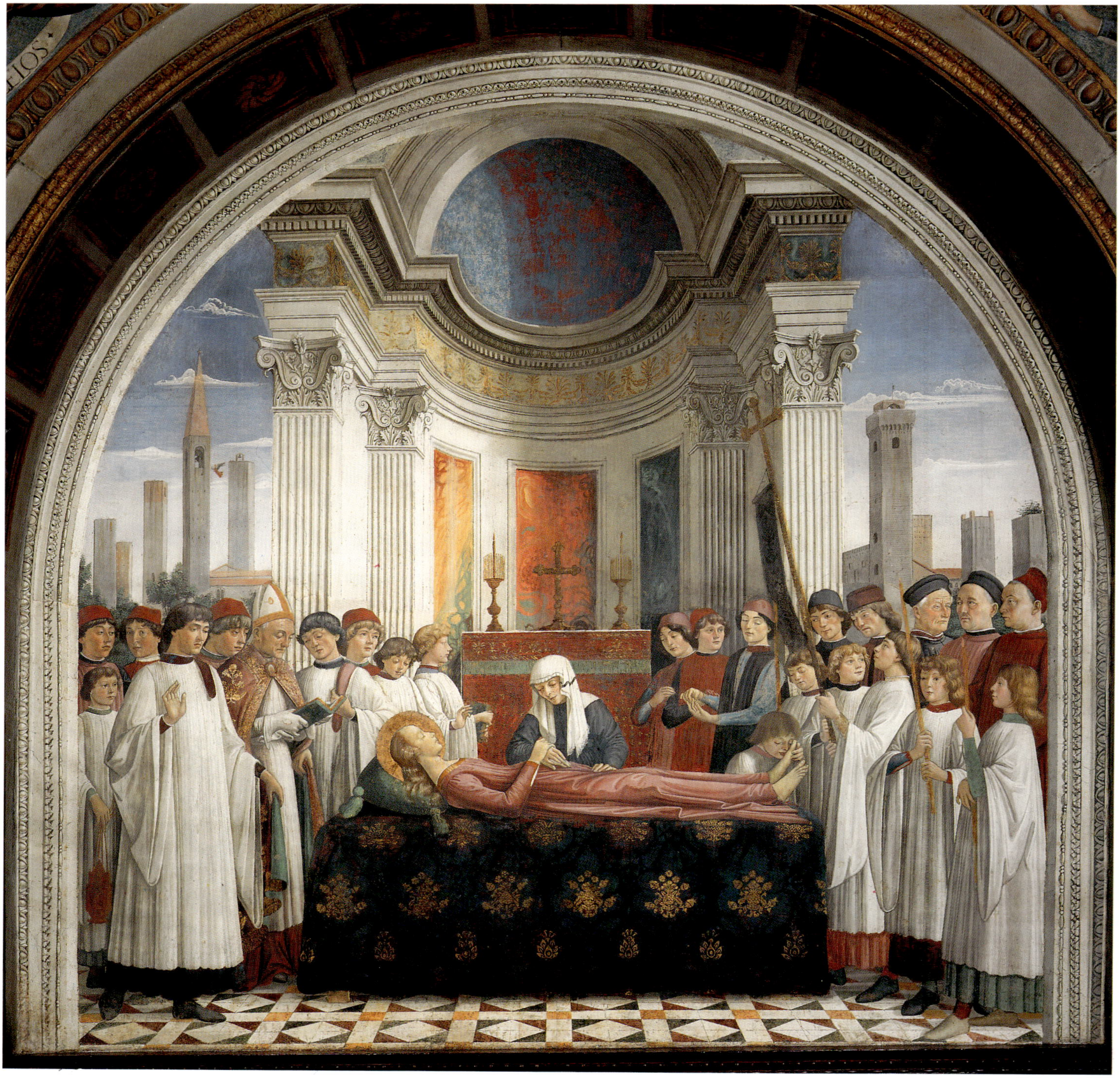

either finished the frescoes, was in the process of painting them, or, much less likely, was planning them. A document of 1475, moreover, mentions a Domenico (surely Ghirlandaio) and a no better identified Piero who were working on the vaults. And from the vaults, the paint-brushes of Domenico and his assistants must surely have proceeded to the walls.
9 There are two "Stories of St Fina": the *Obsequies of*
7 *the Saint* and the *Apparition to Fina of St Gregory who announces her Death*.

The chapel, which was built by Giuliano da Maiano and contains sculptures made by his brother Benedetto, recalls the Cardinal of Portugal's chapel at San Miniato al Monte decorated with frescoes by Alesso Baldovinetti. Ghirlandaio's decorative scheme was a

9, 10. Obsequies of the Saint
San Gimignano, Collegiate church

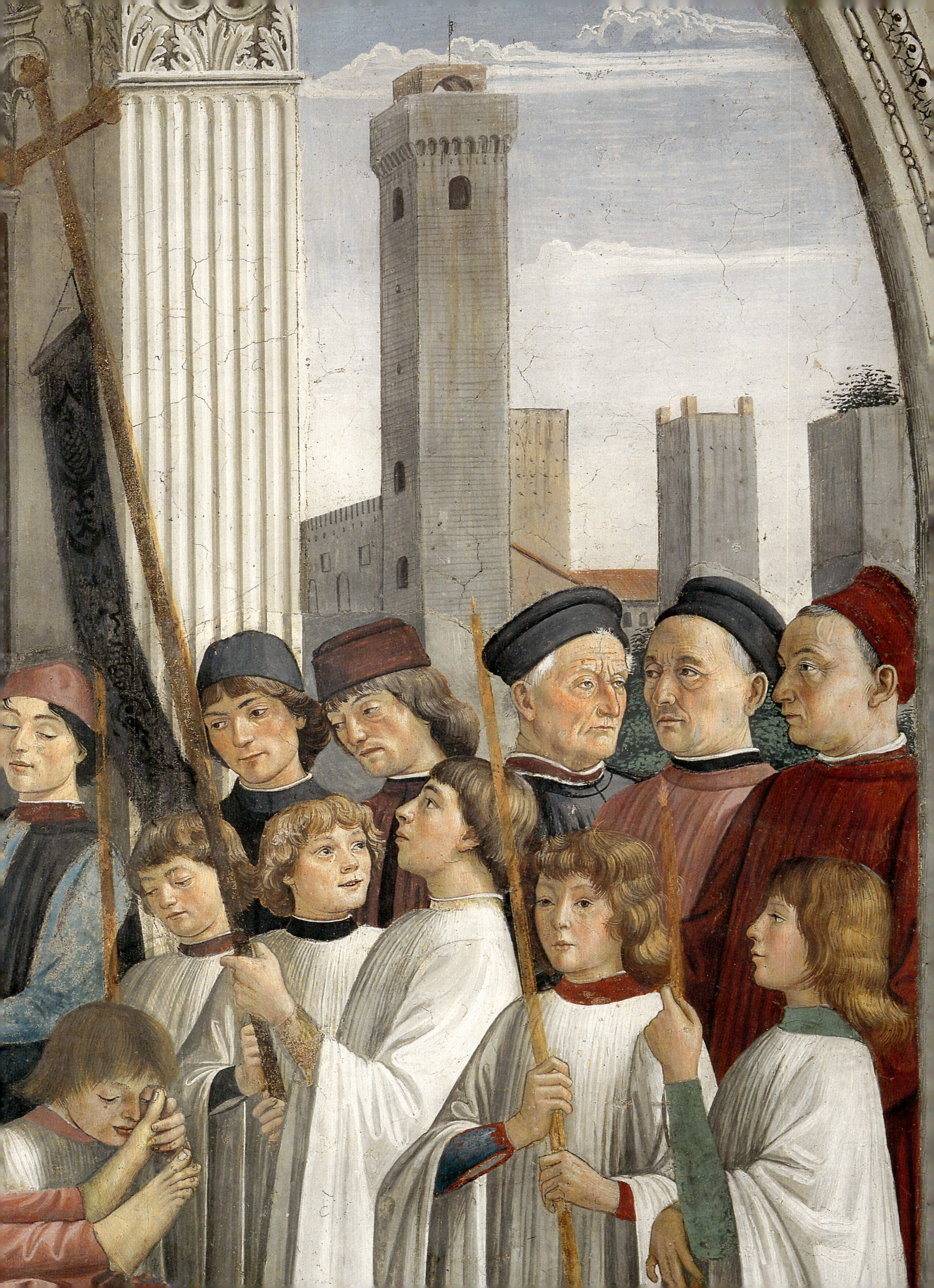

traditional one that started from the vaults and descended across the pendentives onto the walls at the sides of the altar. The painter's imagination, however, had free rein in the narration, which abandons itself to the most ethereal and moving poetry. The result is original and highly pleasing.

The *Obsequies of the Saint* possibly draws more on tradition; between the psalm-singing of the clergy and the choirboys, a sober religious ceremony is conducted against the solemn background of a monumental apse. The figure of the young saint, lying feebly on the rich catafalque, is brimming with tenderness. And yet three miracles take place almost unnoticed: the bells, struck by angels, ring out in the red towers of San Gimignano; the nurse Beldia is healed by her contact with the dead young girl's crossed hands; and a blind
10 choirboy who kisses her foot regains his sight. In the background are the individualized faces of persons we are now unable to identify but who were certainly portrayed from life, either important people in the city, or just ordinary townsfolk. Young men dressed in the latest fashions, almost gallants, join each other's hands in a pleasing play of lines. There is everywhere a limpid air that streams over people and things and lays emphasis on the clear colours, from the complexions of the youngsters to the blond hair of Fina and the blues of the shirts, the greens, and the blood red of the ancient towers, while the horizontal and vertical lines of the reduced setting are harmonized and create their own poetry.

There is more intimacy and concentration in the other story, more immediacy, candour, freshness and order. In the *Announcement of Death to the Saint*, the pathetic figure is stretched out on the floor of her room that is as simple as a cell and whitened by the bare walls and light. Her loose hair forms a halo, while rose bushes peep from the opening of the door that looks onto a garden and the sky. The solemn figure of the saint on a cloud is almost too much in the midst
of so many small things: the decanter and glass, an 8
embossed plate, and fruit which already expresses that knowledge of and harking back to Flemish art. A small window looks out onto a tract of peaceful countryside. The nurse and mother, barely distracted by the vision descending from Heaven, are dressed in almost monk-like habits with white cloths that cover their heads. A ray of the setting sun falls lightly on the face of Fina, the bare floor and the slightly cracked wall behind. There is no doubt here that the influence of Alesso Baldovinetti is all-pervading; however, Ghirlandaio is already speaking another language, one that is softer, almost anxious, where the connection with Domenico Veneziano is closer. Although later his art would be more masterly and stylistically accomplished, perhaps Ghirlandaio would never again attain to such moving poetry. His colours would not be as transparent, limpid and imbued with light. And if here too he was helped by assistants, his own participation is clearer and more immediate. It is no coincidence that his brother David, who would later become his contractor, was in Rome that year (1475).

The Last Suppers

After San Gimignano Domenico returned to Florence and, by now a successful artist, spent some time at the workshop of Verrocchio, where all the reputable artists of the time were converging: Lorenzo di Credi, Botticelli, Perugino and, a little later, Leonardo. They were there to discuss painting, colours, dynamic lines, music. Nonetheless, Ghirlandaio's most successful, genuine and spontaneous moment would remain indubitably the "Stories of St Fina".

The painter had by now won himself a reputation and his painting was popular during that period, when "around the 1480s in Verrocchio's circle, the fine transfigured material was disappearing and giving way to a style that was uniform, obvious, in a word, academic" (Longhi).

The slight decline in Ghirlandaio's art after San
11 Gimignano may be seen in the *Madonna and Child with Saints Sebastian and Julian* in Sant'Andrea a Brozzi, which shows, particularly in the Virgin being placed on a terrace overlooking a broad landscape, a certain drawing on Verrocchio's example. The same
can be said of another painting depicting the *Madonna* 12
enthroned with Saints, painted for the church of San Giusto, and now at the Uffizi, which forms part of the most classical Florentine tradition of the time, with the wall enclosing the Holy Conversation and slender cypresses and fruit-trees beyond. The scene is really rather crowded. This was, albeit in a different vein, basically a return to the earliest Giottesque tradition and to the tradition of Masaccio and the early Renaissance (Filippo Lippi in the Duomo of Prato, the lost frescoes of Sant'Egidio in Florence), mediated by

11. Madonna and Child with Saints Sebastian and Julian
Brozzi (Florence), church of Sant'Andrea

12. Madonna Enthroned with Saints
191 x 200 cm
Florence, Uffizi

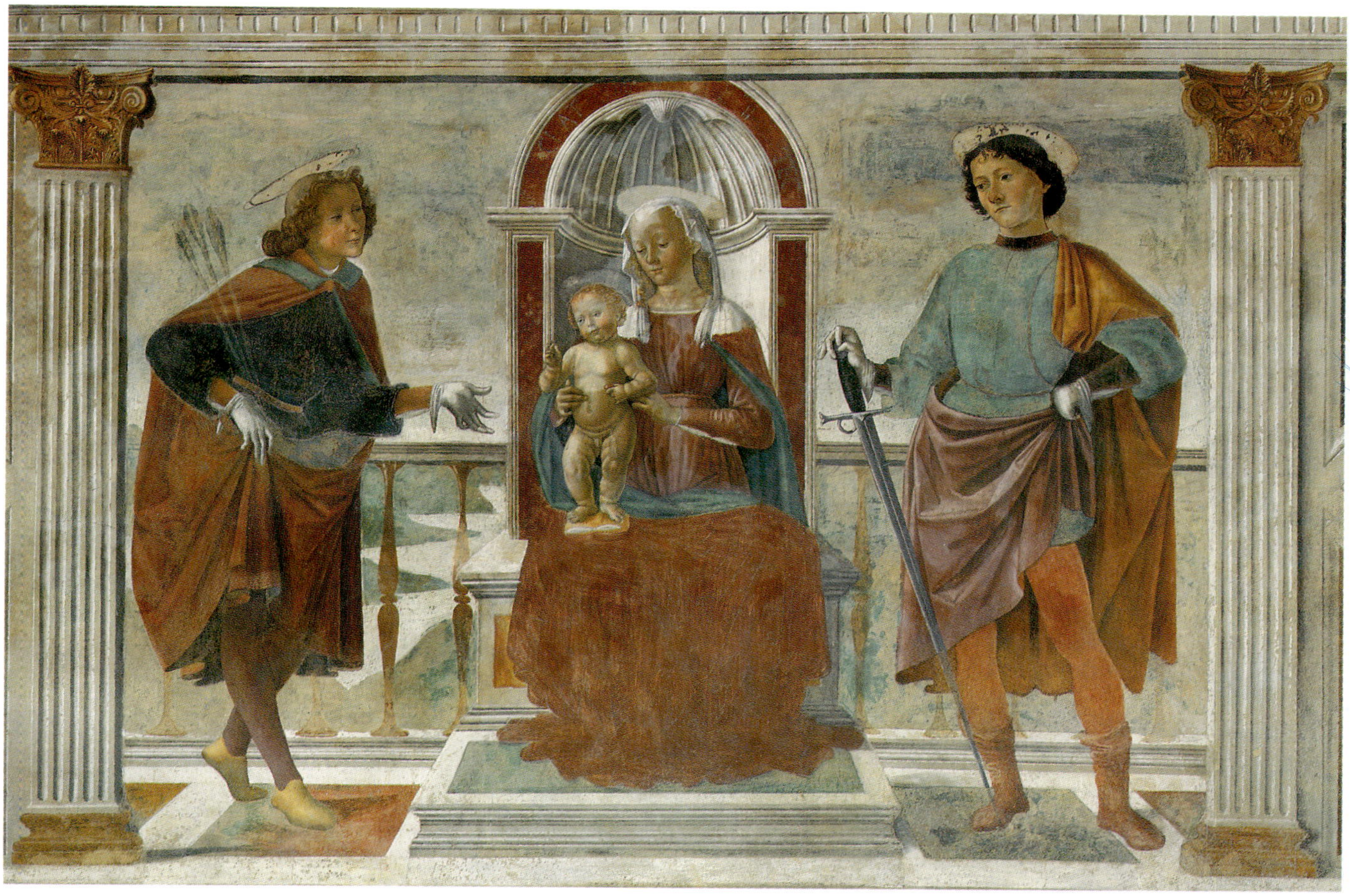
11

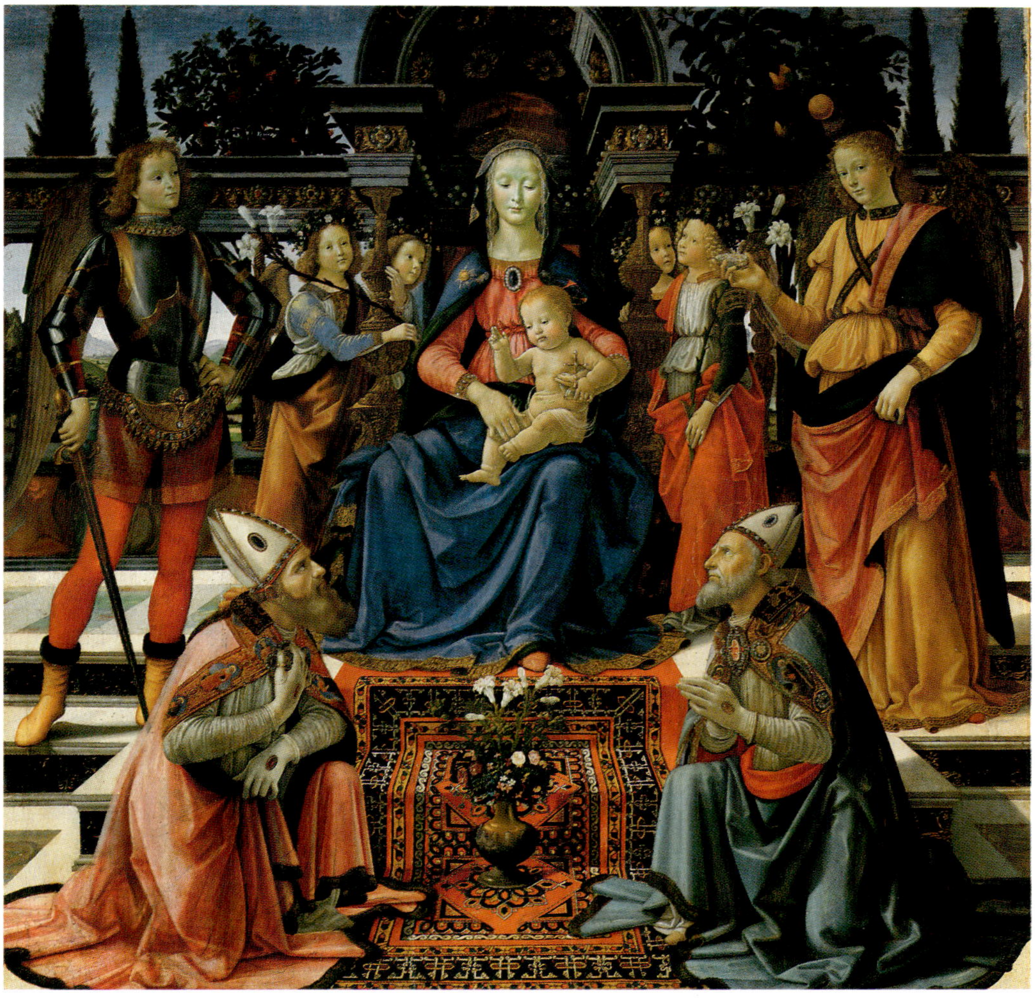
12

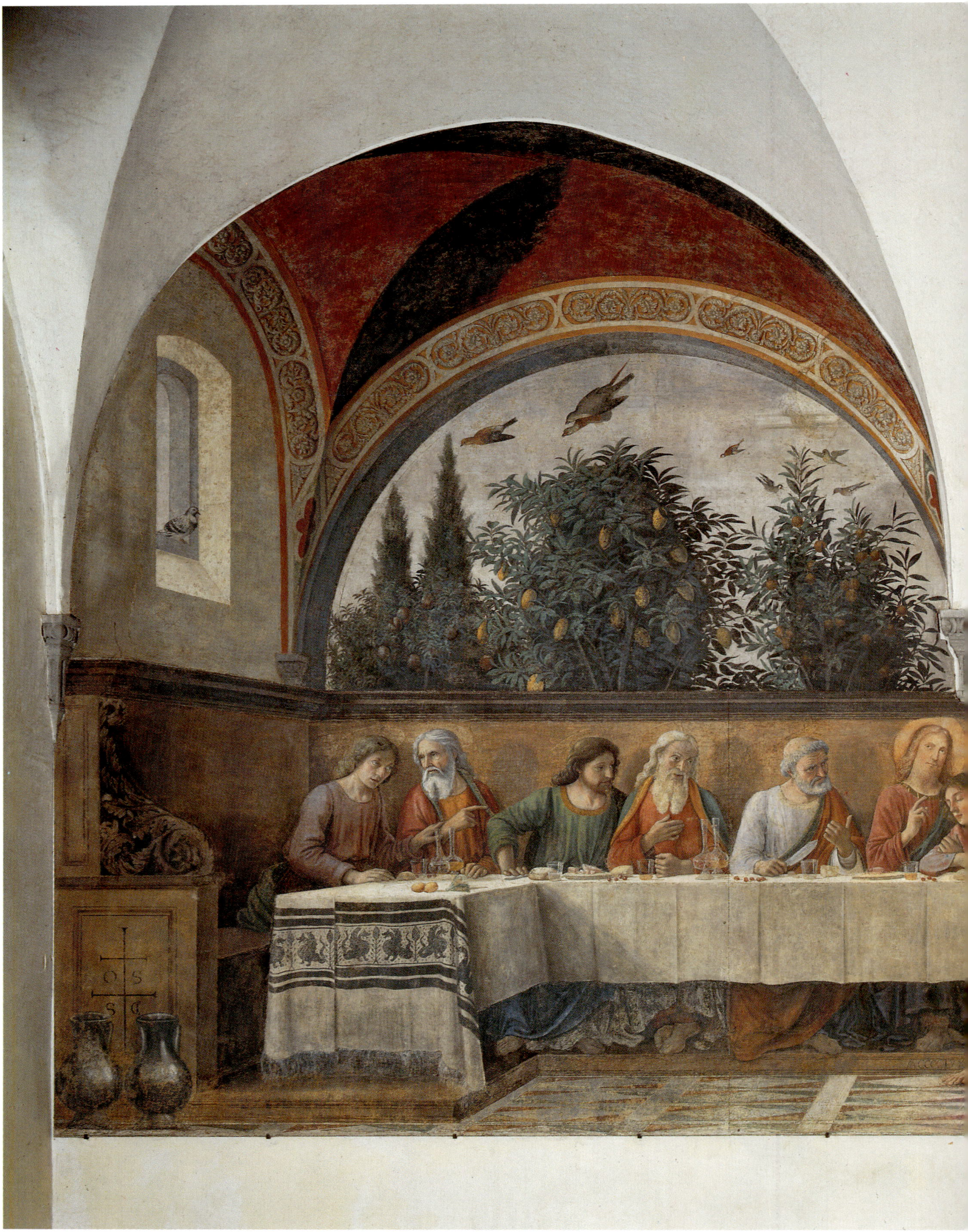

13. Last Supper, Florence, cloister of Ognissanti

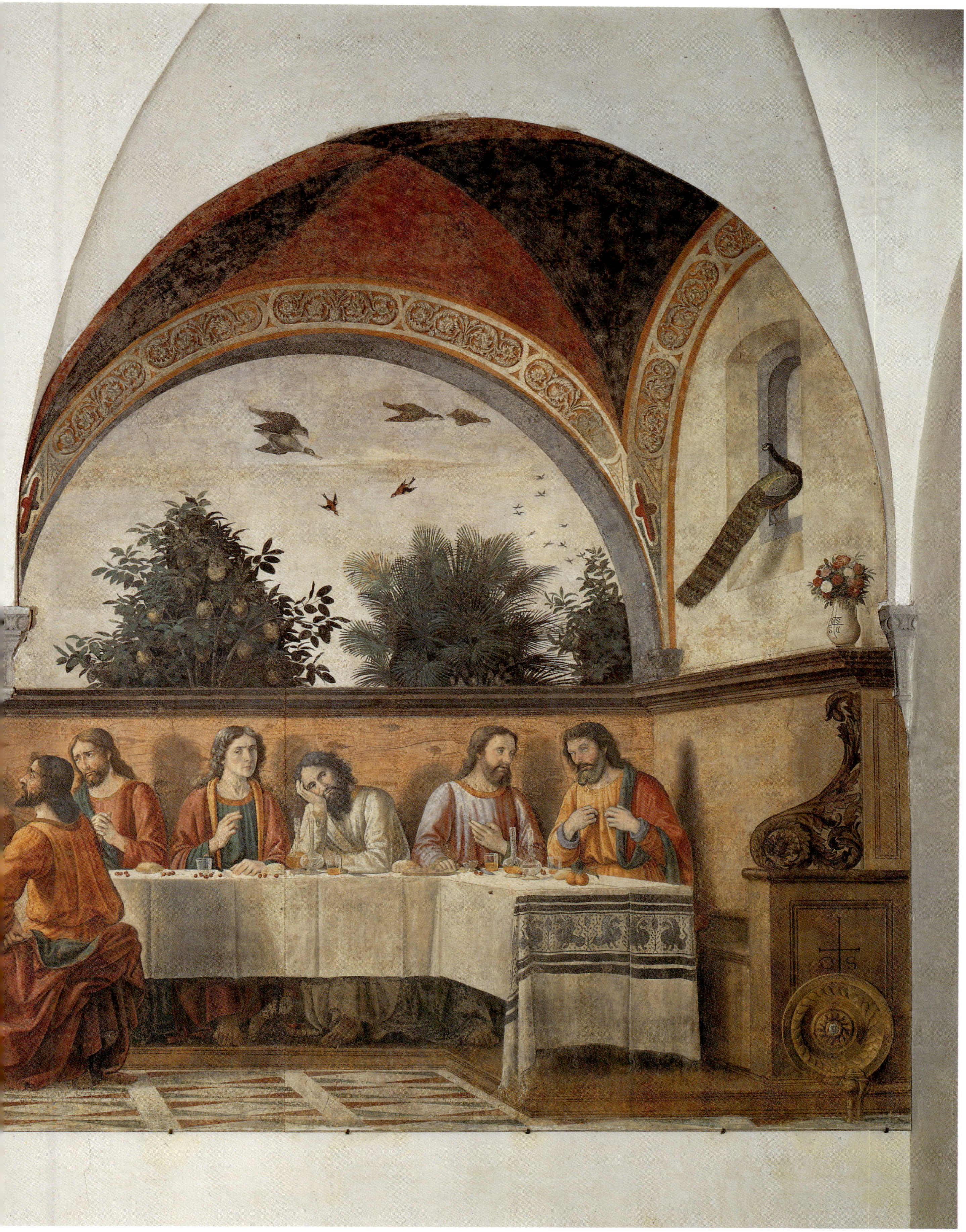

13

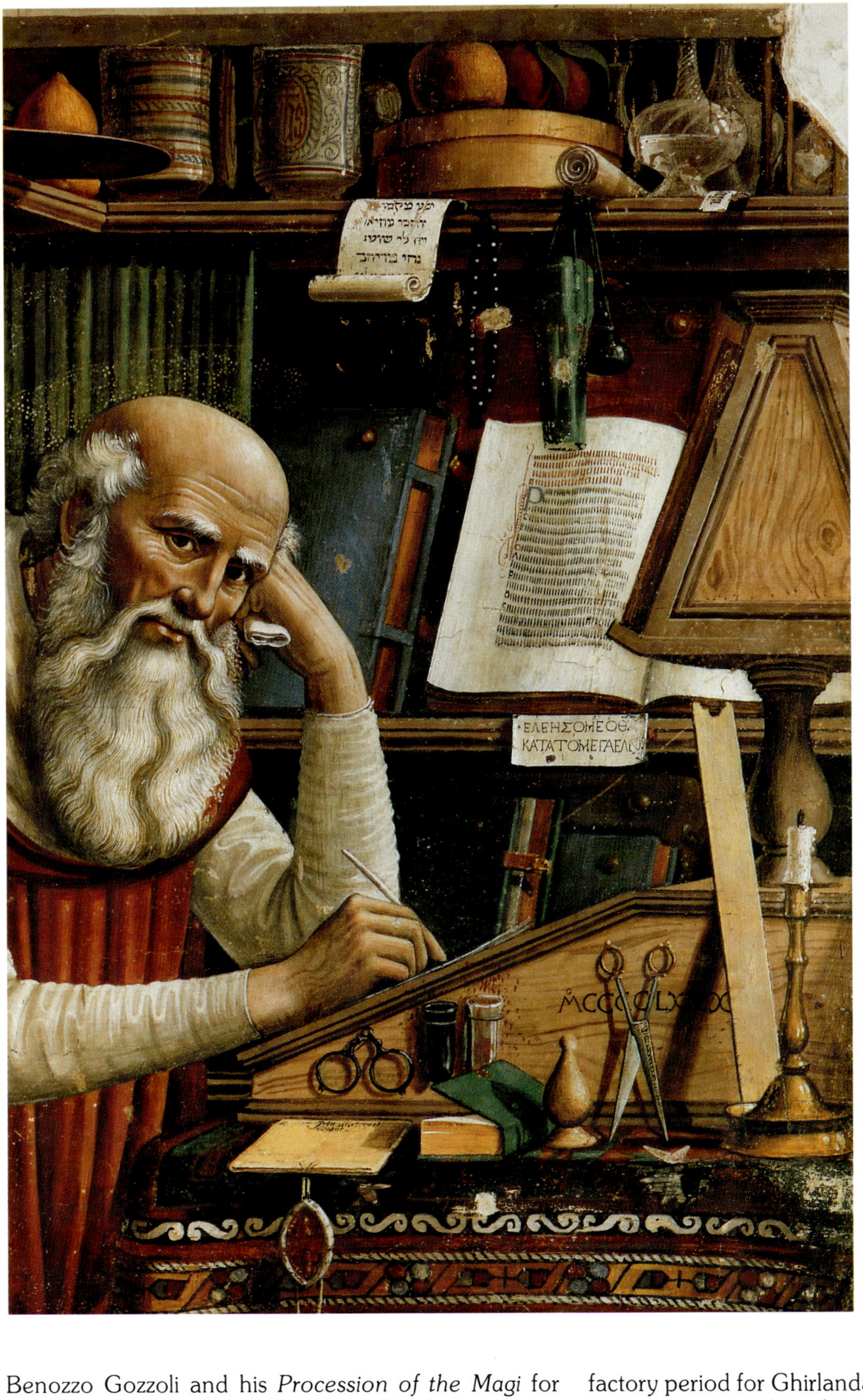

14

14, 15. Saint Jerome in his Study
Florence, church of Ognissanti

Benozzo Gozzoli and his *Procession of the Magi* for the Chapel of the Medici Palace in Via Larga.

In 1480 in "his" church at Ognissanti Ghirlandaio
15 frescoed a *St Jerome* that rivalled the *St Augustine*
which Botticelli had painted there a short time before. This work, which was accomplished with excessive ease, is superficial and full of objects that suffocate and impoverish its impact. The direct comparison with the Botticelli Saint serves merely to underline an unsatisfactory period for Ghirlandaio. His painting of the *Last* 13
Supper, executed in the refectory of the convent in the same year, is yet a further demonstration of it. It was originally a celebrated work, but the otherwise exhaustive Vasari refers to it glibly as "... a Last Supper, in fresco". The scene is ample and characterized by vivid, animated lines, as was his style, but it draws on the structural organization that was characteristic of Andrea del Castagno. The spirit is typical of Ghirlan-

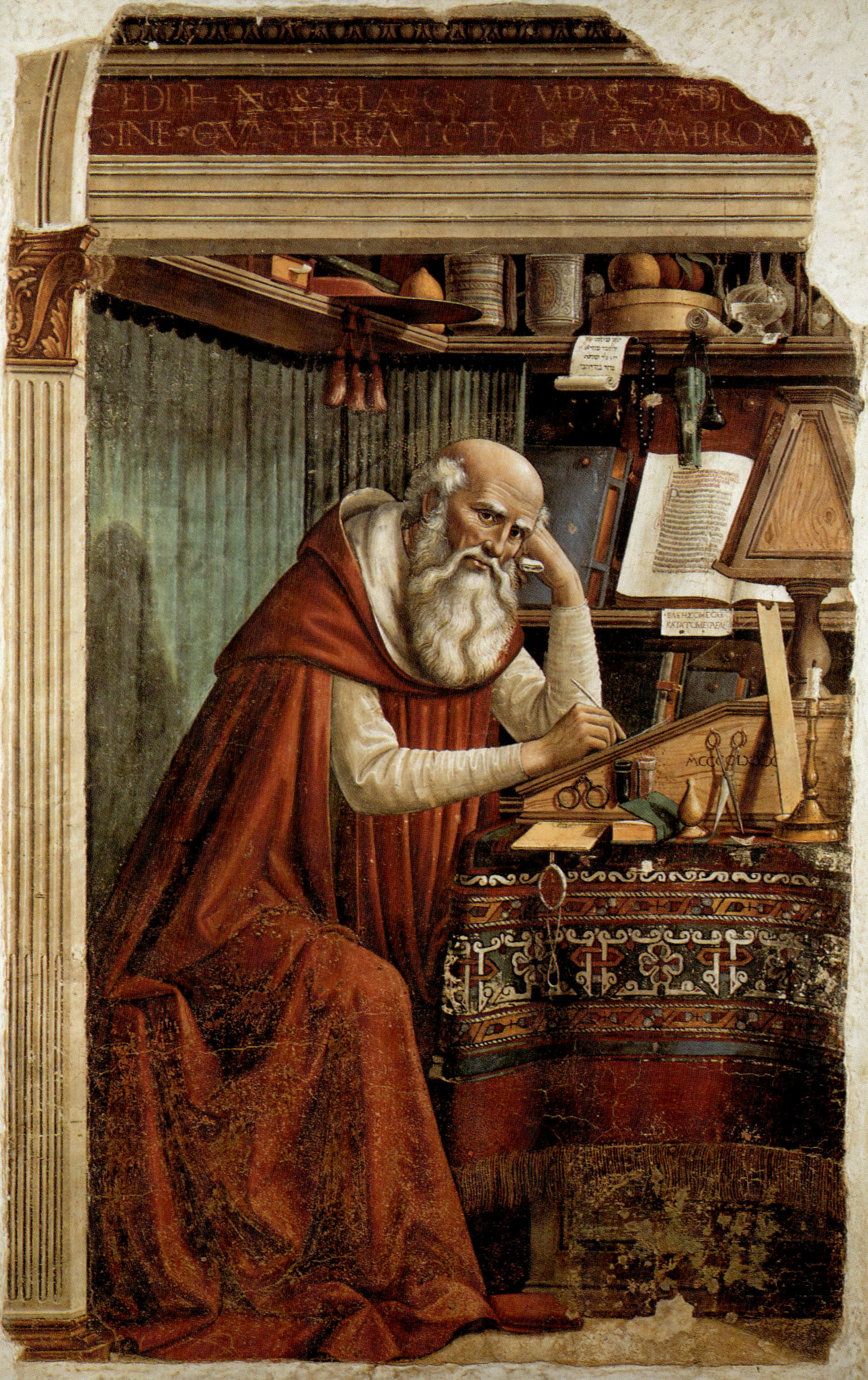

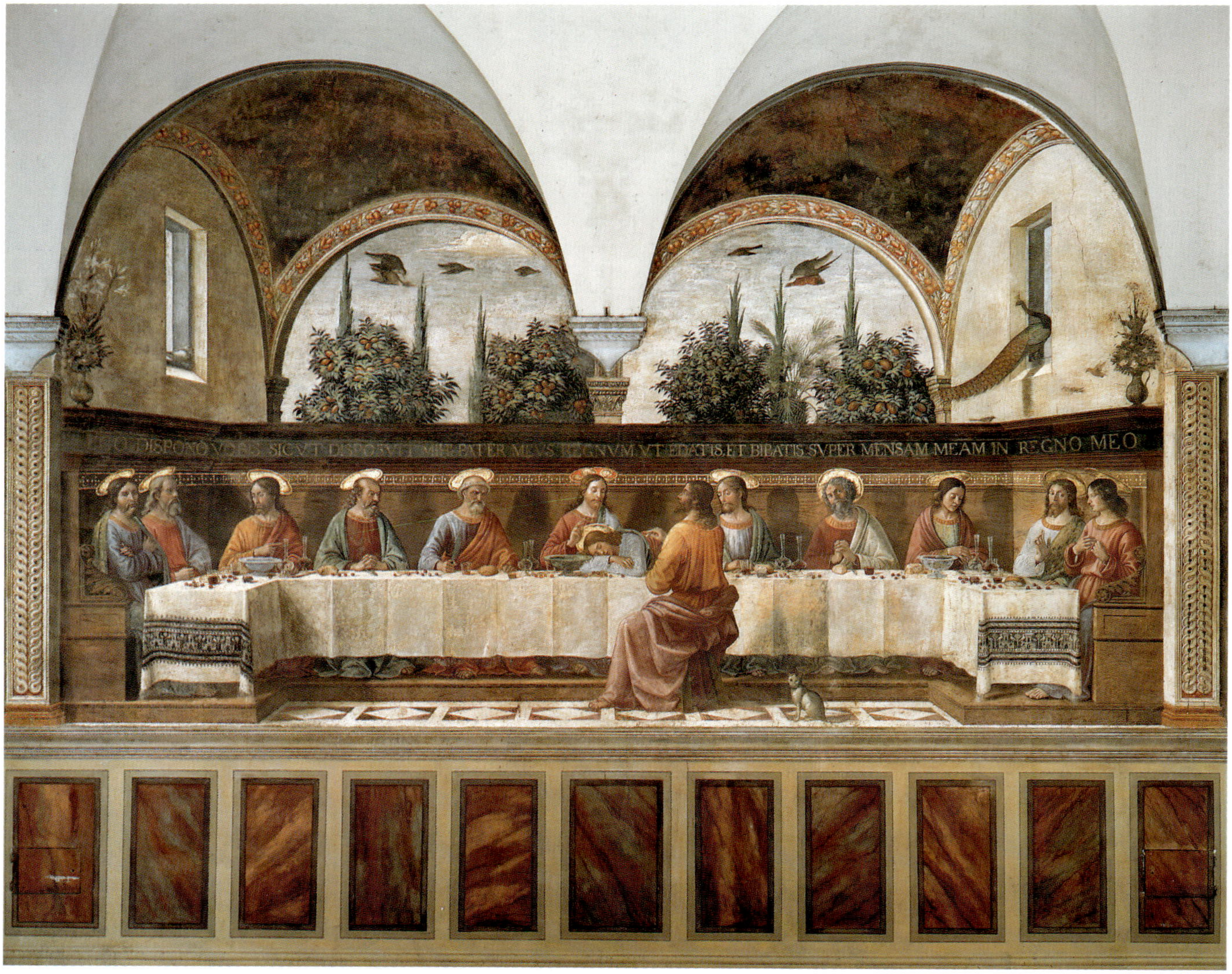

16

daio, who as ever remains rather psychologically superficial and uninterested in any form of dramatic expression. Jesus and the disciples are not particularly characterized and seem peaceful and rather at ease; even Judas, who though seated on his own in front of Christ, according to tradition, has a serene countenance and composed posture. However, the overall effect is agreeable and there are some ingenious touches. The lunettes offer an easy opportunity to the expert painter - a view of trees in a Tuscan garden beyond the wall; fruit-trees, cypresses, and an isolated palm-tree that appears rather incongruous in the surroundings. To the right, a peacock perches on a windowsill, while other birds flutter around in the crystalline air. The table is covered by a white tablecloth with blue embroidery. Plates, decanters, glasses, saltcellars and knives are carefully arranged in front of each table-guest, as are the bread and cherries. It might even be the realistic and serene representation of a Florentine table of the period.

17 Domenico also painted a *Last Supper* in the abbey of
16 Passignano and another in the convent of San Marco,
the latter a few years after the one in Ognissanti which is undoubtedly the most beautiful and where the hand of the master is clearest and most immediate.

16. Last Supper
Florence, convent of San Marco

17. Last Supper
Passignano (Florence), abbey

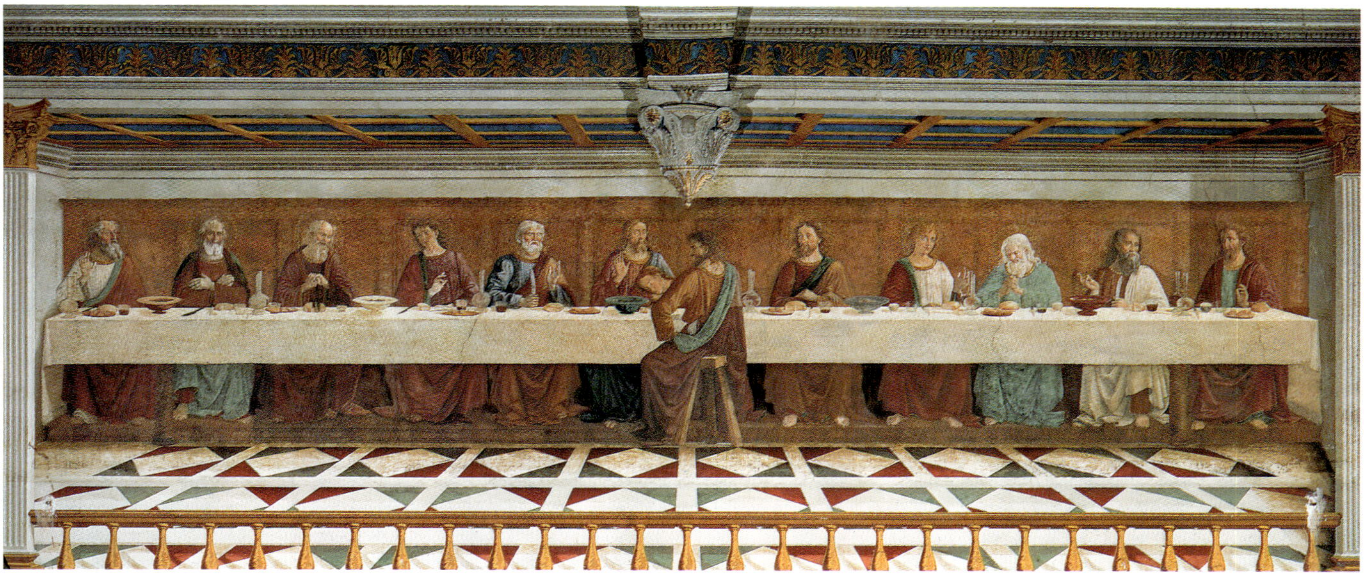 17

Nevertheless, in the San Marco fresco too how pleasing it is to observe that chronicler's narration of his city and the rich bourgeois inhabitants who enlivened it in the middle of the 15th century. It is typical of the work of Ghirlandaio, who certainly sketched out the drawing and, at times, participated directly in its execution. Rendered without resorting to dramatic force, it reveals a serenity and great faithfulness to life. Note the impassive Judas, seated in front of Jesus and almost conversing with him. The supper takes place at a large table with a bright tablecloth, embroidered at the edges. Nothing about it is casual; the crockery, the decanters, the knives, the bread and the cherries, are carefully arranged in front of every guest.

With customary ease, Ghirlandaio fills the lunettes with large trees and birds in flight against a bright sky whose light is reflected onto the right-hand wall where an open window frames a perching peacock. The rest is in shadow. Two flower-displays complete the frame which encloses the space. A cat, waiting patiently for a hoped-for scrap of meat, lends a touch of intimacy and domesticity that is rarely lacking in Ghirlandaio.

The Sistine Chapel Frescoes

The young Ghirlandaio was now well-known, and received the commission to execute two frescoes in the Sistine Chapel. We are in the years 1481-82. Sixtus IV's commission for the decoration in fresco of the chapel that bears his name is the official consecration of Florentine art. In addition to Ghirlandaio's contribution, other stories were executed by Botticelli, Cosimo Rosselli, Perugino (now elected a citizen of Florence), and Luca Signorelli. Domenico "... represented Christ calling Peter and Andrew from their nets, and the Resurrection of Christ, the greater part of which is now destroyed, for it was above the door..." (Vasari). Later, the *Resurrection* vanished completely in the destruction of the wall.

18 The *Calling of St Peter* was certainly a considerable undertaking and Ghirlandaio here takes on a solemnity that is unequalled either before or after. Possibly in some expressions, such as that of the sober Christ or the adoring look of the two who are summoned, we are reminded of Masaccio and his *Tribute Money*. Ultimately, almost every character finds its place and the movement slows and comes to rest in a deliberate, rapt contemplation. Ghirlandaio's distinctive style is again expressed in the group of talkative women on the left, and the curious peeping glances of those who want to see and, perhaps, be seen. The extensive, evocative landscape contains trees, water, and undulating hills that fade into the distance. The painter is clearly influenced here by the ample spaciality of Perugino in the *Handing over of the Keys to St Peter* frescoed in the same room, and certain subtle vibrations running through the countryside and faces are unquestionably the result of his meditations on the art of Botticelli. But Ghirlandaio really comes into his own in the group of characters on the right who are all, or 19
almost all, real portraits. Represented here are the most important components of the large Florentine colony in Rome - figures belonging to the most illustrious families of the city who had opened branches of their Florentine businesses in Rome, but above all

18

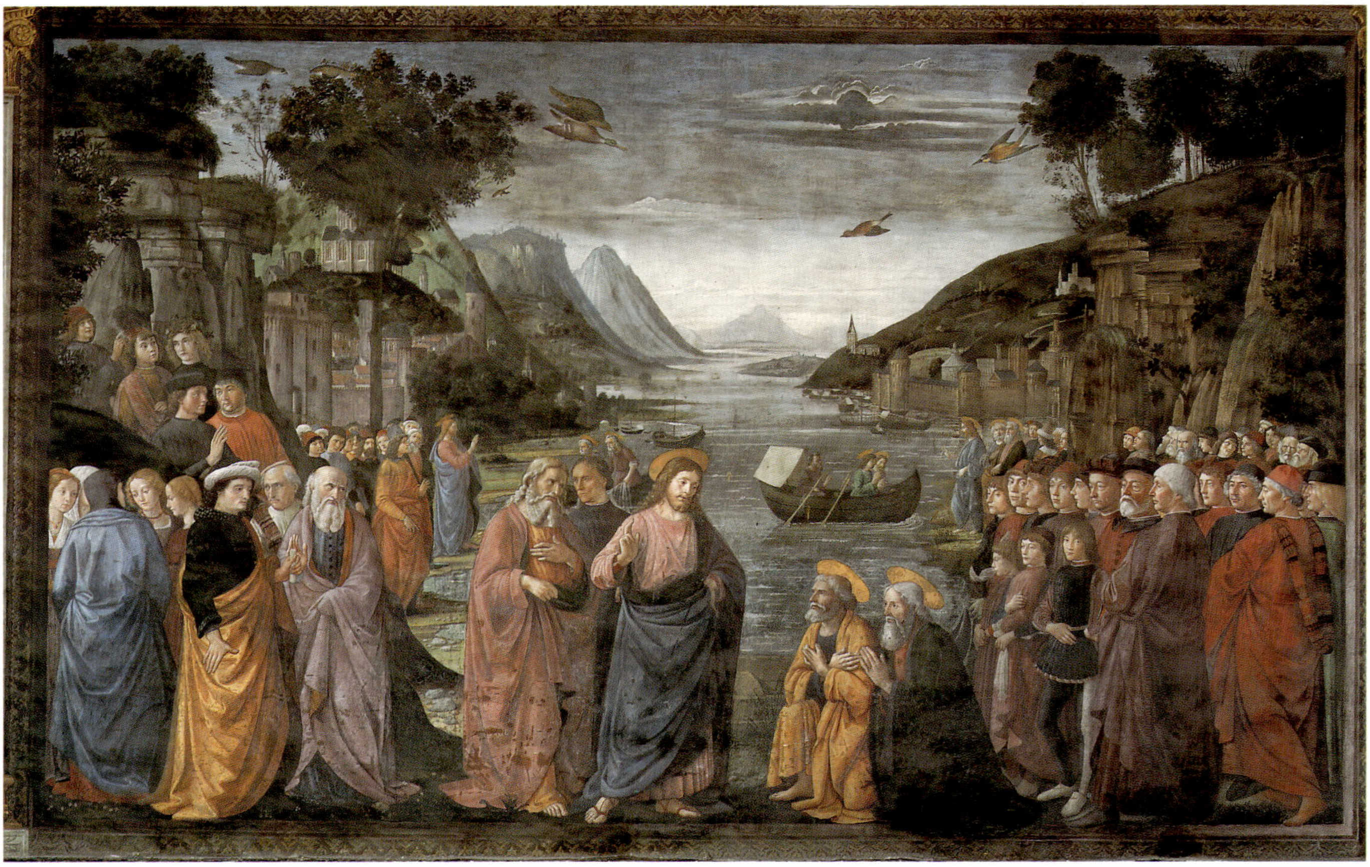

representatives of the Medici House banks of credit and commerce. These people provided a touch of distinctive culture to that district of Rome which they inhabited between Via Giulia and the Tiber, a quarter that had grown up around the church dedicated to San Giovanni, patron saint of Florence, the first area to be paved in the city of the popes and the least gloomy at night.

Ghirlandaio's picture is a sort of chronicle of that world in which Lucrezia Tornabuoni, the wife of Piero de' Medici, went looking for a fitting bride for her son, the future Lorenzo il Magnifico. She was a guest of her brother Giovanni, and had chosen Clarice Orsini as the bride. After the members of the Vespucci family of Ognissanti, these Florentines who had moved to Rome were the first of the long series of portraits that are, in fact, the greatest achievement of the painter Domenico Ghirlandaio. The portrait, moreover, especially in sculpture, became a Florentine speciality in the very years in which the artist was active. It is enough to recall those somewhat idealized works of Antonio del Pollaiolo (and not only in sculpture), the more realistic ones of Mino da Fiesole and Benedetto da Maiano, and those most delicate portraits of the young Desiderio da Settignano which demonstrated a type of portrait that was halfway between idealization and reality, and which was also characteristic of the sculptors of the following generation and of the Della Robbia brothers in their magical glazed earthenware.

Giovanni Tornabuoni, the brother of Lucrezia, figures prominently among the other characters portrayed. Head of the Medici Bank in Rome, he was so expert in financial and business affairs that he became the treasurer of Sixtus IV, the enemy pope of the Medici family, who in 1478 had taken the side of the Pazzi conspirator against Lorenzo and Giuliano. Tornabuoni is now elderly, or so it would appear from his austere countenance and the deep wrinkles that furrow his brow and temples. He bears in his heart the sorrow and still bitter pain caused by the death of his wife Francesca Pitti, the daughter of Luca, who commissioned Filippo Brunelleschi to design the sumptuous Florentine palace that to this day carries his name. His wife had died in childbirth three years earlier, but the void that she left is still evident. The bitter grief of her widower can be read in a letter which he wrote to his nephew Lorenzo de' Medici: "My dearest Lorenzo... I am so oppressed by sorrow and pain for the cruel and unforeseen fate of my darling wife that I myself know not where I am at. As you must have heard yesterday, at ten in the evening, as God wished, she passed away during delivery and the creature she had longed for was extracted dead from her body, which was for me a double cause of grief". Two other sons were left to him, Lorenzo and Giovanni, whom we also know through the paintings of Ghirlandaio. Right here, Lorenzo, still almost a boy, stands in front of his father, his sad face revealing a certain feminine softness. He is downcast, as if almost foreseeing the family's future misfortunes - the financial collapse following his father's death and the death of his young wife.

Further along the line, in profile, possibly another Tornabuoni is portrayed, the noble and cultivated Cecco, who just a year later, in 1482, would die in

18, 19. Calling of St Peter
Vatican, Sistine Chapel

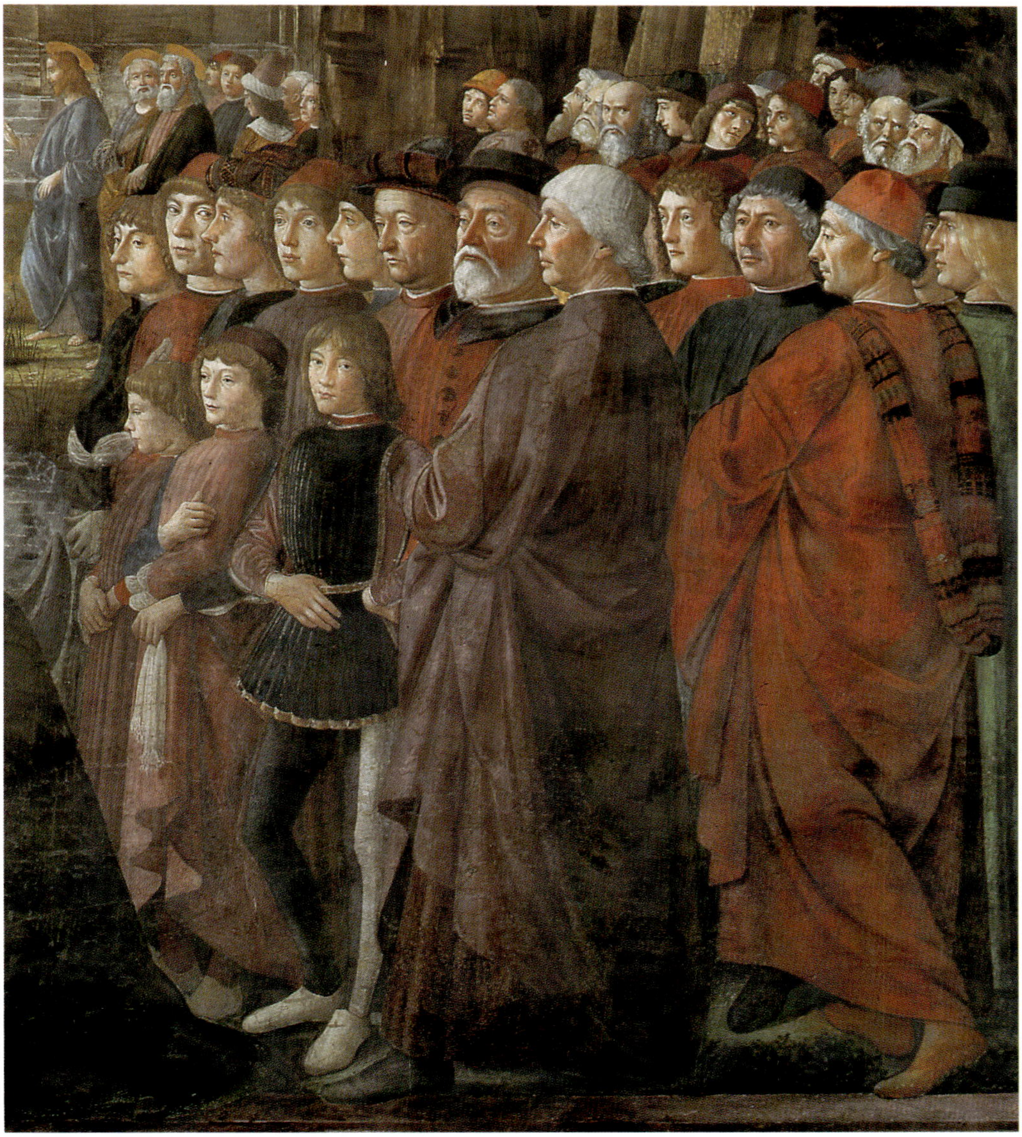
19

Rome and be buried in an elegant tomb built by Mino da Fiesole in the Church of Minerva.

The character on the far right of the group is a member of the Vespucci family, Giovanni Antonio, whose sharp profile is illumined by a bright light that seems almost to lend him the suggestion of a smile. Another bare-headed gentleman, with white hair and a pensive expression that truly emanates a sense of warm serenity, is thought by some to be the Florentine Francesco Soderini, by others the Roman Raimondo Orsini of the powerful family which had strong links with the papal throne. In the very centre of scene, just behind Jesus, is the austere and imposing figure of Diotisalvi Nerone. His grave face, with its piercing eyes and thin, tight-lipped mouth, almost gives the impression that he is harbouring sinister thoughts. His pose is simple, but already reveals the ambiguity of his nature. A long-standing friend of the Medici family, he was a man of such caution that Cosimo il Vecchio had advised his son Piero to keep him near at hand in the silent and somewhat detached administration of the State. Cosimo had intended to entrust the government of Florence to his second-born son Giovanni, for he feared the ailing health and intellectual "distractions" of his eldest son. But fate would have it otherwise. Giovanni died before him, along with the young favourite Cosimo, and Piero was obliged to deal with the government. But he did it well, with sense, intelligence and modesty, singly overcoming even the difficulties arising from the bad counsel of Diotisalvi Nerone. For the latter, Piero should have demanded the restitution of large paternal credits. But the creditors reacted against Piero, not against his bad counseller "... as if that one (Piero) wanted to take from them, not ask for what was his, they took offence, and without any respect talked badly of him and maligned him as thankless and greedy" (Machiavelli). Furthermore, by inciting Luca Pitti against Piero, Diotisalvi hoped to become all-powerful in Florence, but his dark scheming brought him no reward... Having surmounted these obstacles, the Medici re-established their supremacy in the city. For Diotisalvi Nerone Rome was the city of a more or less voluntary exile and he remained there on his own. Perhaps Ghirlandaio portrayed him among the Florentines because of this, though he is isolated, behind Jesus, almost the shadow of Judas. Or perhaps it is our imagination, led on by the painter's easy narrating, that takes over and creates some ghost in the story.

Argyropulus is also among the Florentines, the old man with the resentful expression and rather weak face framed by a short white beard, and with his head covered by a strange, hard, almost prelatic hat. The Greek John Argyropulus, born in Constantinople but driven out by the Turks in 1453, had found refuge in Florence, in the cultivated circle of the Medici, whose guest he was for fifteen years. He had held the professorship of Greek at the university of Florence and Lorenzo il Magnifico had made him a citizen of Florence, which had become the city of his choice. When Argyropulus was called to Rome by Sixtus IV, he continued to regard himself as a Florentine and as such, with the others, Ghirlandaio portrayed him.

In the Roman fresco the colours are vivid and radiant, caressing the delicate flesh tones, the various shades of the solemn robes and fashionable clothes of the young.

The Painting of his Mature Years

The Frescoes in the Sala dei Gigli and Sassetti Chapel

Giovanni Tornabuoni, who had given his wife a most honourable burial in Santa Maria sopra Minerva, commissioned Ghirlandaio to paint the decorative frescoes of the chapel where his wife had been buried with "two stories of St John the Baptist and two of Our Lady, which were then much admired" (Vasari) - paintings which are now unfortunately lost.

Certainly, the frescoes executed in the Vatican had made a considerable impression, especially on those Florentines who had had the honour of being portrayed in the Pope's Chapel. With great praise, they communicated this to relatives living in Florence. When Domenico returned to his native city, now with an even greater reputation, increasingly important and demanding commissions rained down on him.

"On the right-hand of the entrance to Santa Croce he painted the story of St Paulinus. Having thus acquired fame and credit, he did a chapel in Santa Trinita for Francesco Sassetti..." (Vasari).

Then, in 1482 Ghirlandaio received the official commission for the Sala dei Gigli in Palazzo Vecchio. Sandro Botticelli, Perugino and Piero del Pollaiolo had also been assigned to the task, but only Domenico accomplished the undertaking. However, this work is not of a high quality. Already occupied with the Sassetti Chapel, which probably gave him more satisfaction, in the Sala dei Gigli he probably traced the outline of the painting only, leaving a large part of its execution to assistants, almost as if the officiality of the task caused him some embarrassment. These must

20 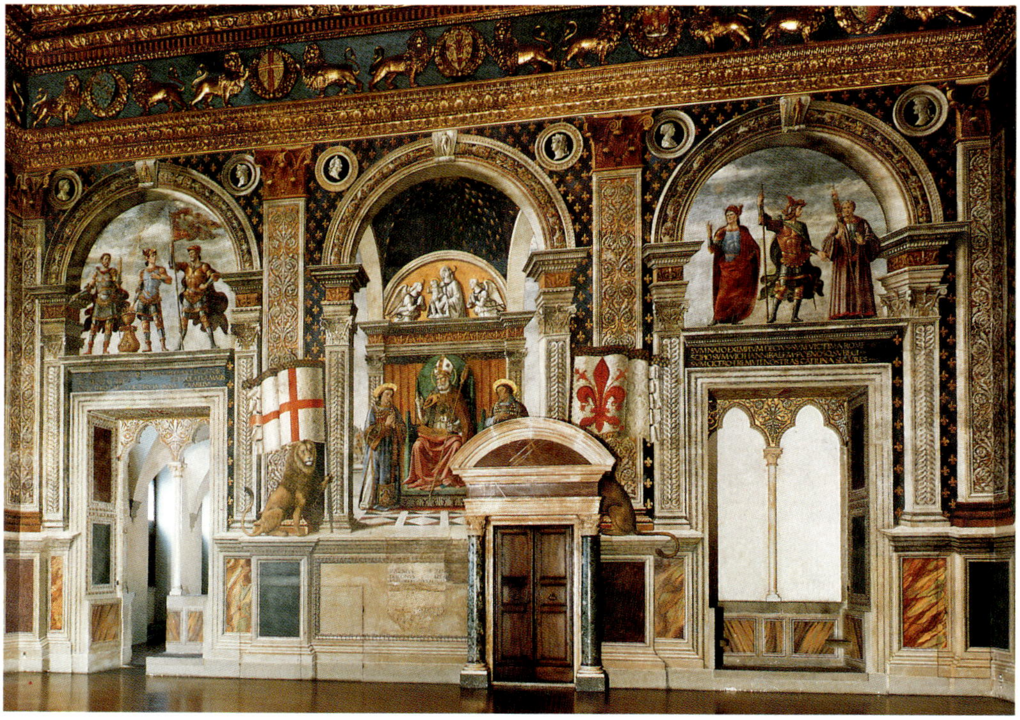

20. Right-hand wall of the Sala dei Gigli Florence, Palazzo Vecchio

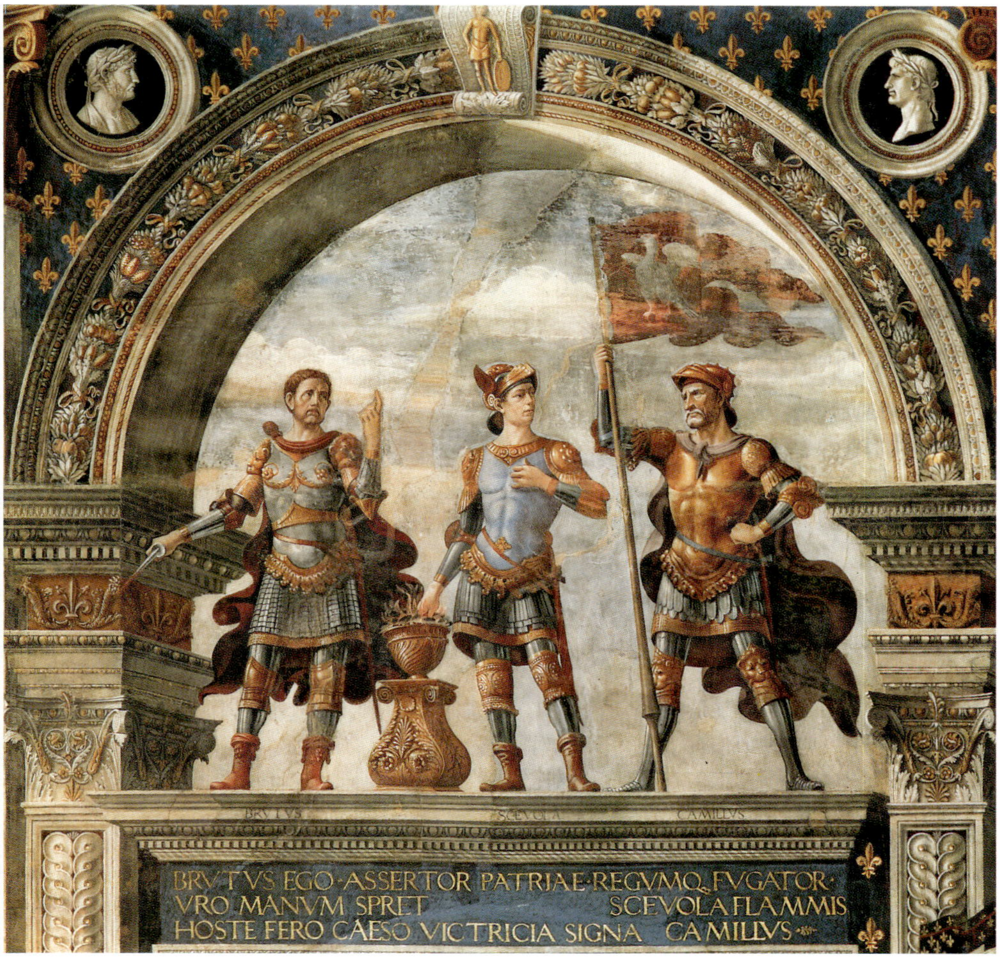

21

21. Brutus, Mutius Scaevola and Camillus Florence, Palazzo Vecchio

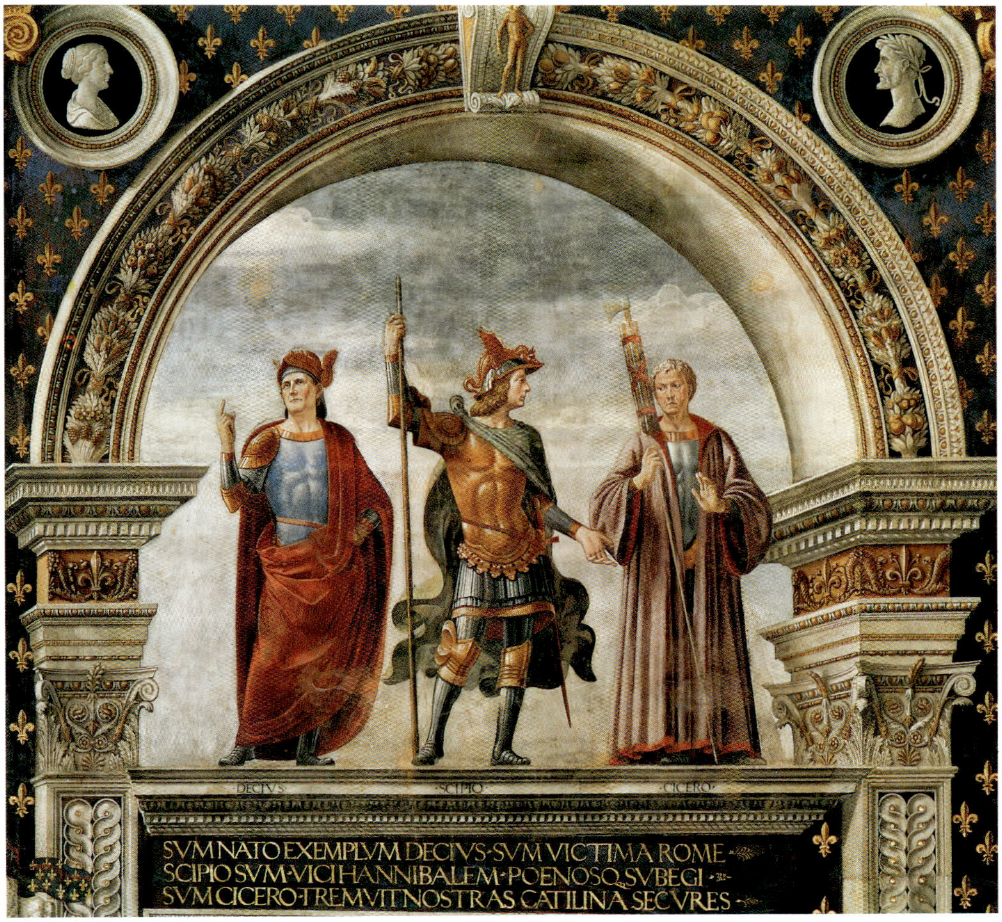

22

22. Decius, Scipio and Cicero Florence, Palazzo Vecchio

23
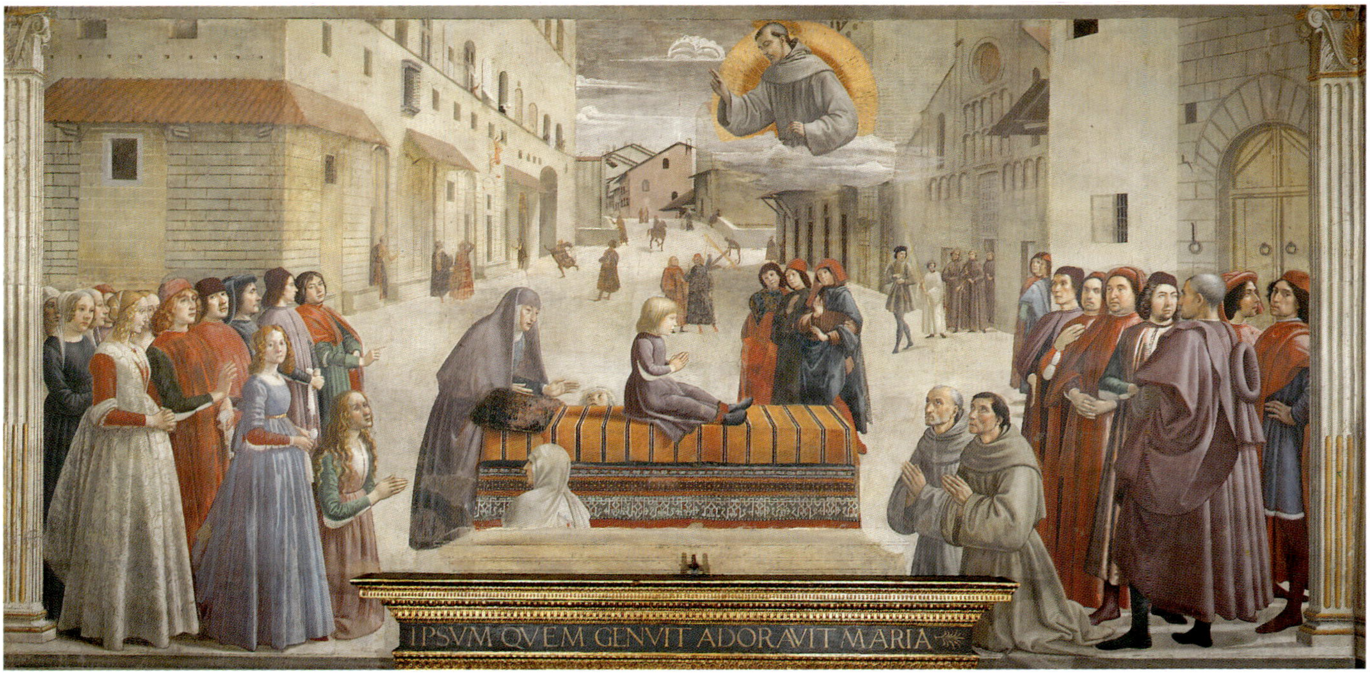

23, 24. Resurrection of the Boy
Florence, Santa Trinita

have been uneasy and disconcerting years for Domenico, who went from one job to another. Divided between Palazzo Vecchio, Santa Trinita, his own workshop, and before long Santa Maria Novella and San Marco, he spent his time supervising, correcting and advising; but where his paint-brush left its mark the scenes and figures took on new life.

20 In the Sala dei Gigli the pictorial scheme is grandiose
21,22 and the ancient figures depicted in the higher part of the fresco have an extraordinary energy. The deacons in the centre, on the other hand, are weak, rather limp and monotonous, even in the colours, which have lost their original brightness and lustre. In this fresco the painter found occasion to portray not living figures but a serene and well-identified corner of the city, beyond the throne of St Zenobius.

Undoubtedly here more than elsewhere his followers had a hand in the work. In addition to his two brothers David and Benedetto, and his brother-in-law Bastiano Mainardi, there were many other assistants: Bartolomeo di Giovanni, Francesco Granacci and Biagio d'Antonio di Firenze (possibly the same as Giovan Battista Utili) to name but the most important. Only two works are known to be by his two brothers: a mosaic in the Museum of Cluny by David, and a *Nativity* in the church of Aigueperse by Benedetto; certainly too little to be able to discern their presence in the projects of Domenico Ghirlandaio. Bastiano Mainardi, on the other hand, is more easily identifiable, if we accept Vasari's attribution to him of the great fresco in Santa Croce: "from a cartoon prepared by Domenico, Bastiano painted in the Chapel of the Baroncelli and Bandini in Santa Croce Our Lady ascending into heaven with St Thomas beneath receiving her girdle, a beautiful work in fresco".

The most important and talented artist is Bartolomeo di Giovanni, who had already made an individual and extremely pleasing impression in the fresco of the Sistine Chapel. He has an intense, almost biting Nordic style, evident in the cartoons of the Galleria Colonna in Rome, and we shall see him again in the small
scenes from the predella of Domenico's *Adoration of* 79-8
the Magi for the Spedale degli Innocenti. Fundamentally he anticipates the rapid and nervous manner of Piero di Cosimo. Granacci developed later as a painter, and it is difficult to identify him in the early works done with Domenico. It is therefore impossible to attribute the responsibility to this or that assistant for the more nondescript and inferior parts of Ghirlandaio's fresco cycles. This would only be a convenient way of judging or justifying certain unexpected lapses in his art. But this would be superfluous, since he was also responsible for the parts that lack the animated style, vitality and mastery of colour that were present in others. From these sometimes considerable discrepancies we must form a judgement about his work that makes him at once a marvellous interpreter of people and situations, a calm, almost monotonous narrator, or a tired and empty artist at times in search of the best, at others yielding to a commonplace routine.

"... He did a chapel in Santa Trinita for Francesco Sassetti with stories of St Francis, an admirable work, remarkable for its grace, finish and delicacy" (Vasari).

Francesco Sassetti was a wealthy banker and friend of the House of Medici. Belonging to that noble Florentine world, with its Maecenastic aspirations, he had the desire to leave an everlasting and tangible remembrance of his own name. He hit on the idea of a funeral chapel, an ancient custom that dated to at least the fourteenth century. The artist most in vogue in Florence at that time was swiftly chosen: Domenico

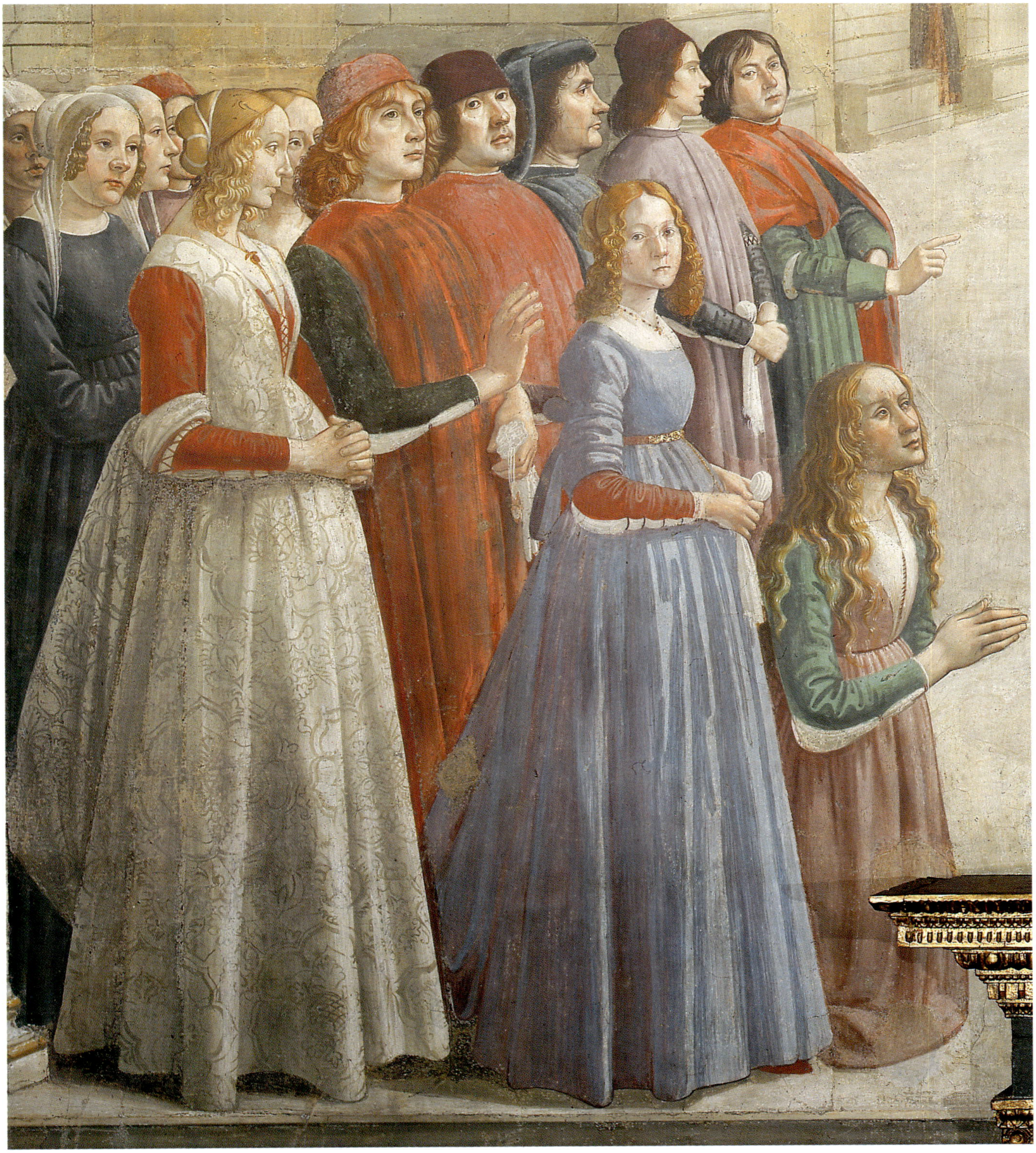

24

Ghirlandaio, who had just returned from Rome and was busy at work on the official commission for Palazzo Vecchio that he had received from the Signoria. The finding of a suitable place proved to be more difficult. Francesco Sassetti had initially thought of decorating the Cappella Grande of Santa Maria Novella with the stories of his guardian saint, St Francis of Assisi. But the Dominicans, who were titular occupants of the basilica and still bitter rivals of the Minorites, would not accept the idea. Sassetti thus opted for the smaller and narrower chapel to the left of the main altar in the church of Santa Trinita. The contract was concluded between 1475 and 1479, at a time when Domenico was still making journeys from Florence and San Gimignano to Rome, with that remarkable ease of movement so typical among artists of the period.

At Santa Trinita, after the "Stories of St Fina", 7-10
Ghirlandaio would give his best, the best of his poetry, the joy of his colours and serene images, a vivid record of the wealthy, elegant, cultivated and refined life of his city. At the base of the stories are the two sar-

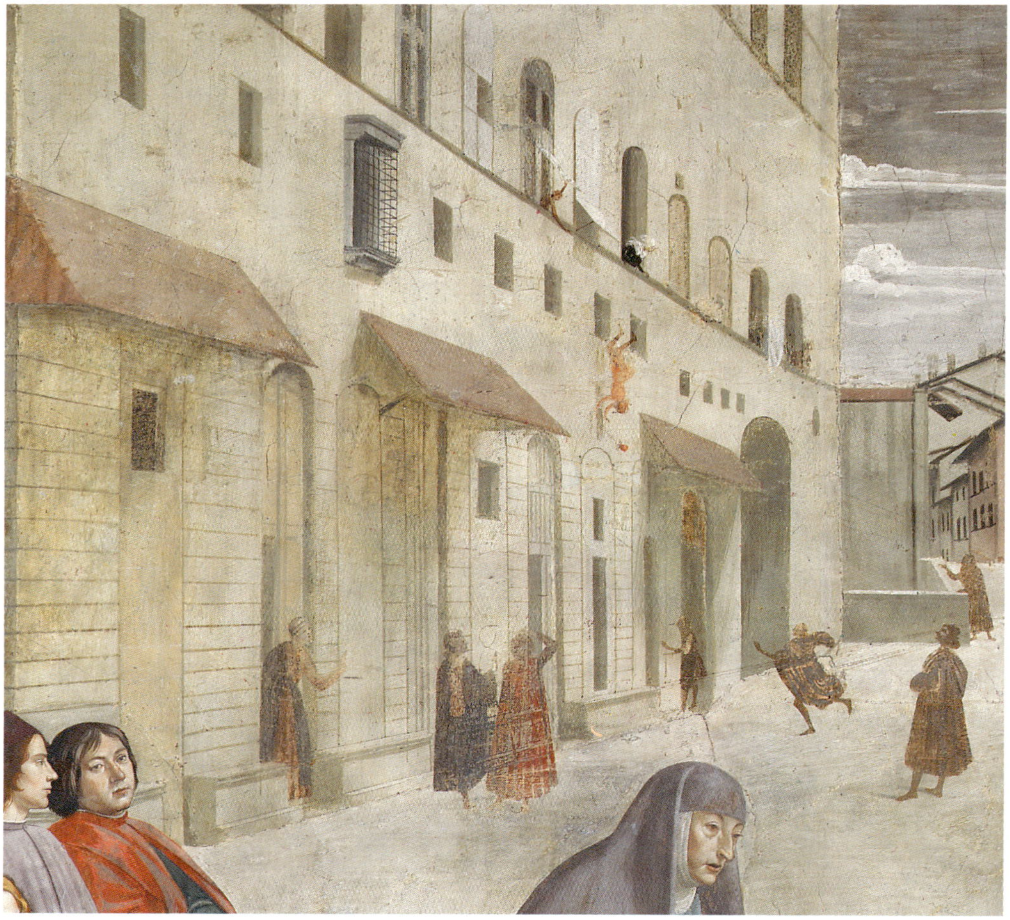

25

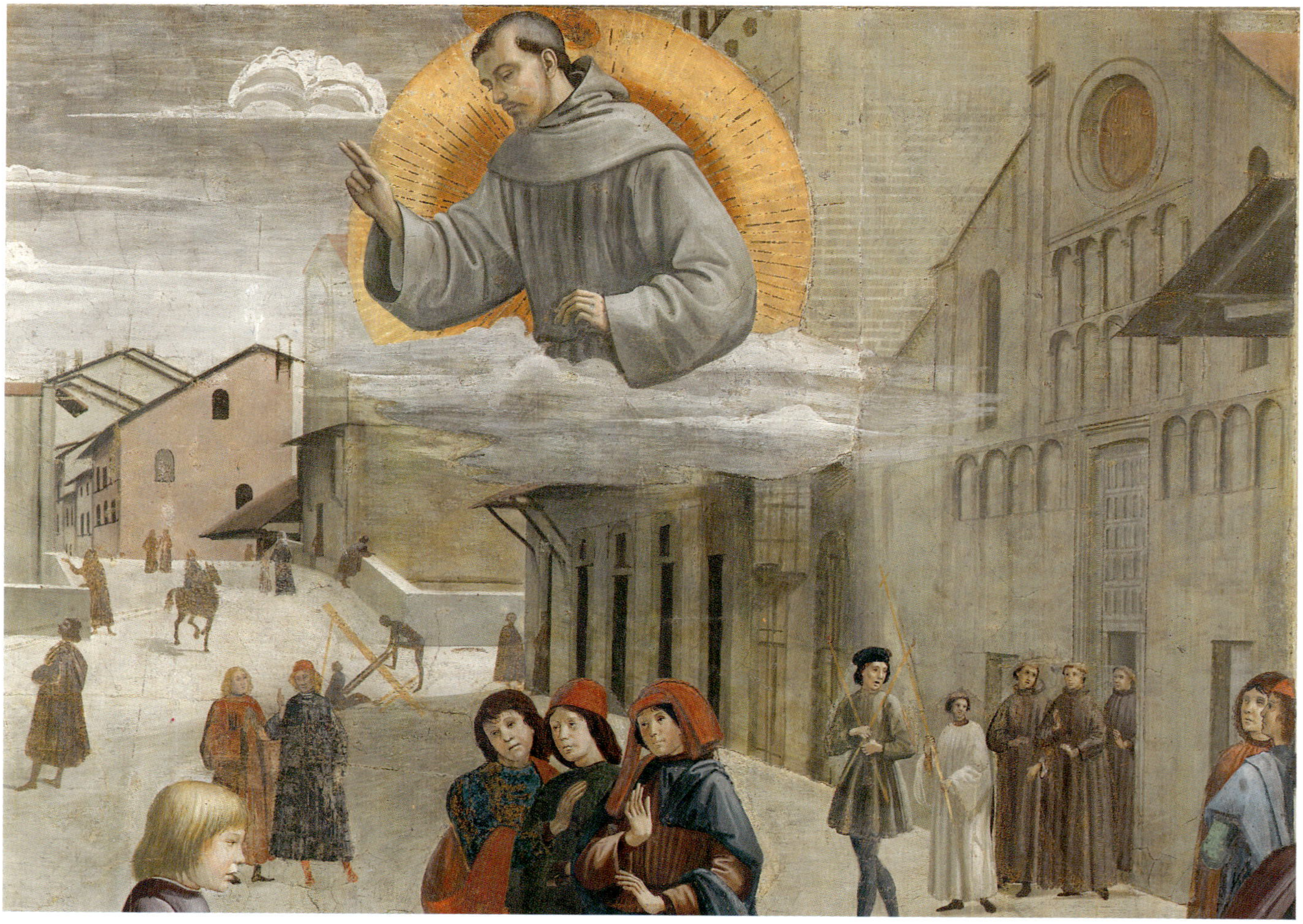

26

25, 26. Resurrection of the Boy
details showing the Spini Palace and the church of Santa Trinita
Florence, Santa Trinita

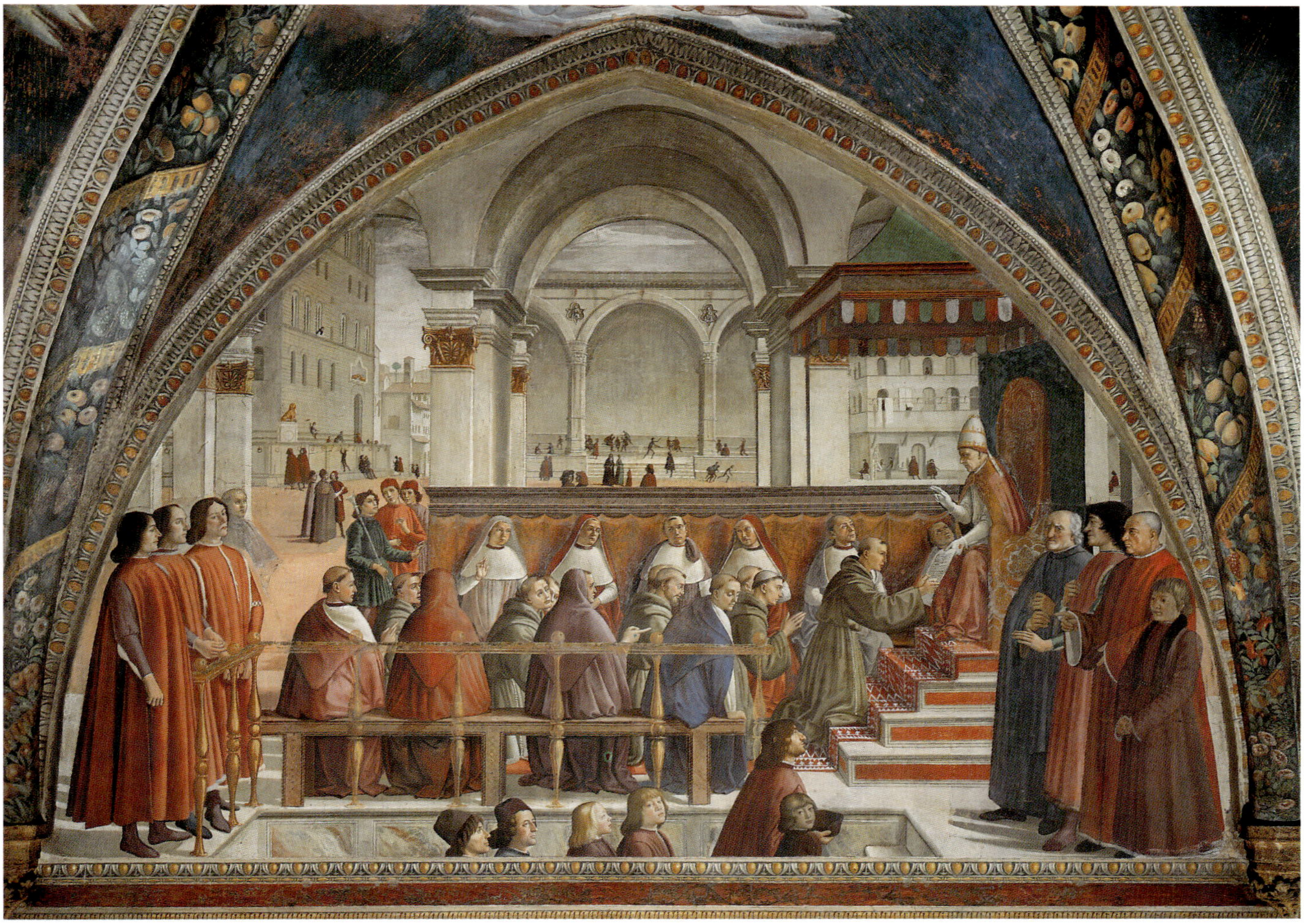 27

27. Confirmation of the Rule
Florence, Santa Trinita

cophagi of Francesco Sassetti and his wife Nera Corsi, possibly the work of Giuliano da Sangallo. In white marble, highlighted with gold and black porphyry, these beautiful sarcophagi are sculpted with all the subtlety of a cameo. On the chapel's facade, above the family's coat-of-arms in glazed terracotta of Della Robbia derivation, Ghirlandaio painted the Sibyl announcing the coming of Christ to Augustus. The prophecy would be fulfilled, as we shall see, in the
39 painted sarcophagus of the *Nativity* that Domenico executed for the altar; thus, the pagan world would gradually blend into the Christian gentleness that pervaded the stories of the saint.

The decorative scheme is traditional: on the vaults, four Sibyls between fruit garlands in vivid colours against a blue background with golden rays, a graceful rippling of pink and white layers.

Following Vasari step by step let us review and com-
3-36 ment on the "Stories of St Francis". These are the stories and miracles of the humble man of Assisi transferred to the streets of Florence. The people that witness and participate in the life of the saint are the most important citizens of the city, with their children and friends. It is a considerable section of 15th-century Florentine life and the society that lived it which unfolds in front of us. At times one has the feeling of entering into the life of the scenes, becoming part of that calm atmosphere, being one of those men of the past who are, through the ability of Domenico's paintbrush, still so alive and present.

Not all the stories are of the same artistic quality. Evidently Ghirlandaio took personal care of the scenes nearest to the spectator's eye, leaving greater freedom to his assistants in the stories higher up. Among the most famous is the one depicting the *Resurrection of* 23
the Boy of the Spini House "... In it he represented the Ponte Santa Trinita (the old one, by Taddeo Gaddi; the present one was built by Ammannati almost a hundred years later) with the palace of the Spini, the first scene showing the appearance of St Francis in the air to raise a child of that family... and other figures who are marvelling and rejoicing at the miracle, affording no little pleasure to the rest of us. Among them are portraits of Agnolo Acciaioli, Palla Strozzi..." (Vasari). The great houses look deserted, because all the inhabitants have come out to witness the calamity of the boy who has fallen from the window and, subsequently, the miracle of his resurrection. In this, as in the other stories, the life and deeds of the saint are an occasion for the painter to represent places, people and surroundings of contemporary Florence. Not for nothing were the Sassetti family connected with the Medici and the powerful bankers of the city. Not long after, the Tornabuoni family would also commission

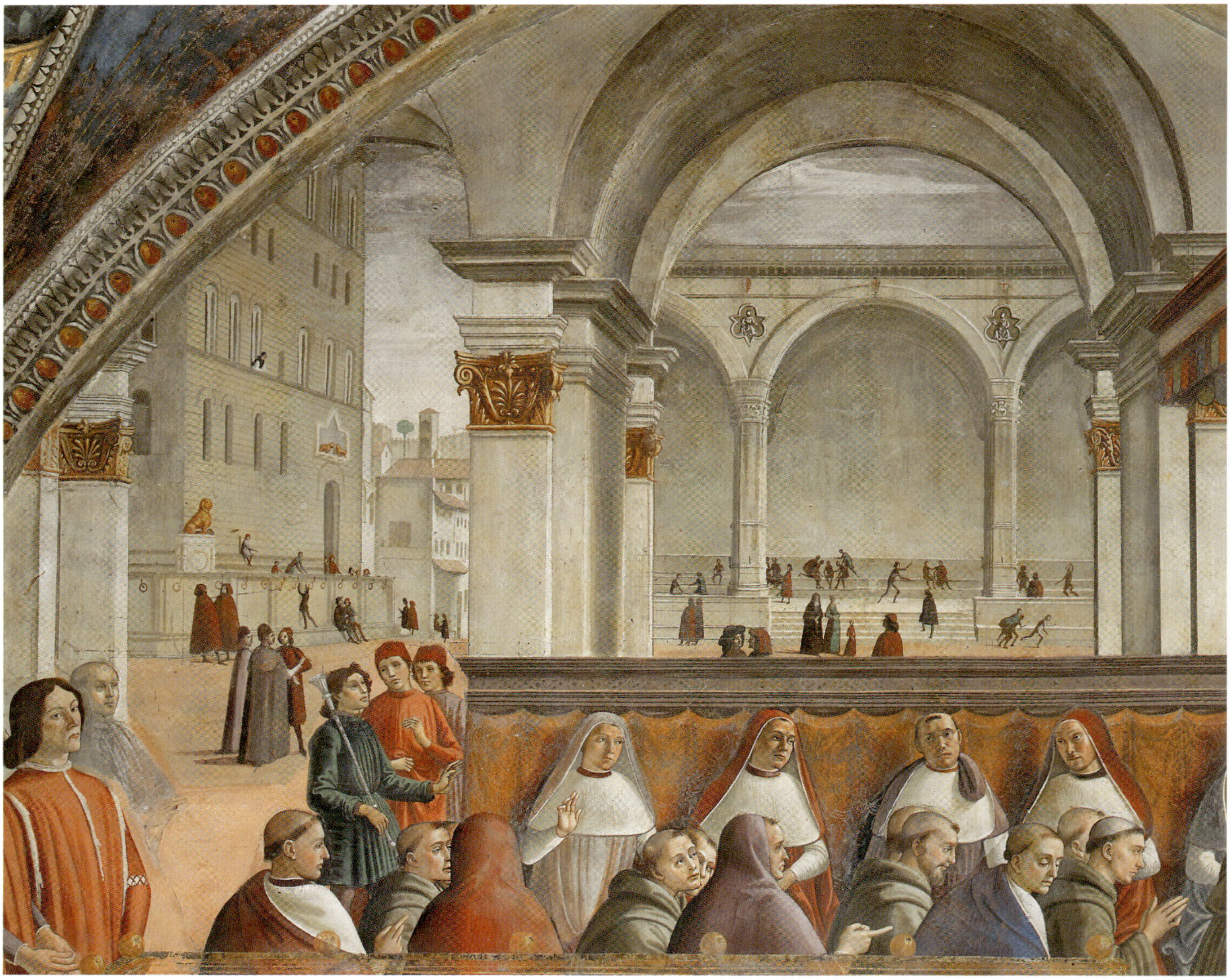

28

28. Confirmation of the Rule
detail showing Palazzo Vecchio and the Loggia dei Lanzi in the background
Florence, Santa Trinita

29. Confirmation of the Rule
detail of Agnolo Poliziano; Piero, Giovanni and Giulio de' Medici; Matteo Franco and Luigi Pulci
Florence, Santa Trinita

30. Confirmation of the Rule
detail of Antonio Pucci, Lorenzo il Magnifico, Francesco Sassetti and his son
Florence, Santa Trinita

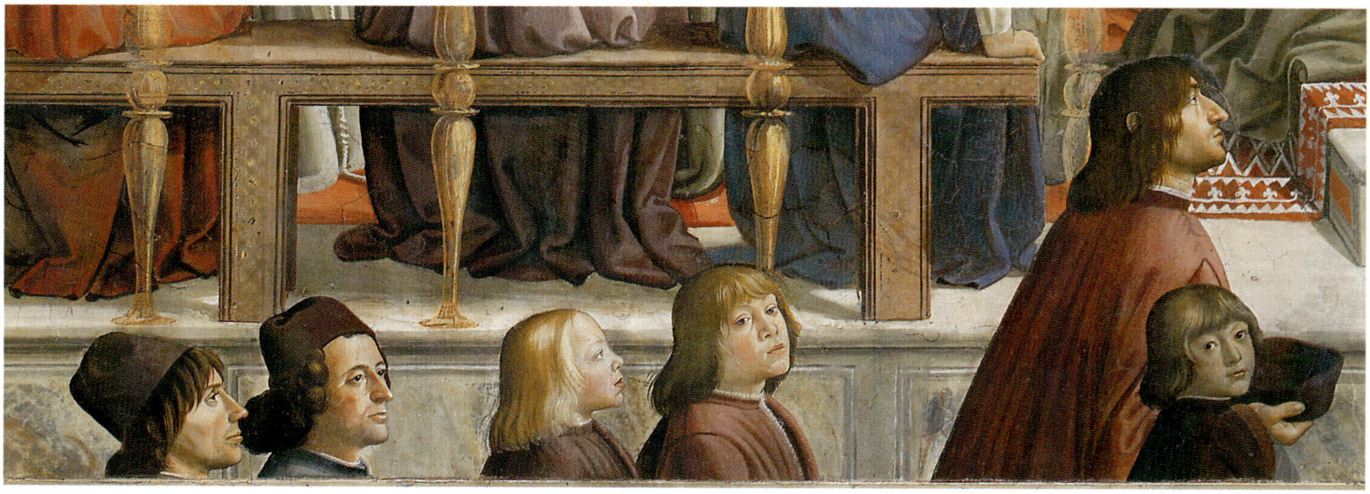

29

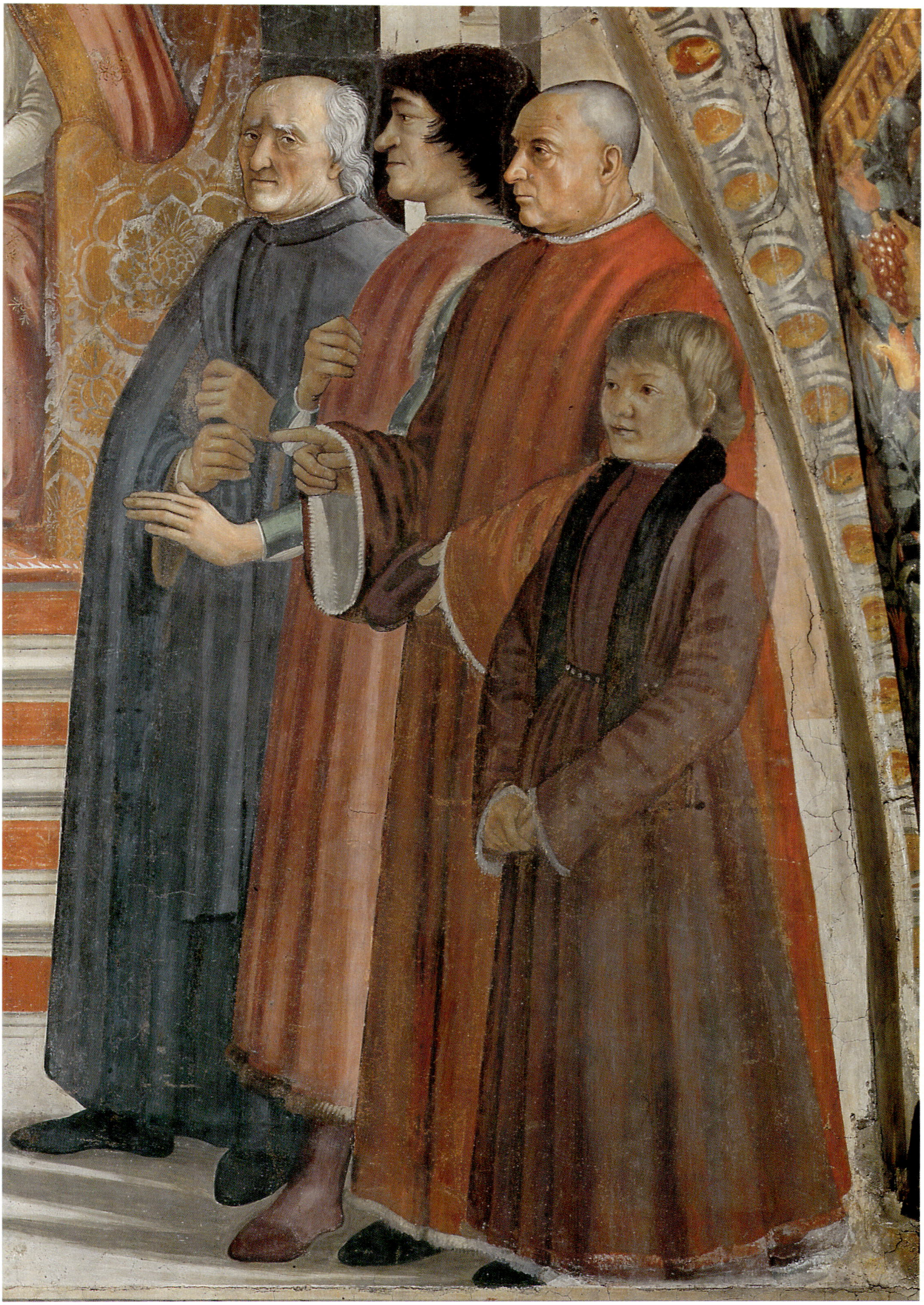

30

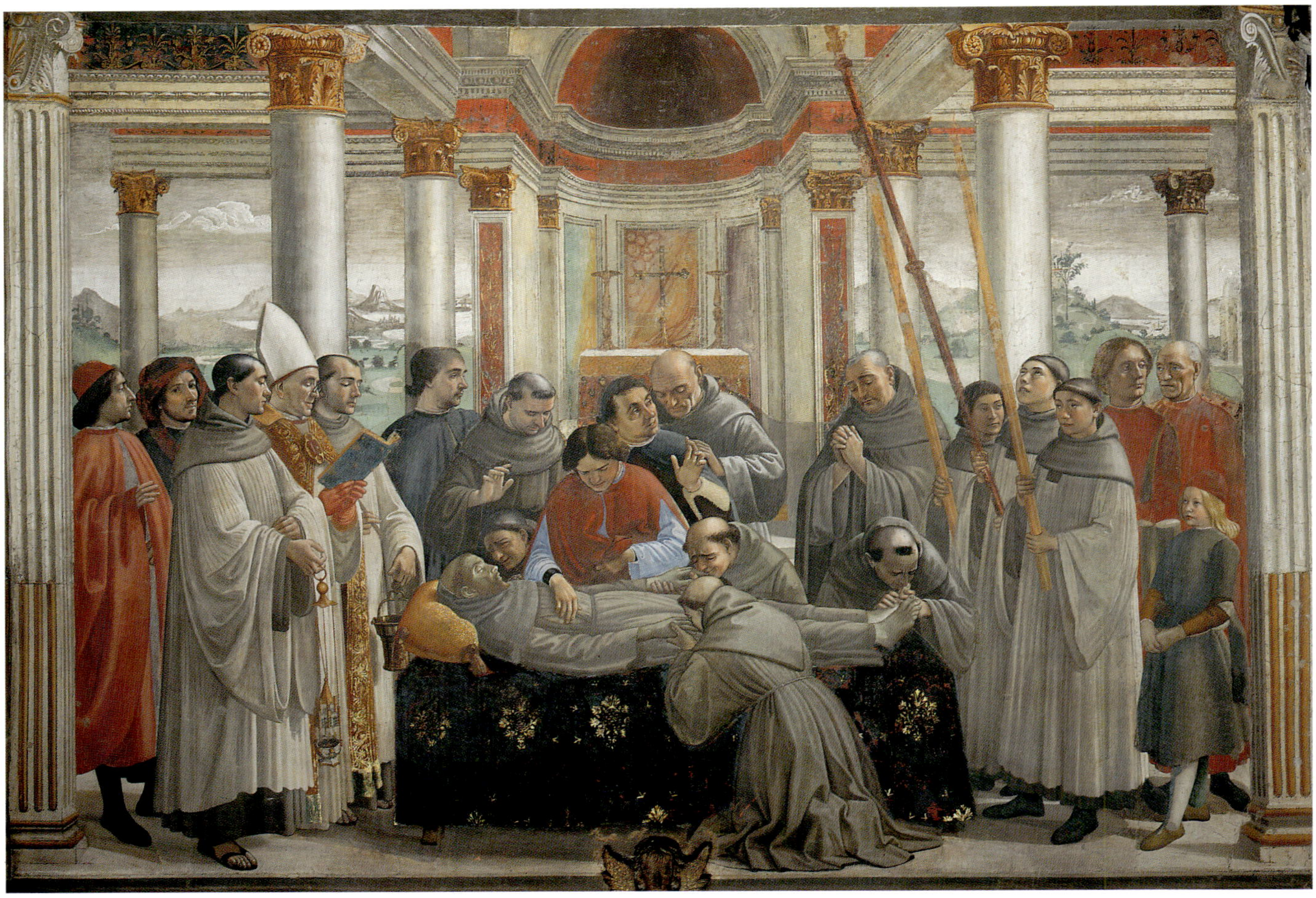
31

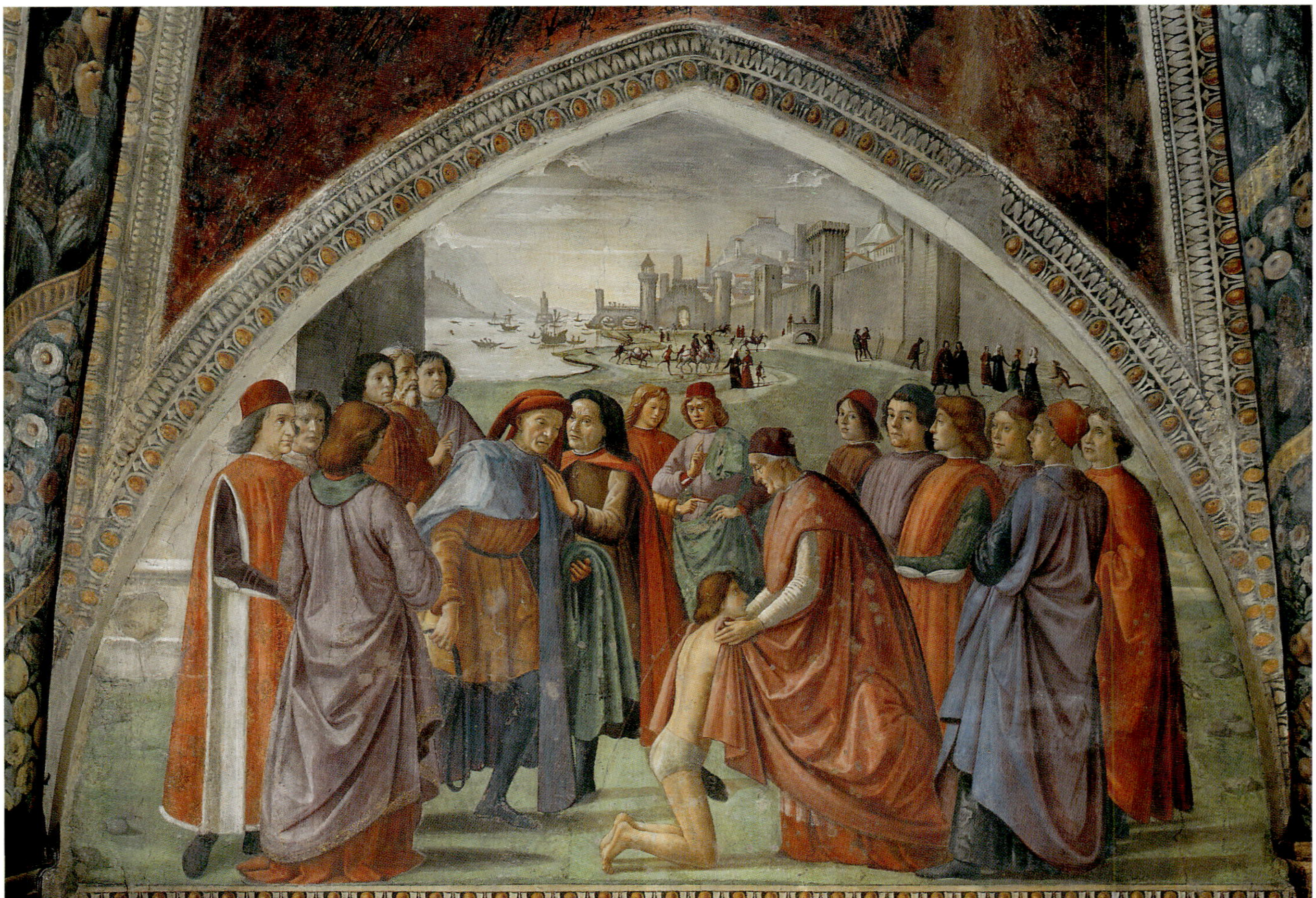
32

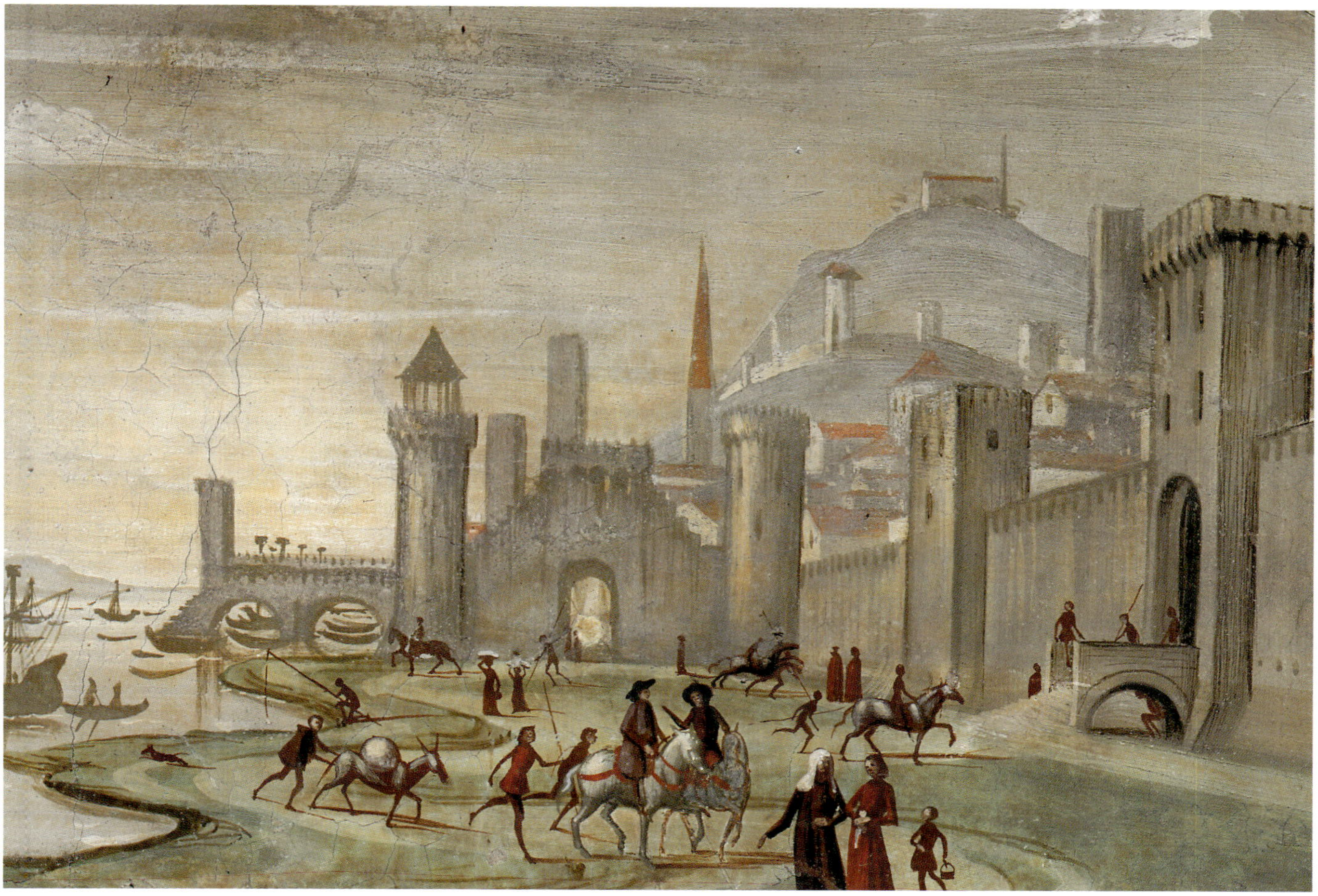
33

31. Obsequies of St Francis
Florence, Santa Trinita

32, 33. Renunciation of Worldly Goods
Florence, Santa Trinita

Ghirlandaio to paint the famous frescoes of Santa Maria Novella. Together with the people is the life of Florence. In the background of the *Resurrection of the Boy*, there are two carpenters, two small figures barely painted in who continue their work heedless of the two events; there are people running, perhaps to give word of what has happened, others riding by haughtily, and by and by the assembled group of personalities. They are in their most splendid clothes, es-
24 pecially those men and women on the left by Palazzo
25 Spini: Maso degli Albizi, possibly, Agnolo Acciaioli and Filippo Strozzi il Vecchio with their wives, sons and daughters, people who ought to be there to witness the events, but who are really posing for their portraits; friends of Francesco Sassetti who was a friend of the Medici. On the other side, just in front of
26 the church with its old facade, there are humbler figures, possibly even rich bourgeois townsfolk not yet at the top of the social scale. The group of three youngsters in the centre, with their headgear and clothes coloured in red, is vital, animated, pleasing. The two kneeling monks in their soft grey cassocks, probably from the nearby Vallombrosan convent, are not well-known enough for Vasari to mention their names, but they are as real and alive as two figures in the flesh.

Florence appears again, this time in its most impor-
tant square, in the *Confirmation of the Franciscan* 27
Rule by Pope Honorius III; this time the Medici family are also present, honouring Sassetti. "... In the middle is his visit to Rome to obtain the confirmation of his order from pope Honorius, presenting a rose to that pontiff in January...". In the centre is the consistory hall decorated with gold drapes, and with prelates and personages witnessing the pope's blessing, "... with cardinals seated about it, and some steps approaching it on which are figures standing, among them being
a portrait of Lorenzo de' Medici the Magnificent, the 30
elder". Lorenzo is easily recognizable, his profile rendered unhandsome by that squashed nose which deprived him (and his mother) of any sense of taste or smell and meant that he always spoke hoarsely, and his olive-complexioned face framed by a brown shock of rather shaggy hair. Lorenzo had been ruler of Florence since 1469, but had never left the family palace in Via Larga for Palazzo Vecchio. He was above all the great patron of architects, sculptors, painters and poets (being a poet himself). He was, moreover, such an able politician, succeeding in maintaining a masterly balance between Venice and Milan, the Papacy and the Kingdom of Naples, that he was called the needle of the scales of Italy. To his right is Antonio Pucci, now somewhat advanced in years, and Francesco Sassetti

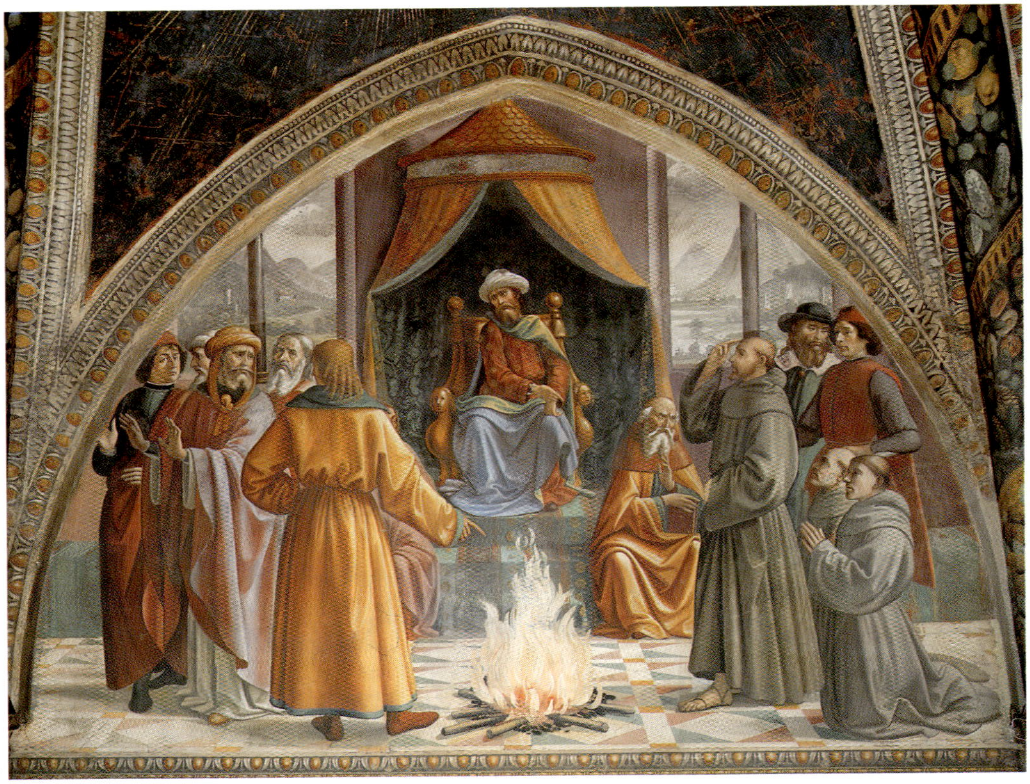

34

34. *Test of Fire before the Sultan*
Florence, Santa Trinita

35, 36. *Stigmata of St Francis and detail of Mount Verna*
Florence, Santa Trinita

dressed in red; his young son Teodoro is by his side. Coming up the steps with their tutor are Lorenzo's two
29 elder sons, Piero and Giovanni, and with them Giulio, the orphan of Giuliano who was killed in the Pazzi conspiracy, with their blond mops of hair, the solemn face of the former and the rather vague expression of the other who follows. Their tutor is Agnolo Poliziano, a man of letters, the composer of the 'Stanze', and a friend of Lorenzo who honoured him in his house; he who taught Italian and Latin to the Medici boys and had them learn Virgil by heart. We know this from the eldest, Piero, who wrote to his father: "I have learnt many verses by Virgil and I know almost the whole book of Theodore by heart and think I understand it. The maestro makes me practise verbs and examines me every day". All that poetry would be of little use to the young Piero, who shortly after Lorenzo's death in 1494 bloodlessly surrendered Florence to Charles VIII, thus decreeing an exile of eighteen years for his family. Piero would later die by drowning in the Garigliano in 1503.

The three boys are with Matteo Franco, the kinder and more favoured tutor, whose descriptions with the pen accompany Domenico's paint-brush that lingers with such affectionate care on the pinkish, childlike features: Piero was "as fresh and vital as a rose, kind, clean and clear as a mirror and always contemplative...". The same precision is repeated by Ghirlandaio in the sharp profile of Franco's sworn enemy, Luigi Pulci, a caustic and irreverent character whose soul was imbued with a violent laical paganism. Harsh, bitter, poor and melancholy, he was protected mainly by Lucrezia Tornabuoni. In the background is
28 Florence, with its most celebrated buildings: the Loggia dell'Orcagna, the facade of Palazzo Vecchio with its solemn raised podium that was later replaced by the present-day flight of steps; the gilded Marzocco lion (symbol of Florentine democracy); a back-drop of houses in the far left-hand corner and a bell-tower (possibly that of San Piero Scheraggio) where the Uffizi would later be built. In the background is a bustling of small figures, citizens and curious onlookers, possibly an opening and closing of shutters and, in places, a glimmering of gold in the capitals and arch of the consistory hall. A faint clear light passes over the soft colours, mellowing even the severity of the stones in the distant buildings. It is the history of Florence, fixed for ever, that passes by and comes to rest in front of us.

"He further painted there St Francis receiving the 35
stigmata, and finally his death and the lamentation of 31
the friars, one of them represented kissing his hand..." (Vasari) and another his feet, and the incredulous Girolamo, dressed in red, who looks for the wound in his chest. To the left are the arrayed clergy and the mitred Bishop (with spectacles) reading the De Profundis. The scene is a veritable swaying of thuribles and stoups. To the right is the Franciscan Order in all its simplicity, and with its kindly, somewhat rustic-looking monks. The church in the background has a sober appearance, though it gives on to a Tuscan countryside lush with rivers and streams. Here too, lesser-known characters are portrayed, undoubtedly either the monks of the nearby church of Ognissanti, so dear to Domenico, or those of Santa Trinita. Ghirlandaio had certainly been to see Giotto's fresco in Santa Croce, since he has used the same composition and distribution of masses in this scene. Indeed, the teachings of Giotto, and his style, must not be forgotten. But here, once again, Domenico is more joyful

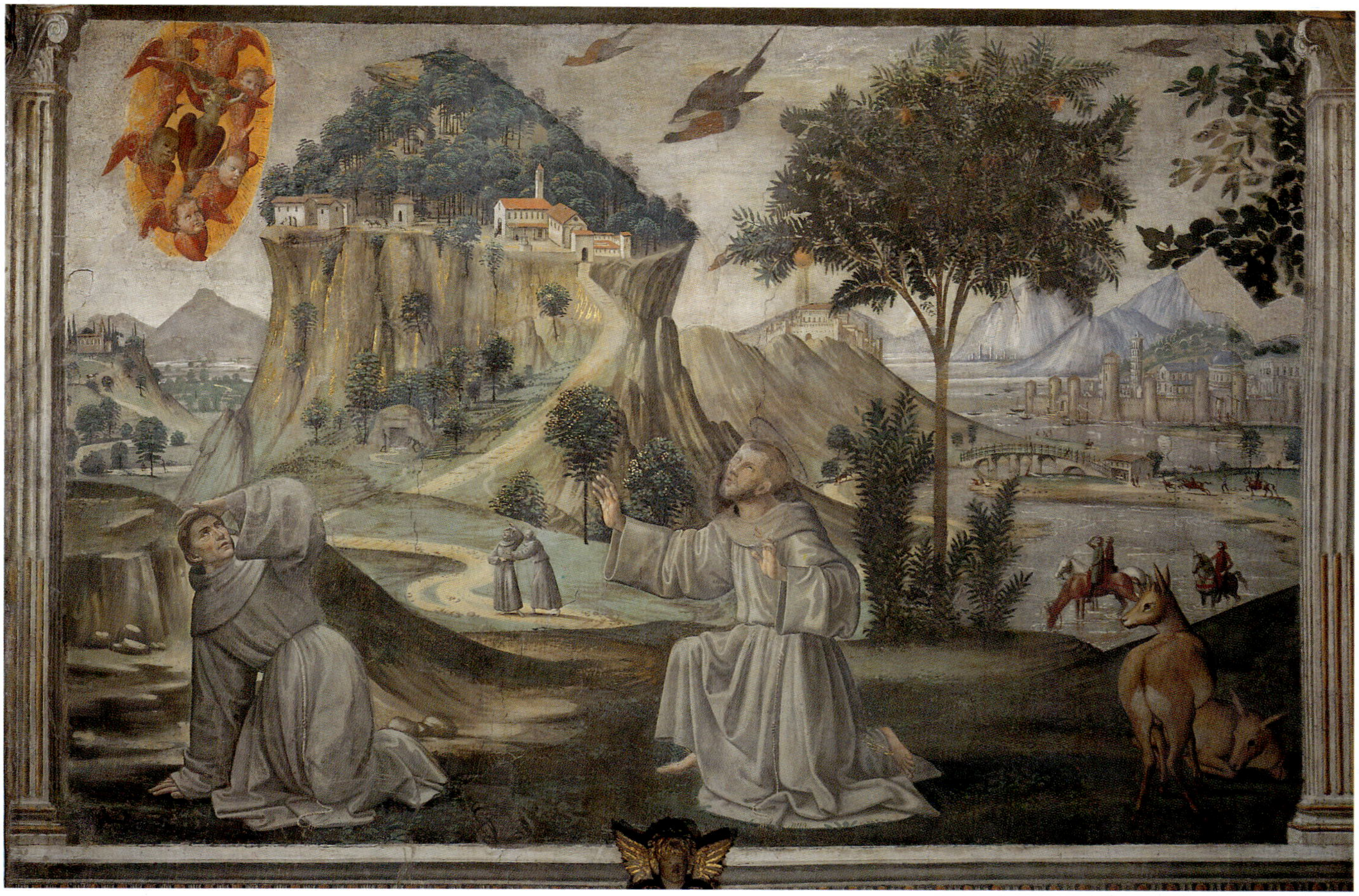 35

and serene. The drama of the event is far from the mind and soul of Ghirlandaio, who is however more present here than critics are wont to believe. The delicate touches of grey and white can only be his. His too is the light that streams over the faces, that gives a warm serenity and infinite peace to the countenance of Francis, motionless in death, and that falls on the gilded yellow of the pillow, on the reds and blues, and on the white clouds in the sky. There is almost a country atmosphere about it, an air of church-square festivity, and there is a masterly touch in the interplay of carefully spaced hands, which assume an almost musical quality through Domenico's artistry. The other stories, which are higher up and further from view,
32 were probably left to his assistants: the *Renunciation*
34 *of Worldly Goods*, the *Test of Fire before the Sultan*
35 and the *Stigmata*. But even here the master's hand and eye return: in a facial expression, in the delicacy of certain effects of light, in a distant landscape, or in some ecstatic abandonment.

At the sides of the altar Ghirlandaio painted full-
38 length portraits of his patron Francesco Sassetti, and
37 his wife Nera. "In two pictures on either side he painted Francesco Sassetti kneeling, and Madonna Nera, his wife and her children, the latter being in the scene above where the boy is raised to life, with some beautiful maidens of the same family" (Vasari). The images are drawn with tight, harsh lines, which contrast rather with the soft lines of the narrated stories. Here we see a recourse to that Flemish taste for a studied reality that is faithful to the subject and makes no concession to imagination or ornamentation. Sassetti is dressed in red with his hands clasped together, his loose-skinned face severe, and his shaven head standing out against the bare splendour of a room faced with marble. Beyond the altar is the corresponding figure of Nera Corsi, who is dressed in black and has her head covered by a simple white cloth, a Florentine usage of the period (especially in the privacy of the home) among women who were no longer young. Her sharp, intense features, which bear traces of a former beauty, are certainly far nobler and more sensitive than her husband's. We see here a couple brought together by long years of communal life and interests linked to the family, patrimony and the house, a couple satisfied with their own well-being and their social position among the most important citizens of the city.

At the base is the painted inscription: *A.D. MCCCCLXXX. XV decembris*. This could be the initial date of the work whose conclusion is in the great altarpiece with the *Nativity*, dated 1485. "He painted 39
in tempera, as a companion to this work, a Nativity of Christ which must excite the wonder of every thinking man, introducing his own portrait and some heads of shepherds, which are considered divine" (Vasari). This work is certainly one of the artist's masterpieces. In it he completes his interpretation of the Sibyl's prophecy to Augustus, in the very inscription on the old sarcophagus that serves as a manger for the ox and ass: *Ense cadens. Solymo. Pompei Pulvi[us] Augur Numen. Ait. Quae me conteg[it] Urna Dabit.* [While Fulvi(us), augur of Pompey, was falling by the

36
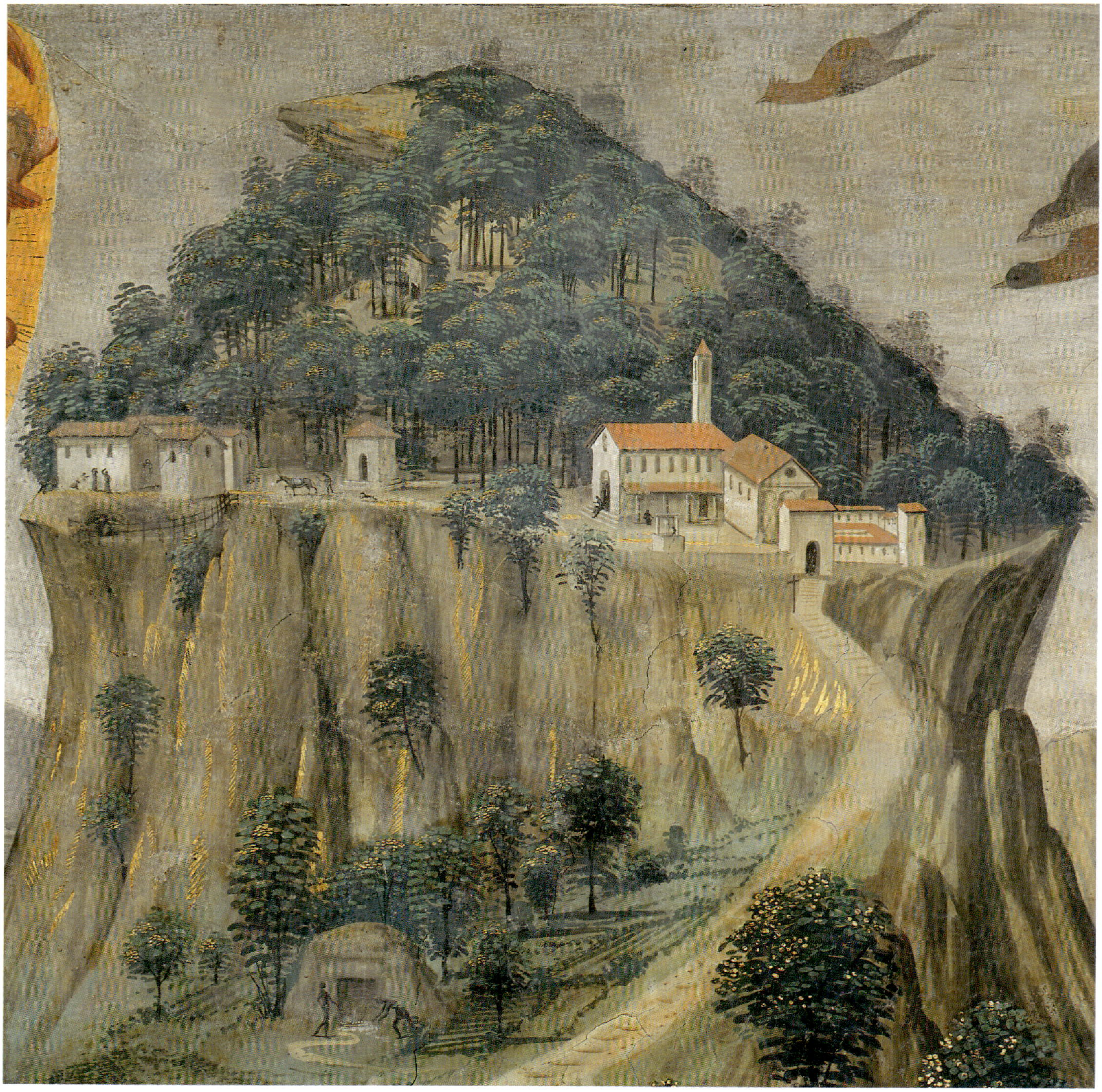

sword in Jerusalem he said: the urn that covers (conceals) me shall bring forth a god]. Thus, Jesus had his first cradle in the old sarcophagus. Here, perhaps, Ghirlandaio expresses the best of himself as a painter, poet and pious man. Re-emerging in his art, one by one, we notice his most distant and most immediate experiences, which are all surpassed and harmonized, though transformed through his sensitivity that now reaches its peak. With its own peculiar vibration, the classical world comes to life in the background pilasters, which seem to bear traces not of ancient Greece or Rome, but of Brunelleschi and the great theorist Leon Battista Alberti. This is Rome, the memory of a Rome which is transformed in the fanciful narrating that is reminiscent of a Benozzo Gozzoli become more eventful and animated. In the same way

37, 38. Nera Corsi and Francesco Sassetti
Florence, Santa Trinita

the long procession that winds along the sloping road 40
reminds us of the one in the *Adoration* which Gentile da Fabriano had painted for Santa Trinita sixty years earlier. In its rather disconnected and episodic progress it also recalls the procession that appears in Mantegna's *Adoration of the Magi*, now in the Uffizi. The Magi are still far away and St Joseph, shielding his eyes with a hand and attracted by voices and noises that rather distract him from his adoration, seeks to foretell their arrival. Mary, utterly absorbed as she is by her tender Child, is not distracted. As we have already said, the sarcophagus, manger and cradle, with its

37 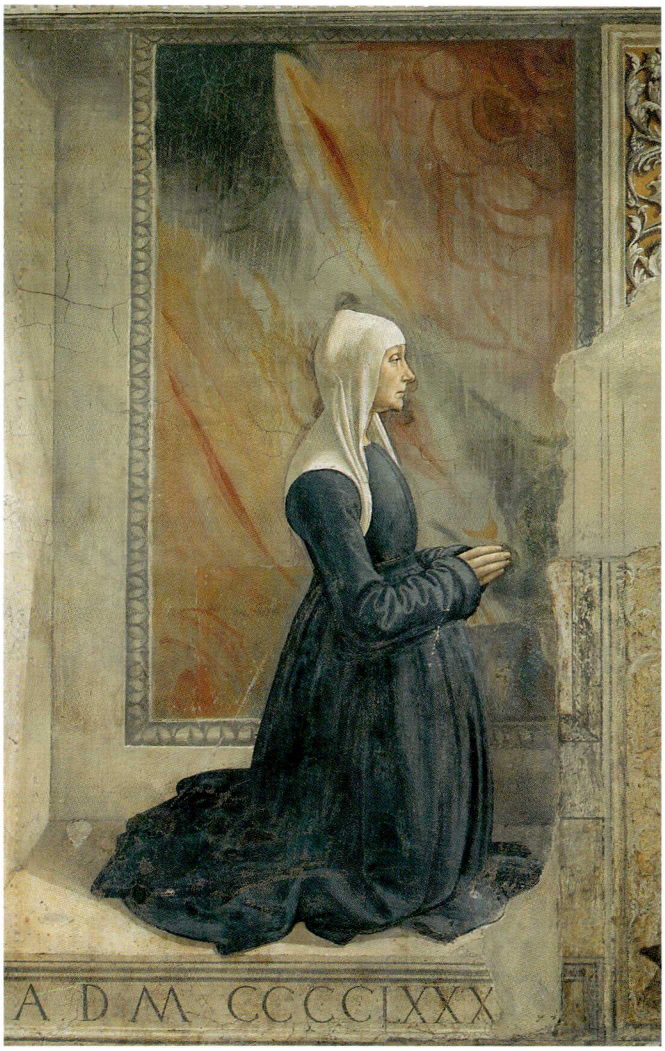

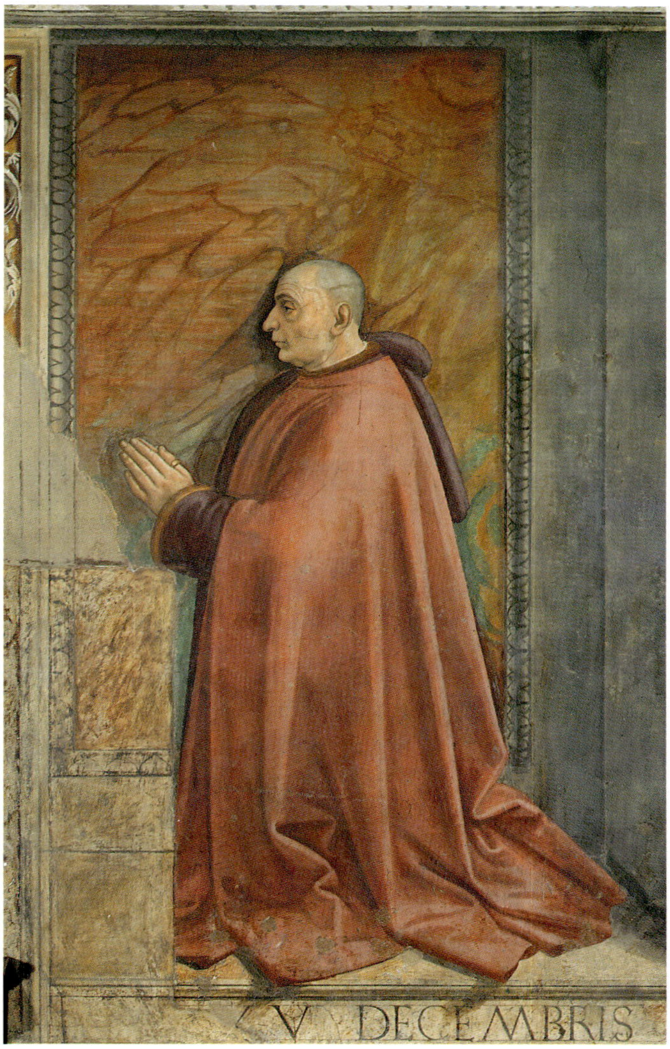 38

embossed festoon so very reminiscent of Donatello and Luca and Andrea Della Robbia, is a classical element. In the distance is a town set in the midst of hills and woods that in appearance would seem to be more Northern than Tuscan. Here there is clearly a fresh reminder of Flemish art, especially that of Hugo van der Goes. The latter had arrived in Florence seven years before, in 1478, and with great ceremony the triptych that the Flemish master had executed in Bruges for Tommaso Portinari, the agent of the Medici Bank in that town, was placed on the altar in the church of Sant'Egidio. This great triptych, now at the Uffizi, is the masterpiece of Flemish art in Florence. In the central panel is the Adoration of the Shepherds, while in the two side panels are Saints James and Thomas with Tommaso Portinari and his two sons, and Saints Mary Magdalen and Margaret with Maria Portinari and her daughter Margaret. This painting, placed between the frescoes of Domenico Veneziano, Piero della Francesca and Alesso Baldovinetti, in an almost deliberate and affected contrast between the two schools, almost immediately became the wonder of the city.

This work in particular, and the innovations that were consequent upon it, influenced a whole generation of Florentine artists, including Sandro Botticelli though perhaps above all Filippino Lippi and Domenico Ghirlandaio. The latter two painters discovered in this new style an assidously observed reality, landscapes studied in detail, and people represented without giving way to the adulation of a non-existent beauty but rather with an attention directed at the soul, at the feeling that showed through in them. Hugo van der Goes' group of adoring shepherds, for example, returns in Ghirlandaio's *Adoration* with very obvious similarities. And yet there is no doubt that there is a difference in the physical culture of the people: Ghirlandaio's shepherds, who at the angel's announcement have just left the fields dressed in old work-clothes with picks and hoes, are more comely. Before arriving at the manger they have been home to put on cleaner clothes; their appearance, faces and expressions are less rough, breathless and astonished. There is more tender adoration in them than wonder, and although they have the posture and gestures of simple folk they are certainly anything but coarse.

The first shepherd, kneeling down, is Ghirlandaio 1
himself. He has portrayed himself for the first time, with his hair and black beard well-kept, his face serene, "... introducing his own portrait" as Vasari puts it. But most striking for the genuineness of his expression and completeness is the old man standing be-

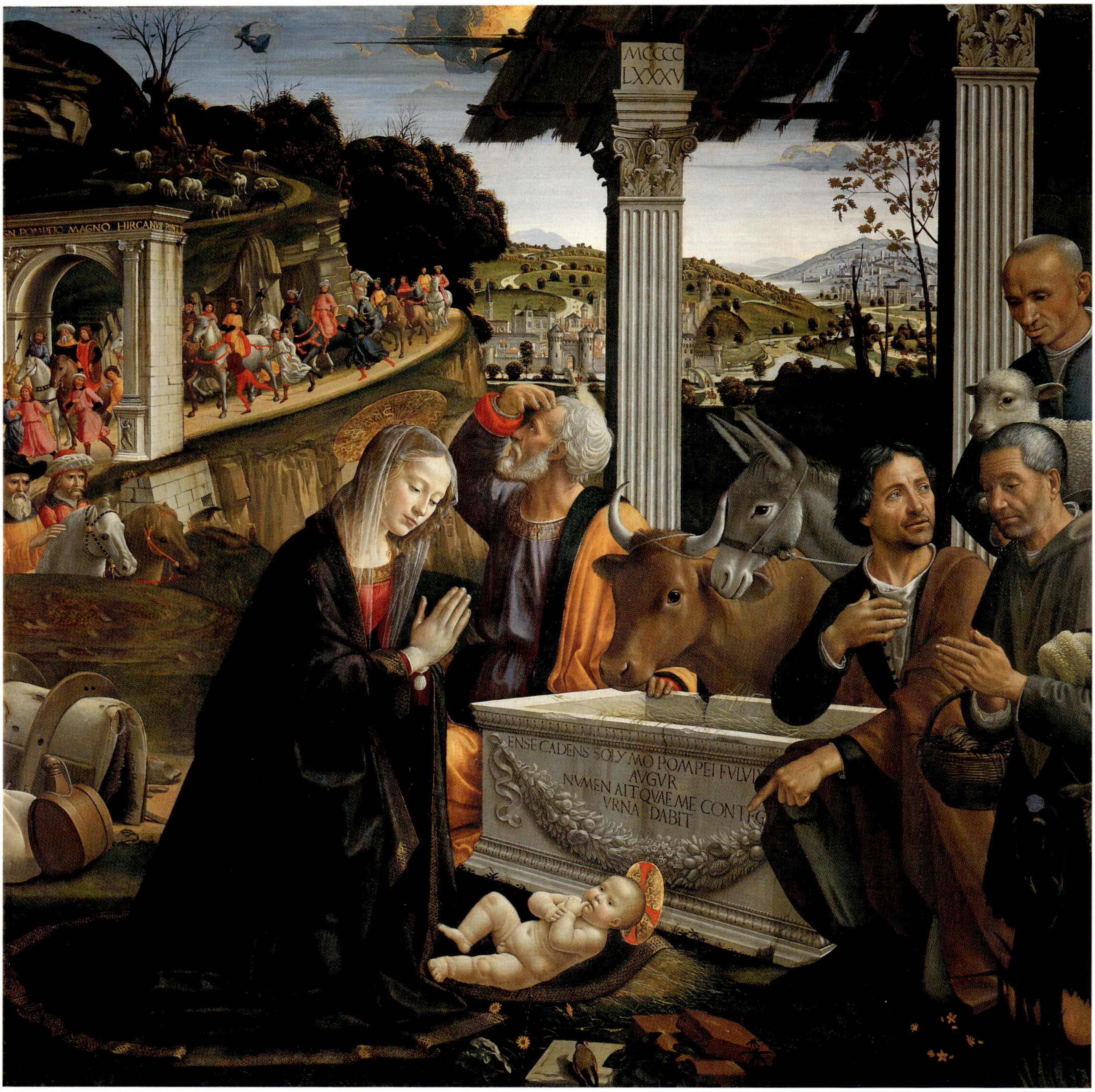

39

hind, who has the simple, honest appearance of a Tuscan peasant, his sharp, good-natured face lightened by his almost shaven-looking white hair. It looks almost as if he is commenting on the event in a low voice.

The reality of small details is there, in the saddle of the ass, lying on the ground near to a basket. A short time before the ass had been carrying it, with its precious load of Mary, in search of a refuge where her Child might be brought into the world. Now accompanied by a providential ox, the ass is warming the newborn Child with its breath. The calm, pensive young Virgin, is absorbed in rapt adoration. We have said that everything in Ghirlandaio's work always appears calm, and invites us to reflect on the serenity of his soul; even the air is peaceful, with the light of the setting sun that illumines and warms the scene. We do not feel the winter, but rather the suggestion of a prolonged autumnal warmth. There are a few bare trees in the background, another vibrant reminiscence of Van der Goes, but the landscape is alive, covered with the green of the meadows and bushes where a flock is grazing. There is a lake in the distance and gentle hills on the far horizon. The foreground is dominated by Mary's large blue gold-edged cloak that falls loosely in soft folds and lightly touches a patch of flowered grass that is undoubtedly of Botticellian inspiration.

Ghirlandaio's *Nativity* does in fact date to 1485; Sandro Botticelli had painted his *Primavera* around 1478. Domenico never refused to acknowledge the sources of his artistic culture, nor would he have wished to

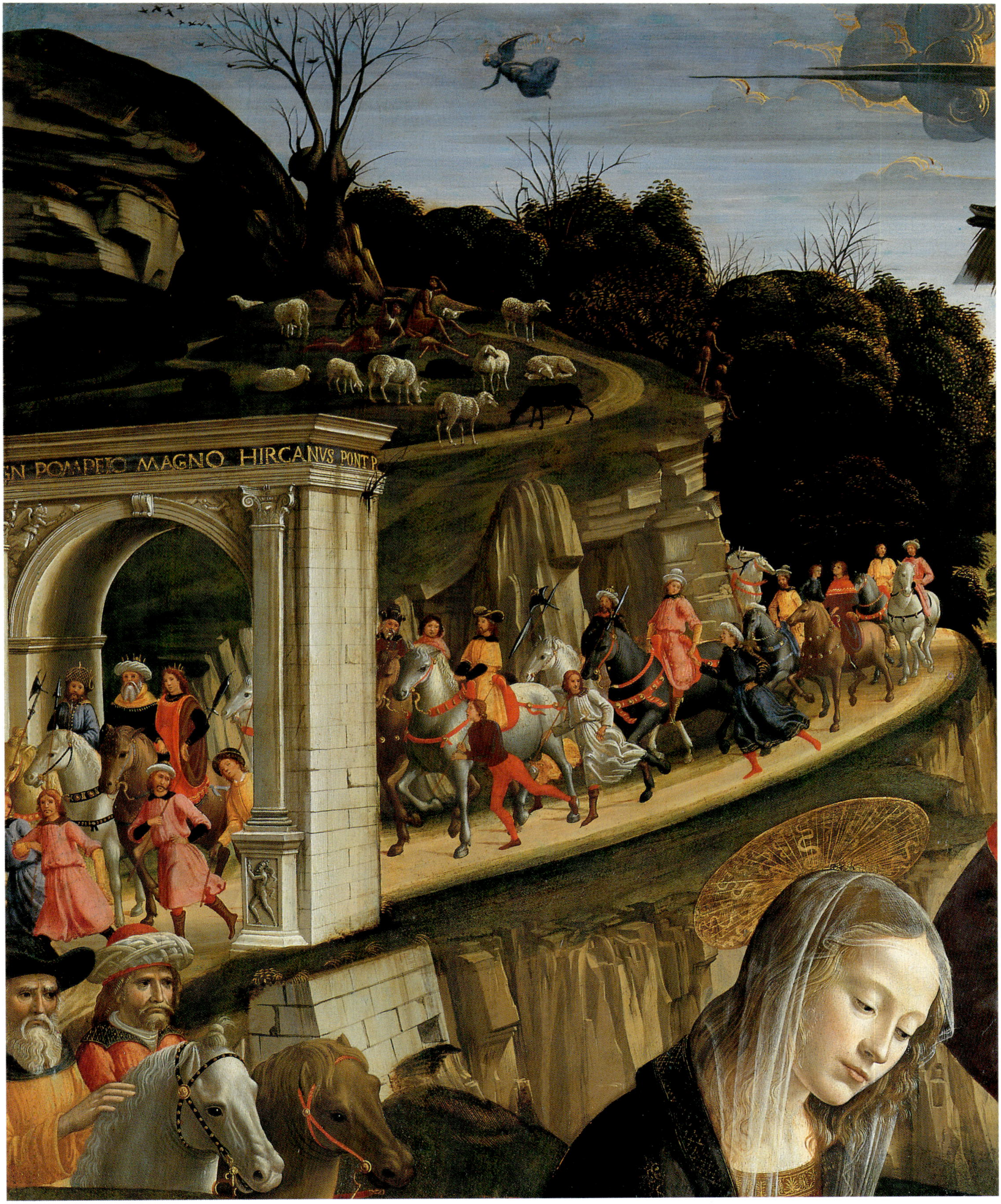

40

39. Nativity
167x167 cm
Florence, Santa Trinita

40. Nativity, detail
Florence, Santa Trinita

negate them. Rather than weighing on him, he felt them by right. Another aspect about Ghirlandaio that has not perhaps been fully emphasized is his piety. This is particularly evident in the *Nativity* which, at first sight, might be a pastoral scene were it not for the light radiating from the Child, for Mary's expression, and for that peculiar air that circulates and streams everywhere over people and objects. Here, in the all-pervading calm, in the absence of every tension, we discover Ghirlandaio's religious faith and the serenity of his soul, expressed without intellectual complication or consequence, in the joy of his colours, the ease of his lines and his participation in events, all of which, even the most dramatic and mysterious, become for him a reason for tranquil acceptance and, almost, the joy of narrating and living his narrations. In him and in his work, birth is serene, death peaceful and sweet. Even in his *Last Suppers* there is a kind of melancholic serenity; it would appear that he never confronted the tragedy of Golgotha.

The Tornabuoni Chapel

By this time Ghirlandaio was famous, possibly the most famous and most highly sought-after painter in Florence. He was popular among men of culture and wealth because he painted them and their families in the most splendid way, as well as the city which through them was embellished and therefore continued to be one of the most important cultural and economic centres in Europe. He was popular with the common people who flocked to see his works in which their own lives were brought to life, the events of the city and its most illustrious characters, the most beautiful women, and possibly even someone of their own acquaintance, a neighbour or the artisan of the workshop nearby. It is rather like us today who, through his painted chronicles, come to know not so much the miracles of St Francis and the stories of St John the Baptist and the Virgin, but that remote Florence - in part similar to our own, but purer, more vivid and more intact - and all its unknown inhabitants who resemble heroes, and those celebrated figures portrayed from life and therefore real and present forever.

In 1486 Giovanni Tornabuoni, who had been portrayed in the Sistine Chapel fresco, turned to Domenico Ghirlandaio for the decoration in fresco of the great chapel of his family in Santa Maria Novella. The story of the decoration of the choir in the great Florentine basilica is a long one, and is narrated in detail by Vasari. "It happened that the principal chapel of Santa Maria Novella, the convent of the Friars Preachers, had been already painted by Andrea Orcagna, but the roof of the vaulting being badly protected, it was almost entirely destroyed by the damp". Many Florentines were eager to have it restored and had come forward to take the expense upon themselves. But the patrons of the chapel, the Ricci family, who were themselves unable to finance such an important project, had never come to an agreement. "Giovanni [Tornabuoni], being anxious that Domenico should paint this memorial for him, tried various expedients, and at last promised the Ricci that he would bear the entire cost, would recompense them in some way, and would have their arms put up in the most prominent and honourable part of the chapel". The agreement was reached and Giovanni undersigned the contract with Domenico Ghirlandaio for the execution of the frescoes; "... arranging that the price should be 1200 gold ducats, and if it should give satisfaction, 200 more". The contract was drawn up in Latin, dated 1 September 1485, and signed by Giovanni Tornabuoni, *civis et mercator florentinus*, and by the brothers Domenico and David Ghirlandaio. It is certainly a highly interesting document, for it provides an insight into the relations between client and artist.

Tornabuoni was a man whose wealth, power and noble descent ensured his position at the side of the Medici, even before close links of kinship joined the two families. His social standing was considerably superior to that of Francesco Sassetti, who was in fact always rather dependent on the Medici Bank. Giovanni's sister, Lucrezia, had married Piero dei Medici, becoming thus the daughter-in-law of Cosimo il Vecchio and the mother of Lorenzo il Magnifico. Therefore, by virtue of this well-born woman of great moral and intellectual power, "more man than men" as Cosimo was wont to say, Giovanni was the uncle of Lorenzo il Magnifico. Tornabuoni was also a powerful figure in Rome - Papal Treasurer and Head of the Medici Bank - and between Rome and Florence he divided his life. As a man of culture he was an open-minded patron. In Florence he had wanted his palace to be built in the same style as the Medici palace in Via Larga, it too possibly designed by Michelozzo. In the contract with the two Ghirlandaio brothers he was very clear in indicating what he wanted. All the stories of the frescoes were planned with stubborn exactitude; furthermore, he wanted there to be columns, pilasters and capitals of marble embellished with gold, and the artist was employed to paint "... figures, buildings, horses, birds and beasts of all kinds...". Already from the draft of

41, 42. Stories of the Virgin: Expulsion of Joachim from the Temple and detail showing Domenico Ghirlandaio, Alesso Baldovinetti and David Ghirlandaio (2nd, 3rd and 4th figures from right) Florence, Santa Maria Novella

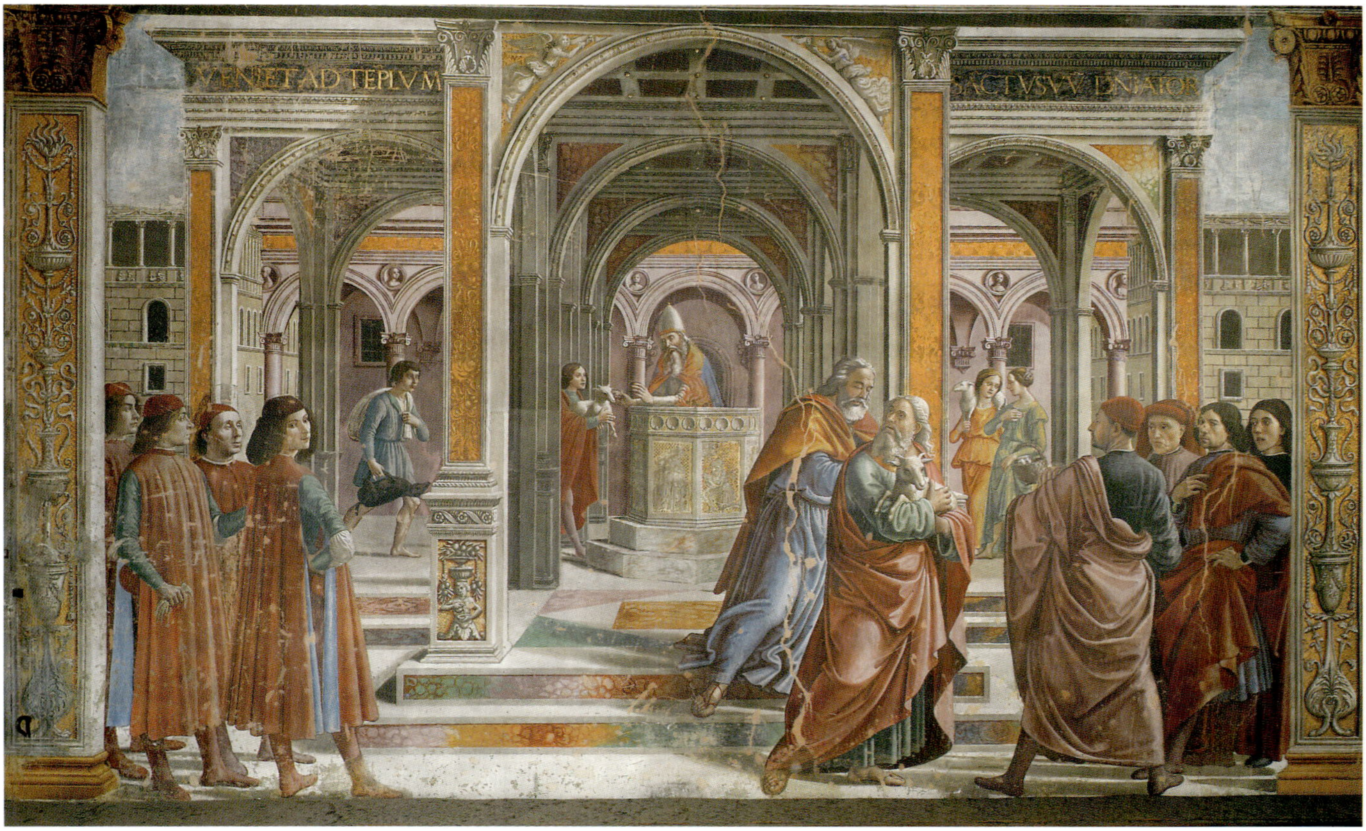

41

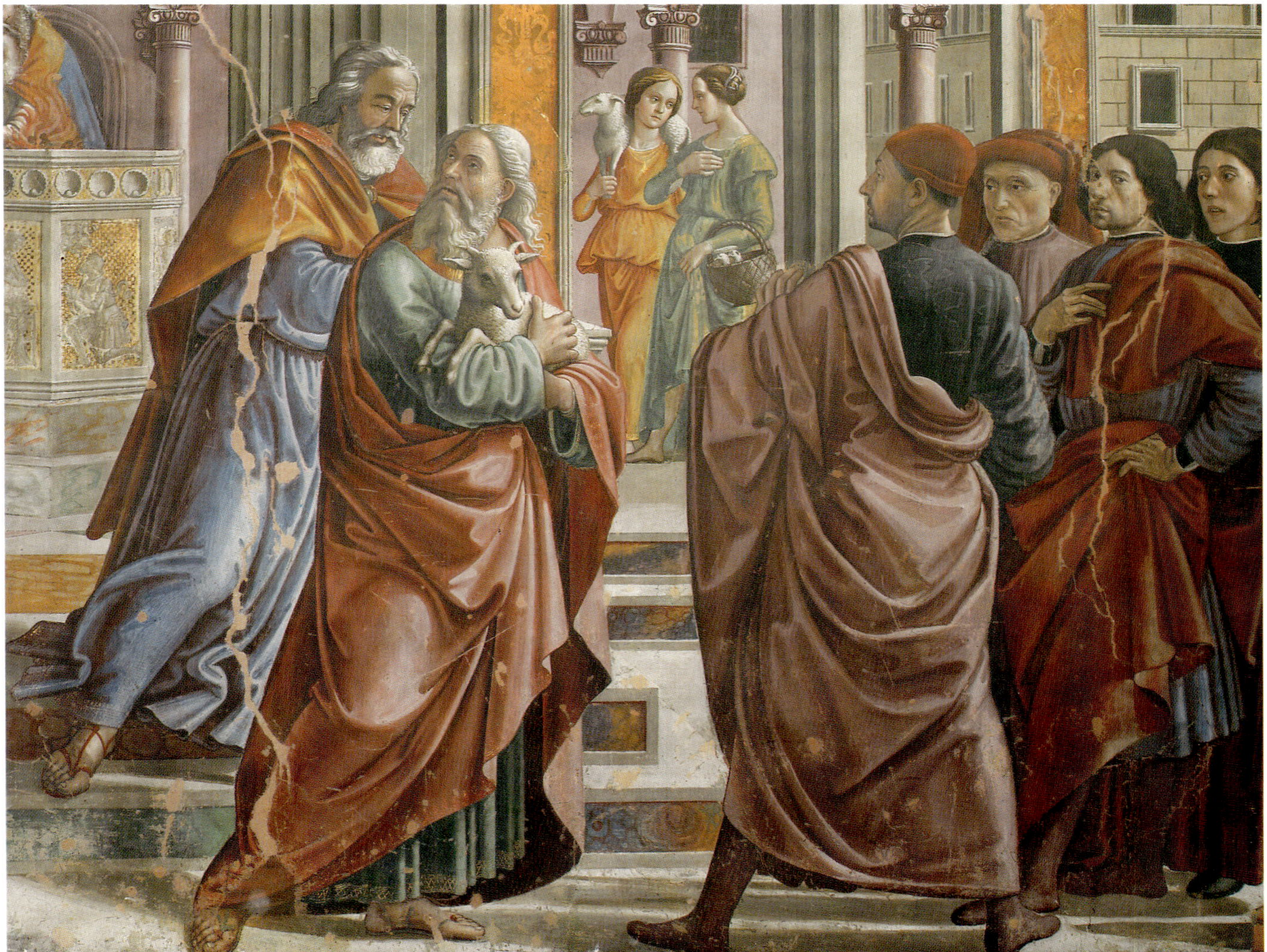

42

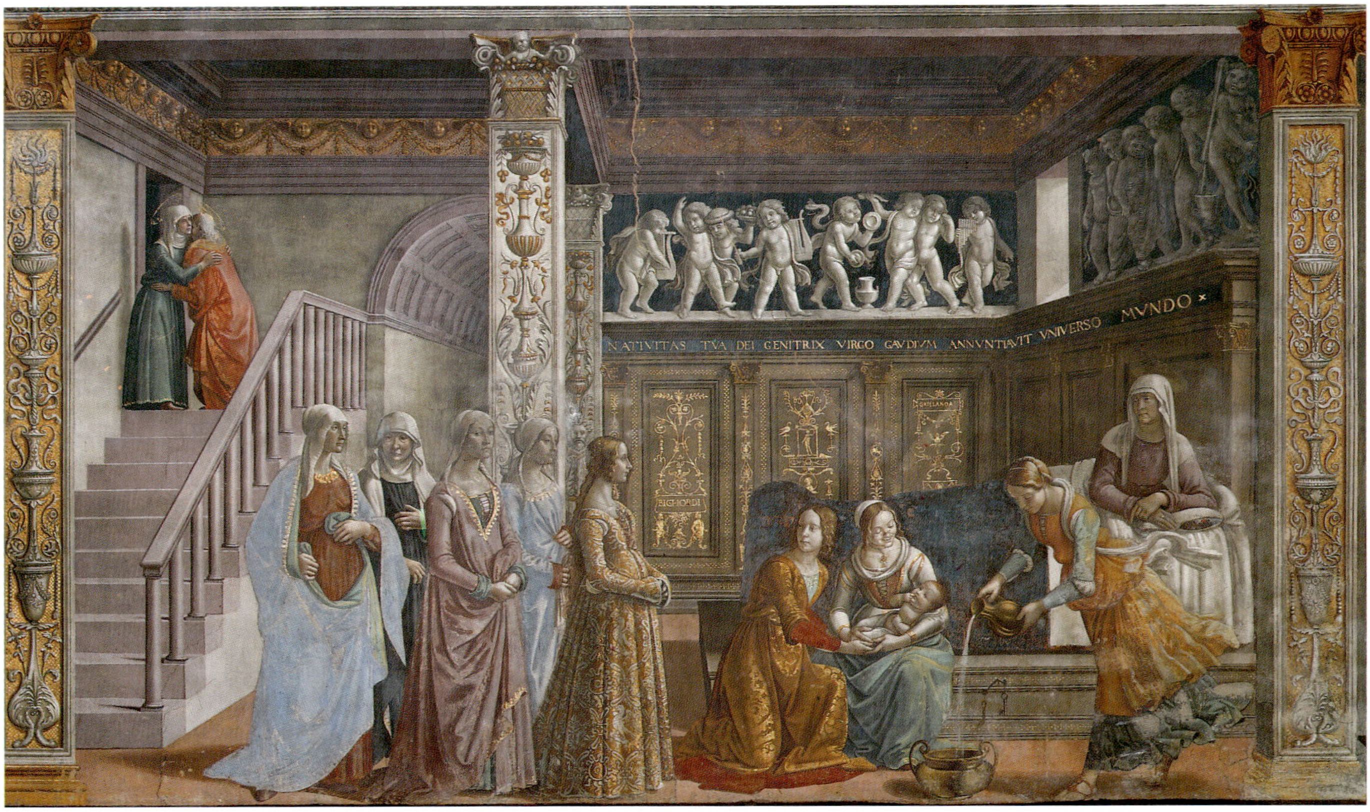

43

43, 44. Stories of the Virgin: Birth of Mary
Florence, Santa Maria Novella

the contract it becomes clear that Ghirlandaio had to enlarge his scale, amplify the reach of his spaces, and find a variety of movements and expressions that now became a whole world, the more vivid and select world of the city. At the same time he had to call on all his technical, cultural and figurative experience in order to give life to stories that would be living pages in the Florentine Chronicle. And it was not the offer of the huge sum, further increased by Giovanni, that spurred Domenico to work so well. "... Domenico, who thought more of glory than of wealth, at once forgave him the extra amount, declaring that he was better pleased at having satisfied him than he could be with any payment that he might receive" (Vasari).

Perhaps something of the former programme was changed, especially in the subjects of the stories, which were not those that had already been painted by Orcagna; but the details requested - "buildings... robes... animals, birds and beasts..." - were all there. The painter's imagination was faithful to the contract and even surpassed it. He introduced a giraffe, for example, possibly the one (the gift of a sultan) that wandered around in the gardens of Lorenzo il Magnifico and died by hitting its head against an architrave, as well as the rarest birds, glimpsed one supposes in some aviary. In accordance with Tornabuoni's wishes, and again even exceeding them, he painted a profusion of ancient monuments that were presumably drawn from his notebook containing sketches of the Forum ruins, compiled in Rome during his stay in that city of 1481-82.

The vaulting of the chapel contains the Evangelists. On the left wall Domenico frescoed the stories of Mary, on the right the life of St John the Baptist. Here more than anywhere else Ghirlandaio was influenced by the need to adopt an enlarged scale, since the chapel is vast and the light that enters from the elaborate window prompted him to emphasize further the subtlety of his colours and use of light which, sovereign, diffuses over everything. Undoubtedly, these fresco cycles are the most famous and most celebrated work of Ghirlandaio, his reputation being based principally on them. Taken as a whole, they give us the impression that he actually amused himself while painting them. Moreover, as we have already mentioned, his art always revealed such ease and fluency that it never gives the sense that he suffered from any inner torment but rather that he succeeded in overcoming certain difficulties that he must surely have encountered along the path of his prolific output. Although he also painted on wood and laid out mosaics he was above all, as a good Florentine, a great painter of frescoes.

The stories of Mary and the Baptist unfold so smoothly, and in the context of the purest Christian tradition, that it is unnecessary to look for their guiding principle and inspiration outside the Bible and the most elementary religious teaching. The narration, executed more precisely and carefully from the bottom where it begins, gets freer and easier as it rises up; though less attentive to details, it becomes increasingly airy and far-reaching with a delightful series of brief annotations in certain small barely outlined figures or in the invention of various landscapes. Here there is

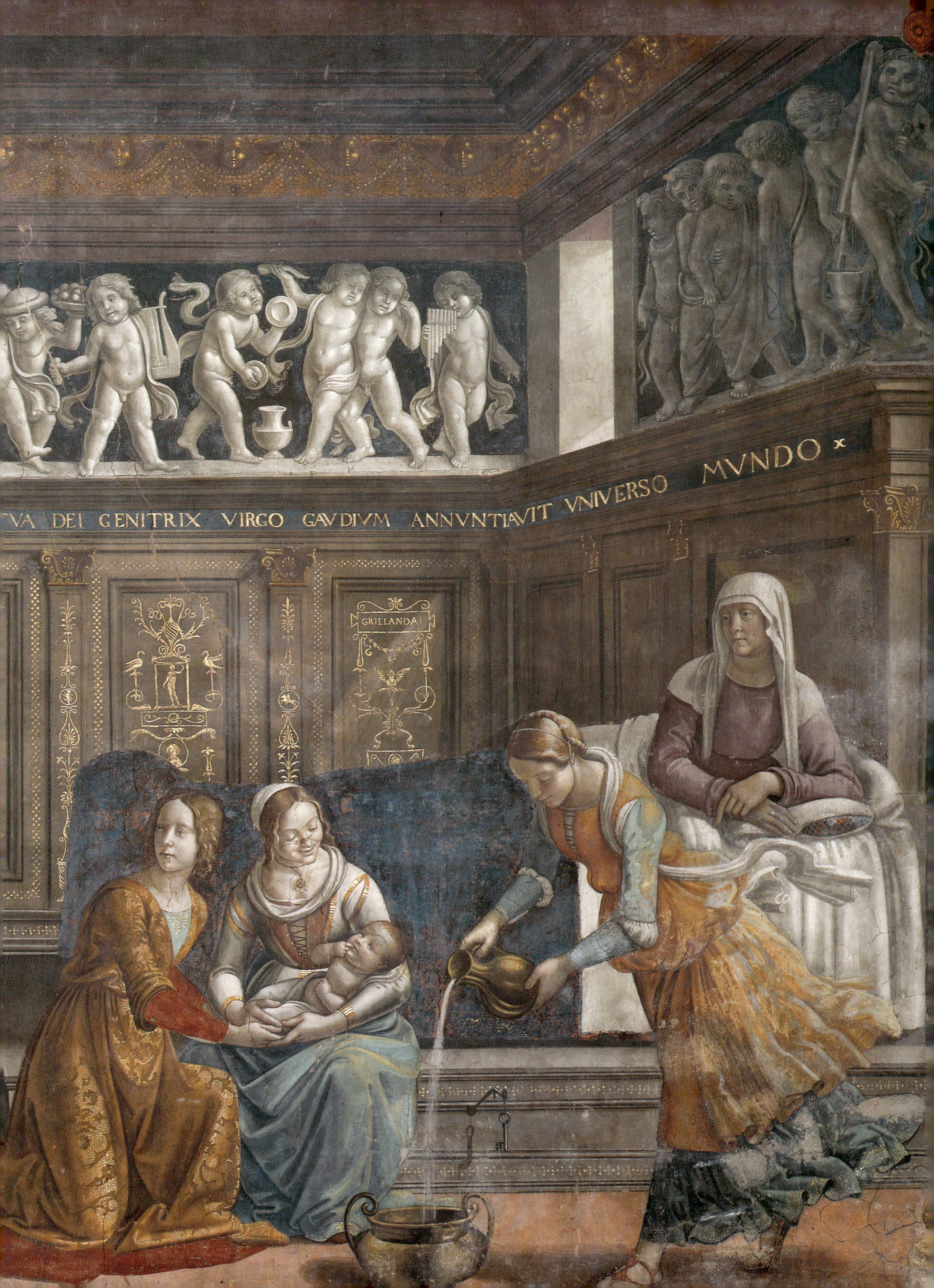

MVNDO
VA DEI GENITRIX VIRGO GAVDIVM ANNVNTIAVIT VNIVERSO
GRILLANDAI

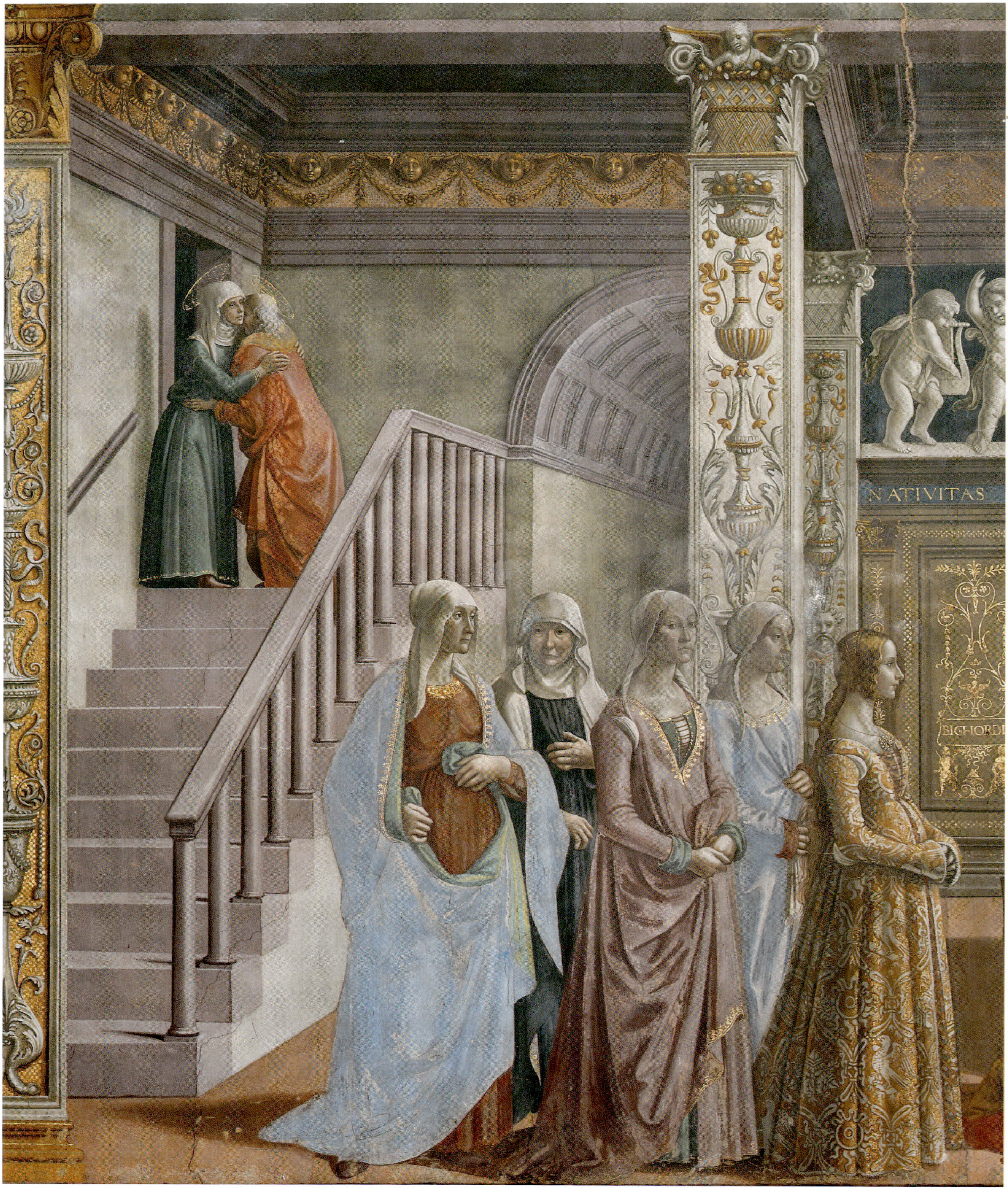

45

45. Stories of the Virgin: Birth of Mary detail of the group of visiting women Florence, Santa Maria Novella

none of the untidiness of which critics have sometimes accused the painter, who often left too free a hand to his assistants. It is as if, confronted with the desires of Giovanni Tornabuoni and his commission, Ghirlandaio had felt renewed, and added something more

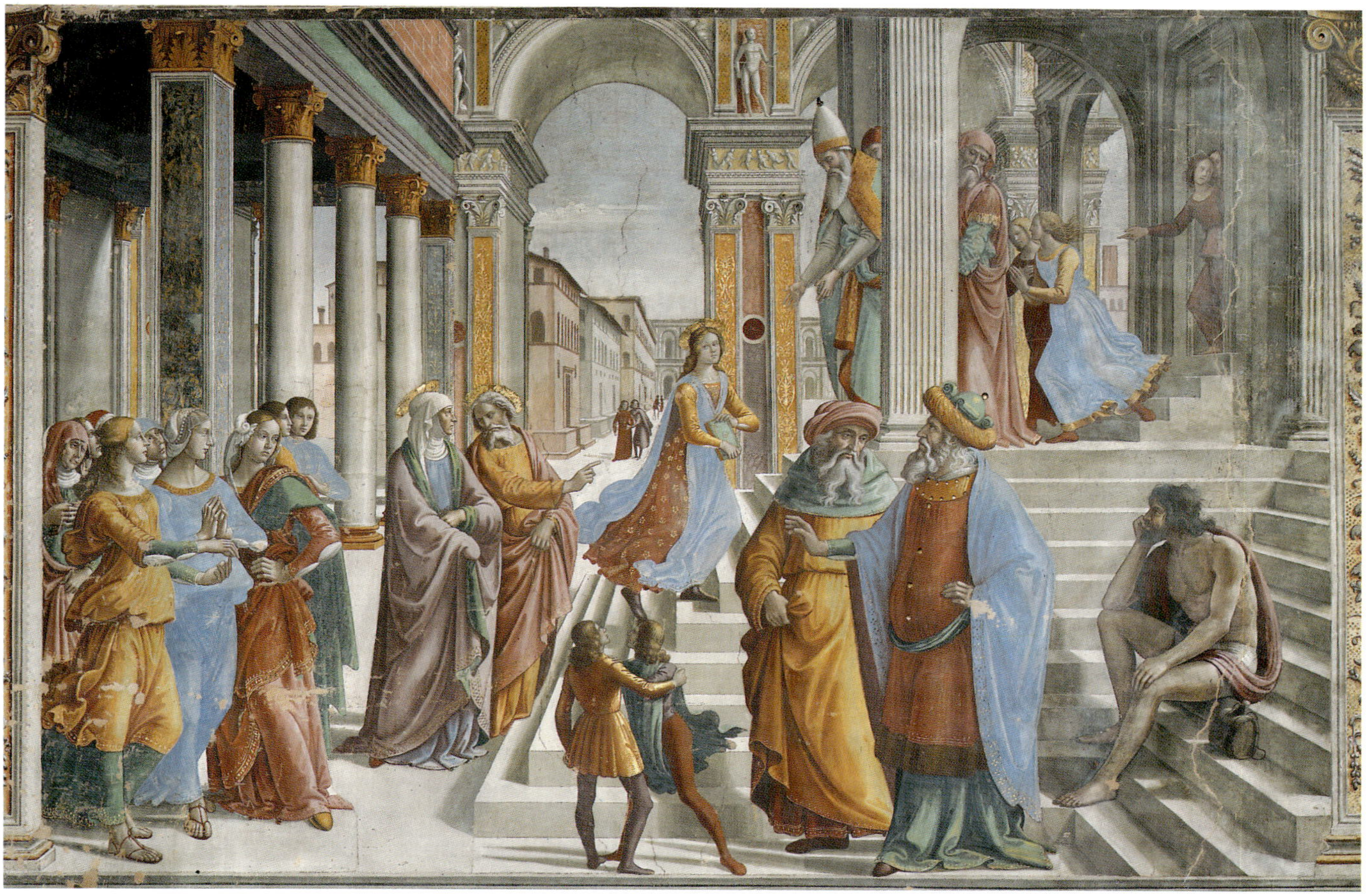

46

46, 47. Stories of the Virgin: Presentation at the Temple
Florence, Santa Maria Novella

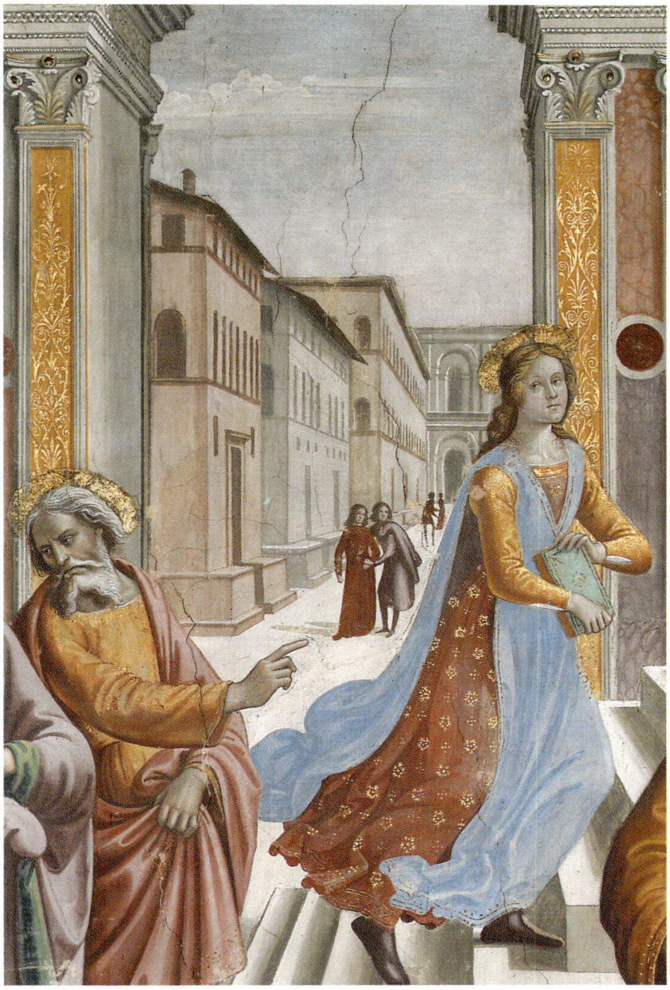

47

poetic and sincere to his everyday chronicle. The
events, surroundings and characters must have some-
how affected him, and, now more mature and accom-
plished, in this great basilica he seems at times to
-10 return to the felicitous spontaneity of the "Stories of St
Fina" at San Gimignano. Here, as formerly in the
-50 Sassetti Chapel, and especially in the "Stories of the
Virgin", it is Florence that provides the backdrop, a
backdrop that is as vivid and present as ever. Here we
see the roads, squares and churches of the city, and
particularly Santa Maria Novella, another district of
the city which though close to Santa Trinita was slight-
ly more suburban; it too was familiar to the painter,
who portrayed the buildings he had within eyesight.
41 The *Expulsion of Joachim from the Temple* takes
place in the characteristically Florentine square of San-
ta Maria Novella. In the background the facade of the
San Paolo hospital is easily recognizable, with its log-
gia that was built in those years on the Brunelleschian
model of the Loggia degli Innocenti. The interior, on
the other hand, open like stage scenery and confident-
ly executed with a rigorous and measured perspective,
is the painter's architectural invention. Once again, the
chronicler Ghirlandaio does not miss the opportunity
to represent the witnesses of his age; this time it is the
42 turn of those artists who were famous in Florence at

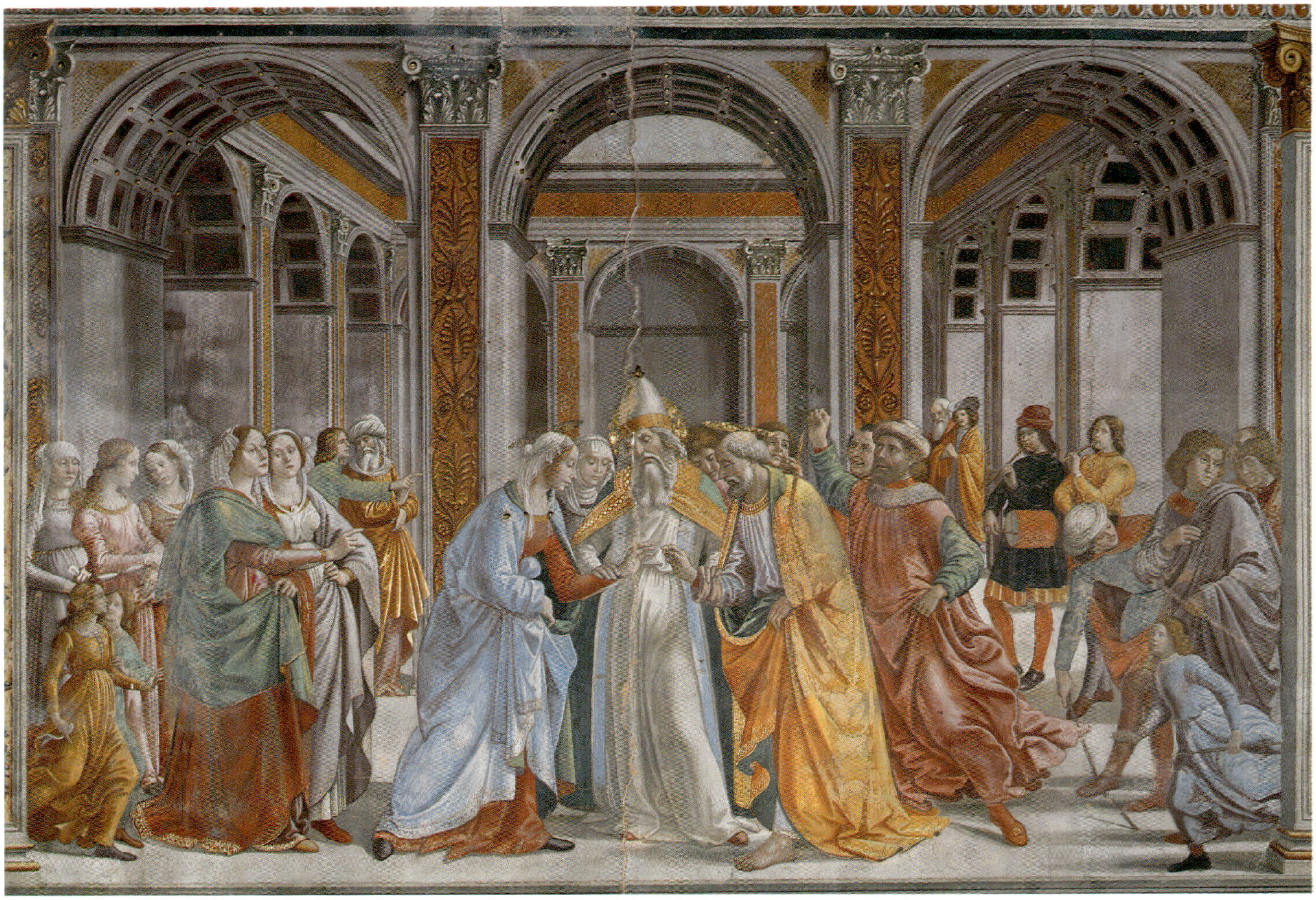

48

that time. Vasari recounts that "one of these, the old, clean-shaven man in a red cap, is Alesso Baldovinetti, Domenico's master in painting and mosaic...", who was probably portrayed from life since he died later, in 1499. "... Another, standing bareheaded, his hand at his side, in a red mantle, with a blue vest beneath, is Domenico himself, drawn with the help of a mirror...". He is the most aristocratic figure, with a well-combed shock of straight brown hair. We have already seen him in the Santa Trinita altarpiece, and we shall
76 see him again in the great *Adoration of the Magi* of the Innocenti. He exudes the same calmness that pervades his paintings and that made him so liked by Florentines who, besides being wealthy and influential in the arid realm of business affairs, were also inclined to indulge their aesthetic predilections. He seems rather detached, totally absorbed by that painting which he loved above all else and which he turned into such a free and easy affair, as smooth and pleasing as the Tuscan dialect in its most refined expression. "... The man with black hair and thick lips is Bastiano da San Gimignano, the artist's pupil and brother-in-law" (Vasari). It is possible that he became part of Ghirlandaio's circle at the time of the "Stories of St Fina". Subsequently he married Alessandra, Domenico's sister, and became his most well-known and recognizable disciple. "... and the other, with his back turned and wearing a cap, is Davitte Ghirlandaio, his brother, the painter". David, portrayed here in a defiant pose, was in charge of the administration of the family concern. He demanded that respect be shown to his brother and colleagues, and was himself responsible for discussing business and seeing to the observation of agreements, but he worked under Domenico's artistic guidance just like the others.

Mary is born in a large room that certainly lacks the 43
humbleness one would expect in the house of Joachim and Anne. It is a large room which the artist had seen again and again in Tornabuoni's house, with the walls divided by pilasters carved with elaborate candelabras, which are repeated, perhaps on leather but more probably on wood or pietra serena, in all the panels of the background. Along the cornice, in gold lettering, runs the inscription: *Nativitas tua genitrix virgo gaudium annunziavit universo mundo* [Your birth, oh Virgin Mother, announced joy to the whole universe]. "Bighordi" is written in the first panel; in the third, "Grillandai". The frieze, filled with the frenetic movement of a row of naked putti, carrying fruit and playing lyres and flutes in a gentle fluttering of veils and ribbons, is a clear and deliberate reference to Donatello.

"The second scene is the Nativity of the Virgin, executed with great diligence. Among other remarkable things it contains a window which lights the chamber and actually deceives the beholder...". From that window set into the frieze a bright warm light enters and floods the interior, throwing into relief the entrance
stairway by which a group of visiting women have just 45
entered. The women have been placed in the scene to

48. Stories of the Virgin: Marriage of Mary
Florence, Santa Maria Novella

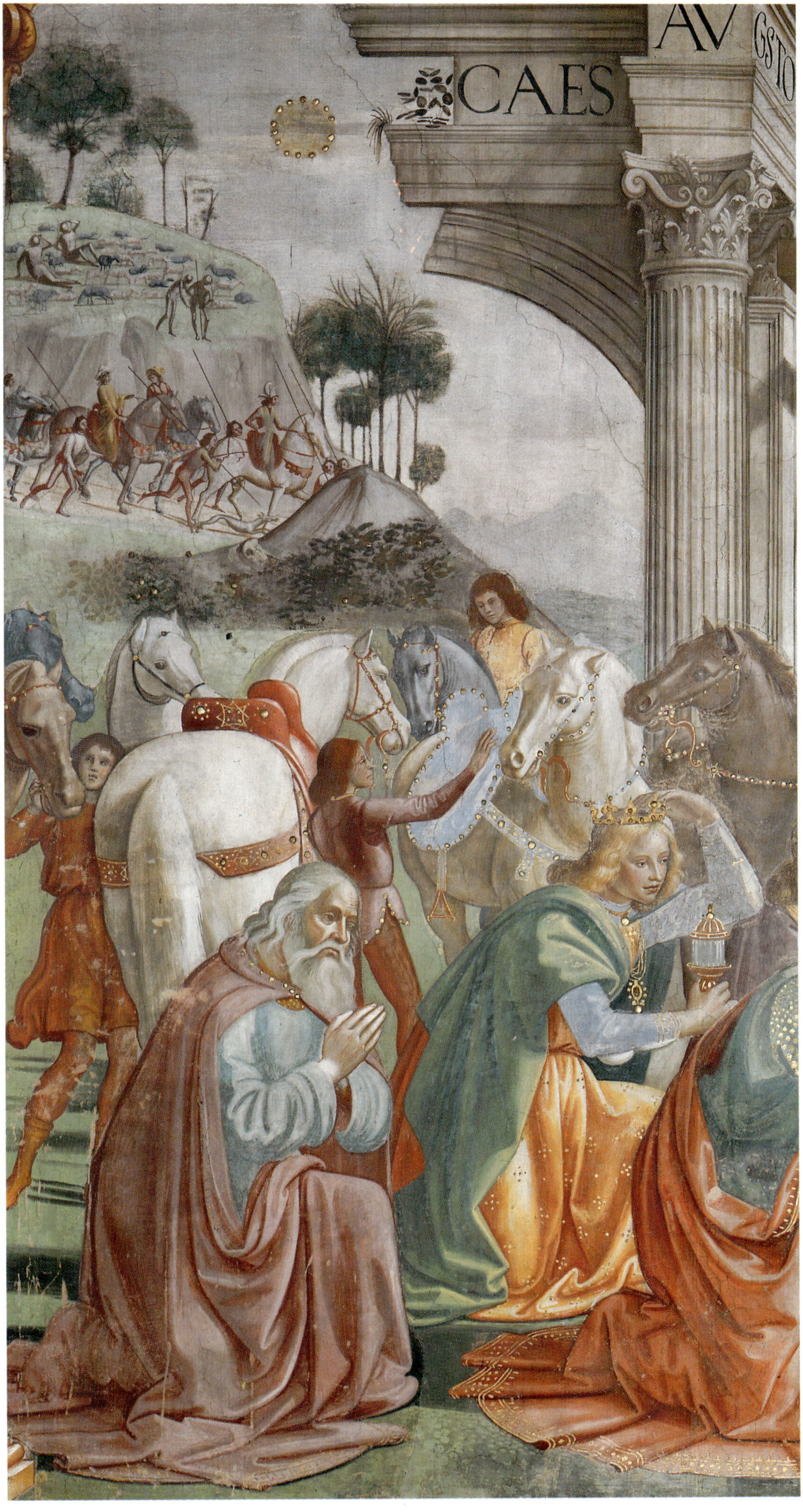

49

49. Stories of the Virgin: Adoration of the Magi, detail
Florence, Santa Maria Novella

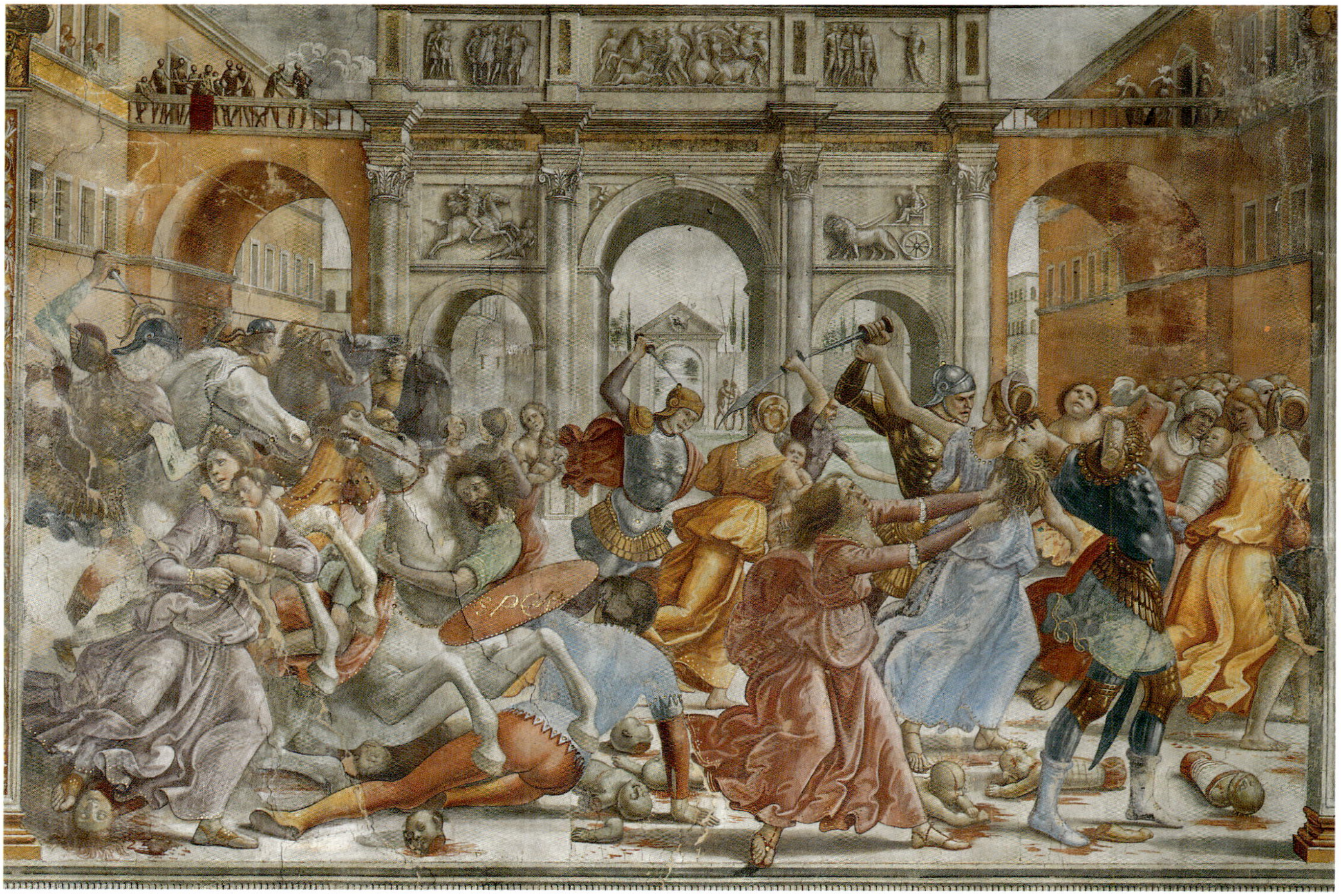
50

50. Stories of the Virgin: Slaughter of the Innocents
Florence, Santa Maria Novella

51. Stories of the Baptist: Angel appearing to Zacharias
Florence, Santa Maria Novella

serve as public spectators, detached from any action like devotees at the threshold of a temple. Standing out from the others in profile is a young woman, almost a girl, wearing gold embroidered brocade, possibly for the first time dressed like a lady and a little embarrassed by the stiffness of the garment and its large, rather long sleeves. It might be Giovanna Tornabuoni, the banker's only daughter, here acting out her first official role at the ceremony in the place of her dead mother. Behind her are four older women, uninhibited in their postures and gestures. It may be that the mother is portrayed here *in memoriam*, or perhaps the aunts Dianora or Lucrezia. The most important figure, however, is the young maiden who
44 provides a contrast with the figure of the old St Anne in her large bed. The wet nurses busy themselves with preparing the bath of the soft, pink, newborn baby, which seems to respond to the tender smile of the young woman holding the infant in her arms, while light invests the women and babe and turns the poured water into a sparkling stream. "... One of (the women) holds the Child in her arms and makes it laugh by smiling, with a feminine grace truly worthy of a work of this great genius, each figure being distinguished in its various expressions" (Vasari). In the upper left-hand corner at the top of the stairs, almost un-
45 noticed, is the biblical meeting between Joachim and Anne, no longer at the Golden Gate of Jerusalem, but in a familiar embrace at the house door.
46 The *Presentation at the Temple* follows, in which the figures reveal a certain stiffness and the architecture is more schematized - a series of columns, arches and stairways, against a background with a sharp perspective that recalls the illusive devices of Piero della Francesca. Here too, in the old bearded men and the delicate-featured youths, Ghirlandaio and his assistants undoubtedly portrayed the Florentine nobility who had their houses in that district.
And so it is in the *Marriage of Mary*, where he shows 48
"... the youths angrily breaking their rods, which did not flower like that of Joseph. This scene contains many figures and a good building" (Vasari). It is true. This may be the scene most crowded with people in different costumes and poses: players of drums and fifes, children running about and men drawing close in order to see the prodigy. The unknown woman indicating the couple to friends is beautifully portrayed, so much so that the bride and groom almost become a secondary image and not the protagonists of the event. It all takes place in an interior, possibly a temple with cross barrel vaults, a kind of foretaste of 16th-century monumental painting.

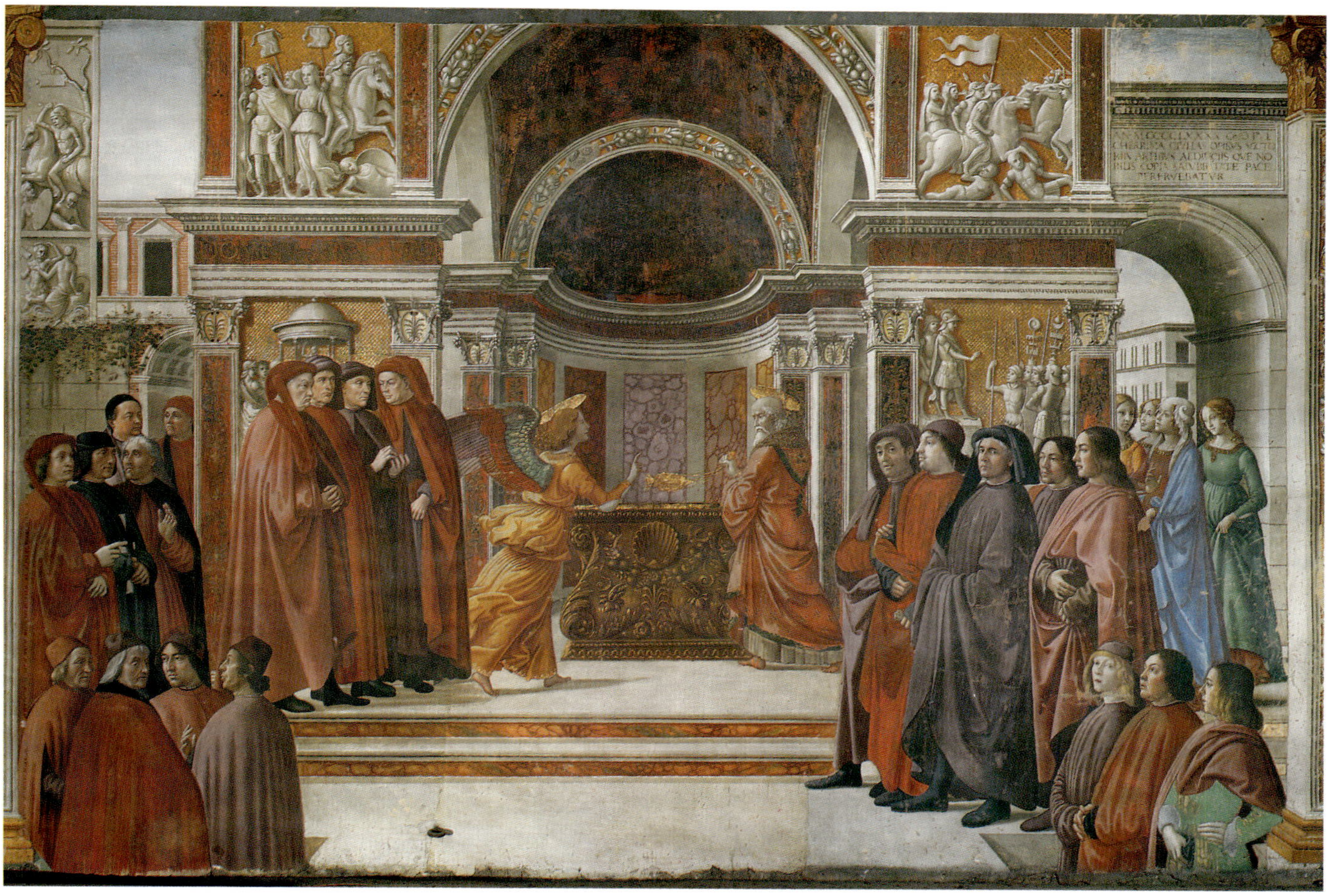

51

49 "The fifth shows the coming of the Magi to Bethlehem with a number of men, horses, dromedaries and other things, a very well-arranged scene" (Vasari). The adjective "well-arranged", which occasionally crops up in Vasari's description, probably implies a less free and spontaneous execution on the part of the painter, who kept to a precise iconography associated with the corresponding gospel story. Meanwhile Ghirlandaio's participation in carrying out the work was becoming less marked. Undoubtedly, a freer hand was given to his assistants, although here and there he may have tidied up a landscape, adding to it the poetry of some cypress or various barely perceptible shafts of morning light. The fragmentary Roman arch is less convincing and, especially on the left, seems to be standing up with some difficulty. The figures in the foreground, in addition to their lack of homogeneity as a group, show a certain rigidity in their poses that does not belong to Ghirlandaio. And there are no portraits.

50 In the *Slaughter of the Innocents*, so highly praised by Vasari, "... we see the cruelty of those who at Herod's command kill the poor children without pity for their mothers... Many other emotions are also represented, so that no beholder can doubt the excellence of the master".

In the last story, on the highest section of the wall, as if in a niche, "... is the Passing of Our Lady and her Assumption, with troops of angels, a number of figures, landscapes and other ornaments, in which Domenico's easy and skilful style usually abounds".

In the *Dormitio Virginis* we see a partial resumption of the framing used in the *Funerals of St Fina* at 9
San Gimignano and the *Funerals of St Francis* in the 31
Sassetti Chapel. The overall effect, however, is more solemn. There is neither the psalm-singing of the monks, nor the distracted grace of the young choirboys, portrayed from life. Here the protagonists of the event are taken from the Gospel and the Acts of the Apostles, not from the streets of Florence or San Gimignano. They are dressed in large cloaks with ample folds; absorbed by a great fervour, or a calm, rapt contemplation, they do not tell a story, but capture it in the very moment of the passing of Mary. They are saints, apostles and fathers of the Church, whom Giotto and Masaccio had painted in another form and with another force. The choirboys of St Fina have become angels that move in undulating lines and an almost dance-like rhythm.

A vast landscape of villas and Tuscan houses bathed in light, interrupted by delicate saplings and rocky peaks against a clear sky, divides this scene from that of the *Assumption of Mary* which is depicted, miraculously, in the top of the arch. In the centre, still in an almost Gothic mandorla, is the Virgin, transparent with light, surrounded by angels and received by Her Son who like the Eternal Father stretches his arms out to her. The forms are a little archaic, especially the Madonna, almost motionless in the circling of the angels and the Christ, whose perspective is rather distort-

52 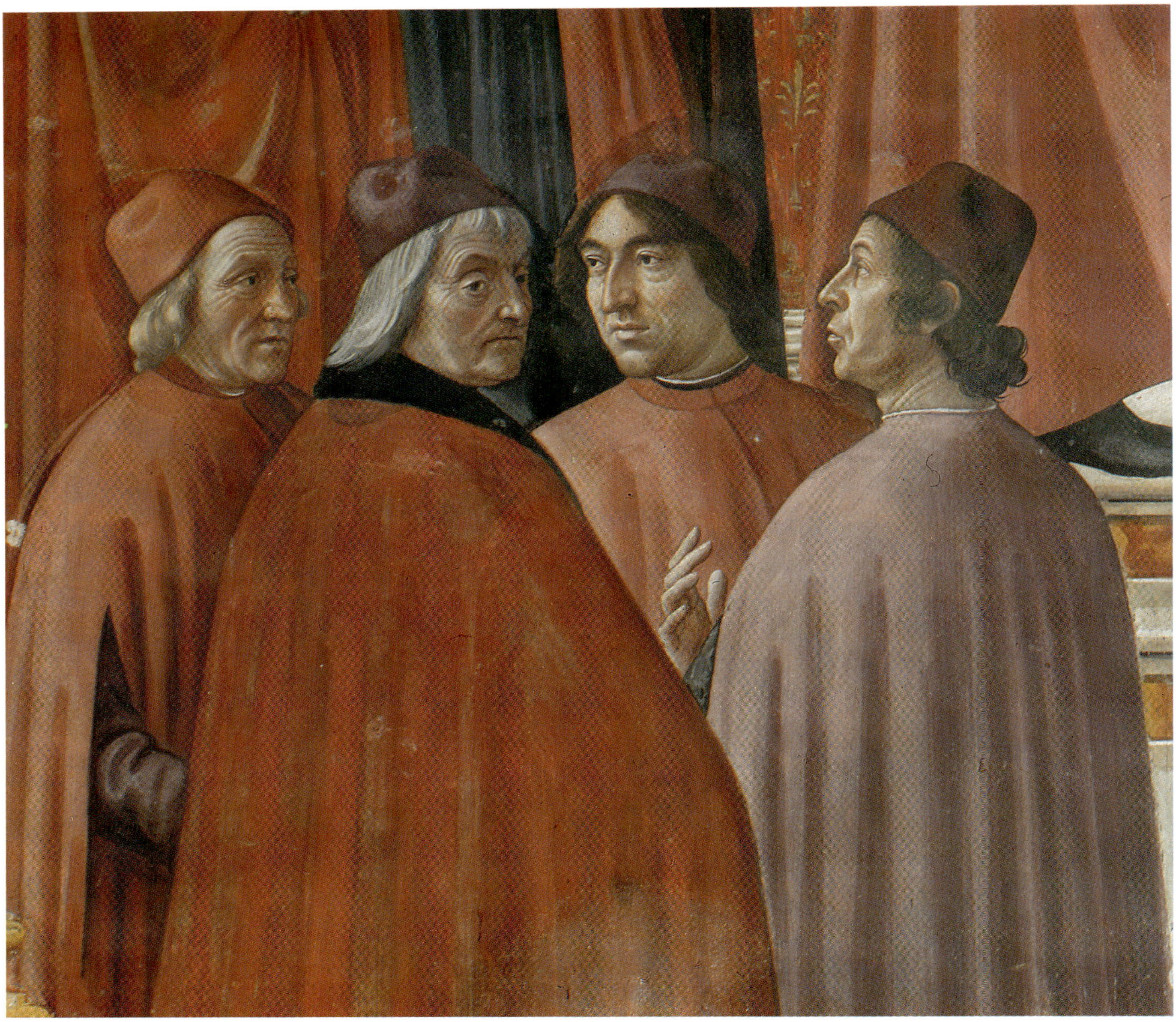

ed by the excessive length of his arms and the reduced dimensions of his body. I would say that nothing here is the work of Ghirlandaio, only the depicting of Our Lady of the Assumption as an ancient "Animula", taken up into Heaven not by her son but by her own mortal remains, and without the ecstatic wonder of the disciples. Indeed, none of the onlookers are distracted away from the deceased and do not see her as she is carried up into the Kingdom of Her Son for all Eternity. The two scenes are connected and at the same time divided; one is a part of the other, but each is quite distinct.

51-64 On the opposite wall the "Stories of St John the Baptist" unfold in a similar harmony of warm colours and lighted atmospheres. Here too Ghirlandaio's presence is more assiduous and obvious in the scenes nearer to eye level. The compositions, poses and pictorial effect are more precise.

51 The *Angel appearing to Zacharias* is represented in the first scene starting from the bottom, in which "Domenico introduced a goodly number of Florentine citizens, who were then members of the Government, and especially all the members of the Tornabuoni family". The event takes place, in a rather crowded and somewhat static setting, against the wall of a temple decorated with classical motifs and inscriptions, battles, cavalcades and warriors. On the right, beyond an archway, is the sky and a house in Florence. Giuliano 53
Tornabuoni, Giovanni Tornaquinci and Gian Frances-

52. Stories of the Baptist: Angel appearing to Zacharias
detail of Marsilio Ficino, Cristoforo Landino, Agnolo Poliziano and Demetrius the Greek (from left to right)
Florence, Santa Maria Novella

53. Stories of the Baptist: Angel appearing to Zacharias
detail of various members of the Tornabuoni and Tornaquinci families
Florence, Santa Maria Novella

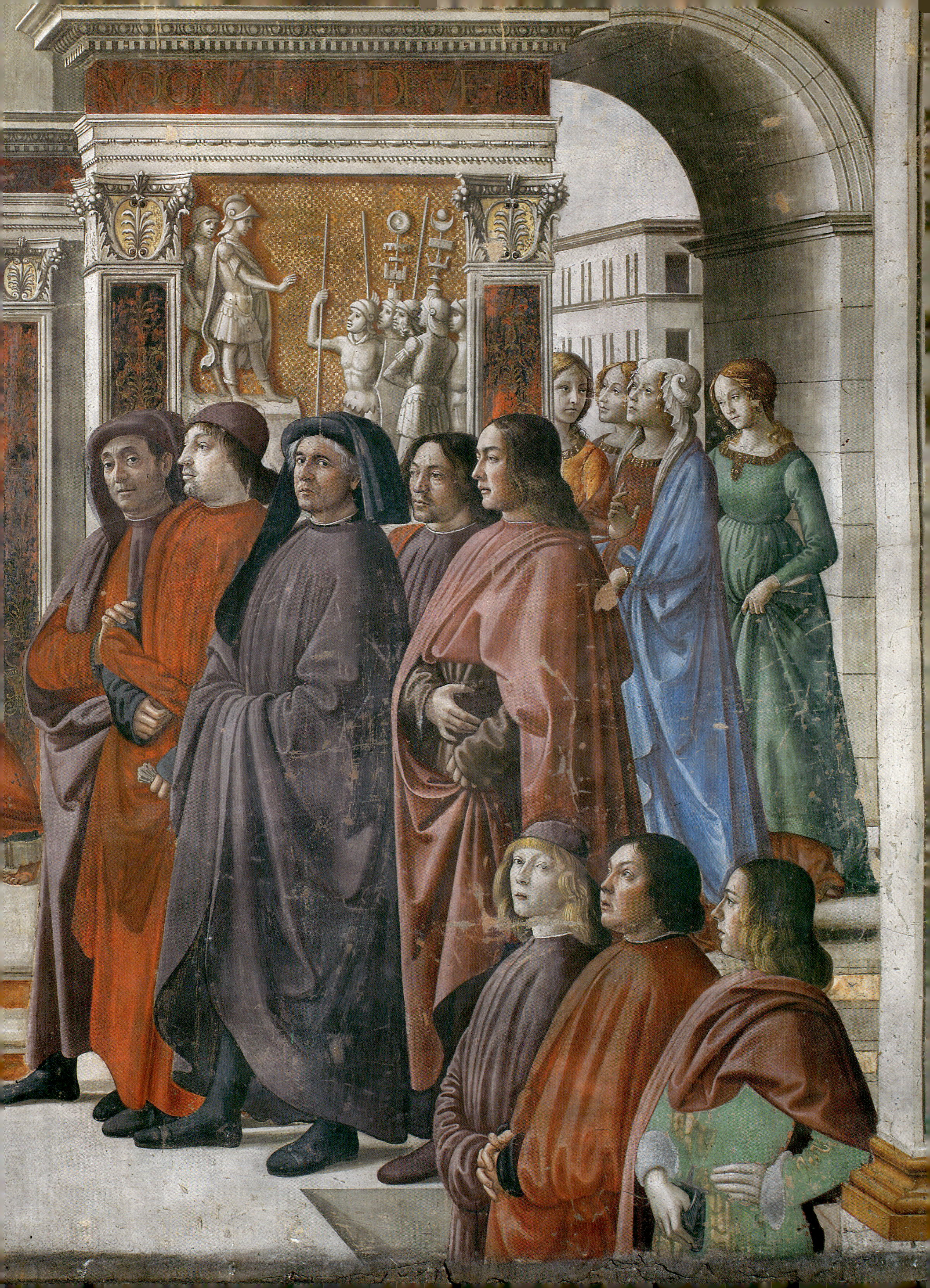

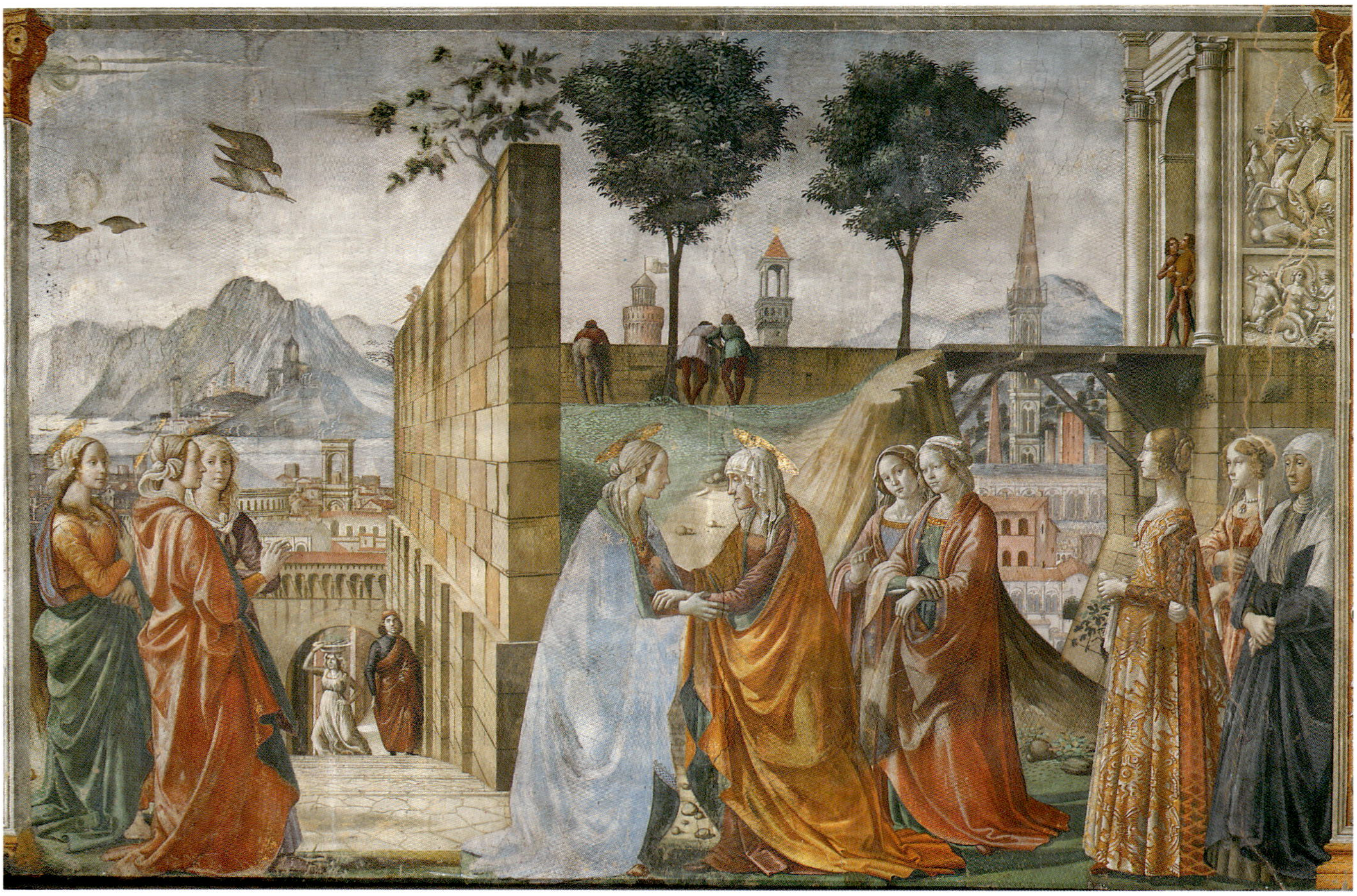
54

co Tornabuoni are standing on the right, posing in front of the painter; on the left is another Tornabuoni, Giovanni Battista. These well-to-do bourgeois Florentines are not at all interested in the stories, and only make us curious to know more about them. Here Ghirlandaio really seems less sincere "in describing with sustained measure" a certain high-ranking social class in the city - his clients, in other words. Yet the artist's masterly skill is alive and present. Those half-length figures of young men below, with a contrite and rather embarrassed air about them, are more vivid and more endearingly represented. They may be employees of the bank, made uneasy by the ostentatious presence of their superiors. Blending in with the background is a group of women, mere damsels passing curiously by.

52 On the left is the fine world of contemporary Florentine culture. "... These were the most learned Florentines of the day, namely Marsilio Ficino in a canon's dress; Cristofano Landino next, in a red mantle and a black ribbon round his throat; Demetrius the Greek in the middle, turning round and lifting his hand slightly; Angelo Poliziano, all full of life and energy" (Vasari). Vasari's description is so vivid that there is little to add to his comments on these portraits from life: Marsilio Ficino, the Platonic philosopher and founder of the Medicean academy that received Cristoforo Landino, tutor of poetry and oratory, scholar of Virgil and Dante, and erudite commentator of the Aeneid and Divine Comedy. With them is the poet Agnolo Poliziano, a friend of Lorenzo il Magnifico and tutor to his children, whom Ghirlandaio had already portrayed in the Sassetti Chapel. His 'Stanze' were probably the inspiration for Botticelli's *Primavera*. The fourth figure is perhaps not Demetrius the Greek, scholar of Platonic philosophy, but Gentile de' Becchi, in his own time tutor to Lorenzo de' Medici; he later became the bishop of Arezzo, but remained among the friends of the Florentine Platonic academy and was venerated as a teacher in the Medici household. Overall, this crowded scene is the least successful. The artist, evidently anxious to produce something pleasing that would satisfy Giovanni Tornabuoni's overriding ambition, did not dare thin out the crowd of relatives, friends of the house and "clients" of Palazzo Medici who imparted lustre to Tornabuoni. The people do not fit in well with the architecture; they cut a fine figure, but exist on their own. Fundamentally, there is little poetry and excessive affectation, almost a certain overdoing it that is rather disturbing and unpleasant. Better, then, to move on to the following scene representing the *Visitation* "... the Visitation of Our Lady and St Elisabeth, accompanied by women wearing the costumes of the day..." (Vasari). 54

54, 55. Stories of the Baptist: Visitation
Florence, Santa Maria Novella

The Visitation is one of the most moving gospel stories in artistic iconography - the meeting between two women who carry within themselves two miracles: the already aged Elisabeth who through divine will con-

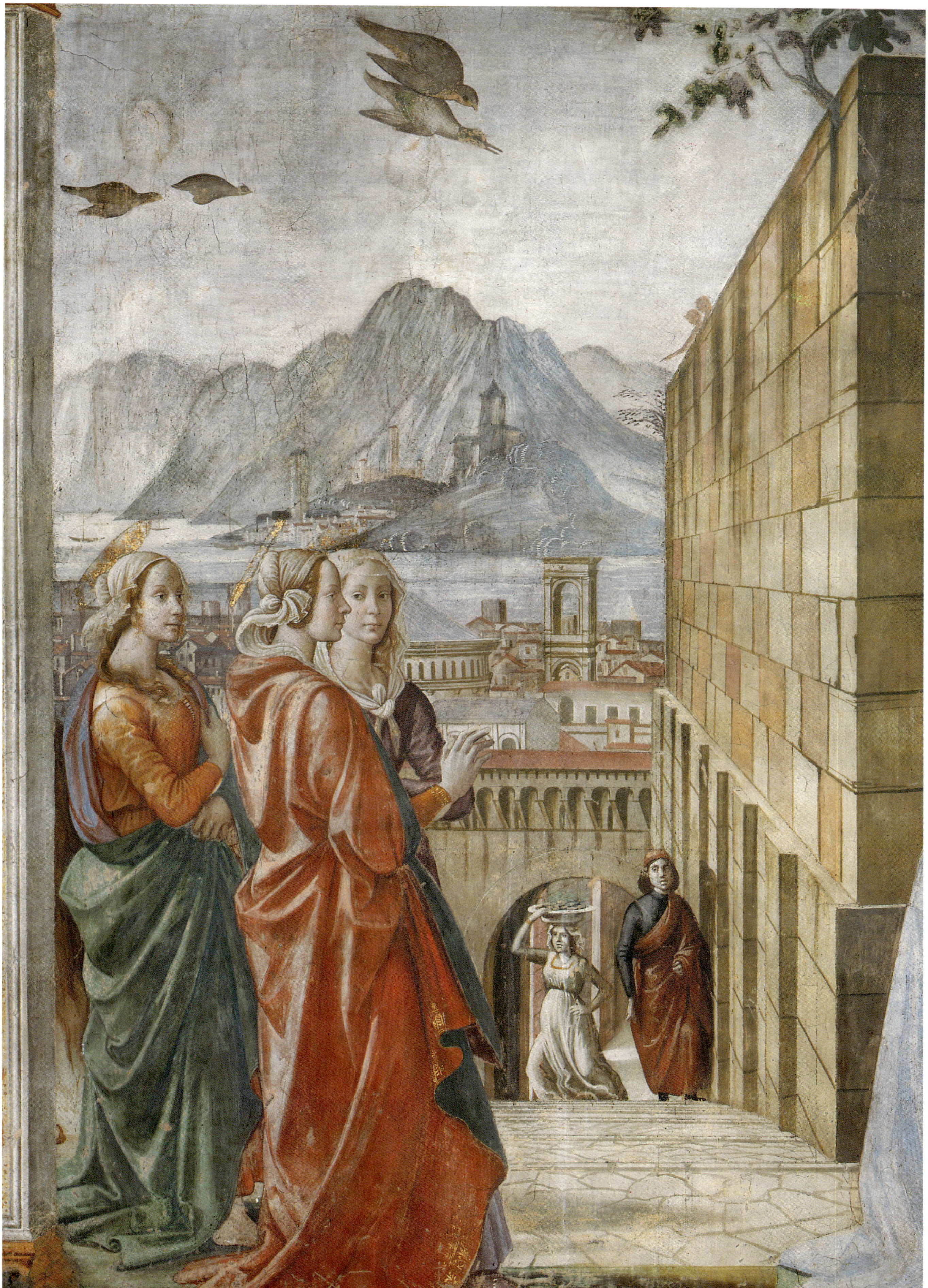

55

56 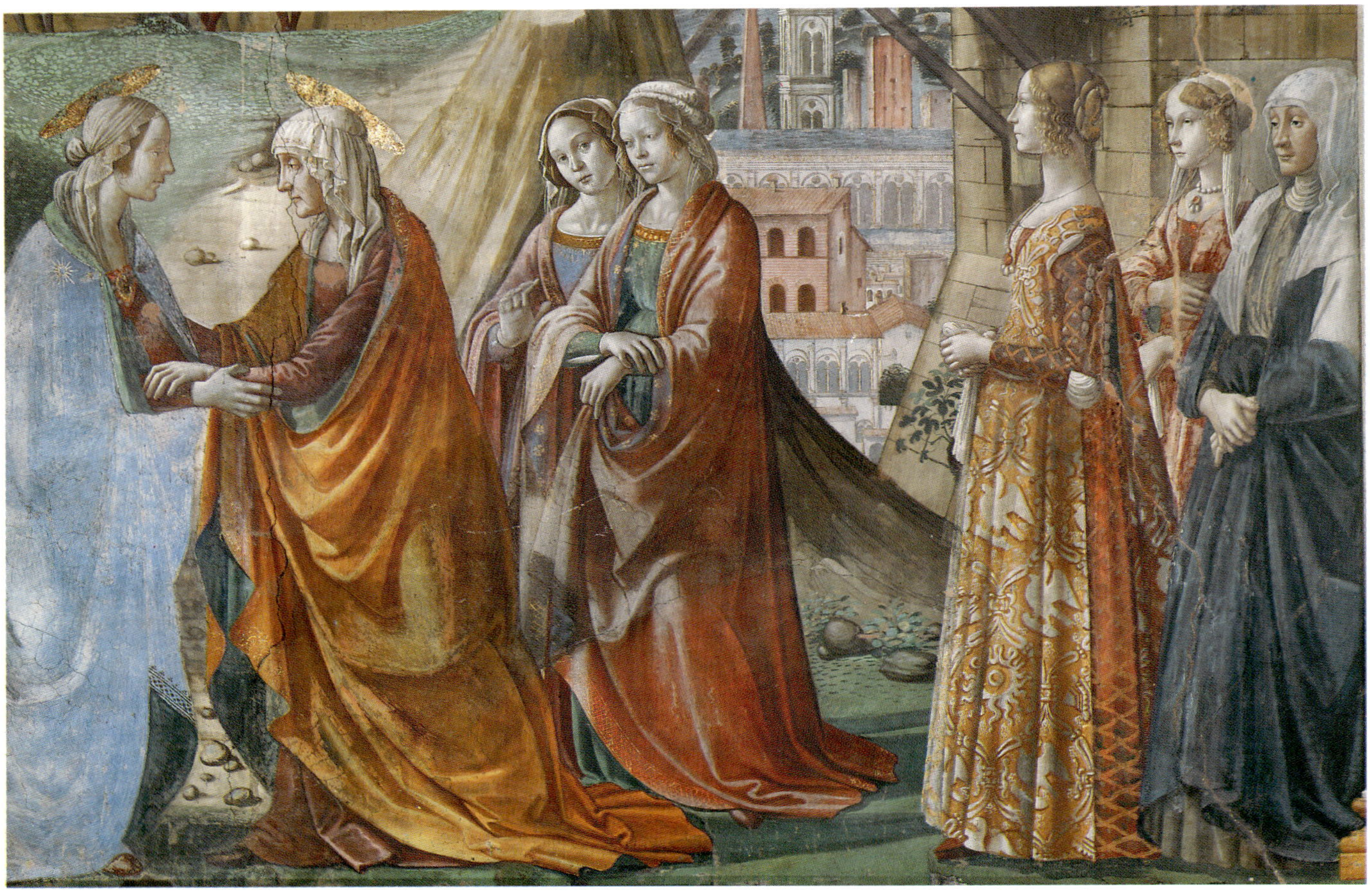

ceived a son who would be the precursor of Christ; and the young Mary, who "knew not man" and conceived Jesus through the Holy Spirit. All these scenes, from Giotto's solemn meeting in the Scrovegni Chapel in Padua, to Pontormo's exultant *Visitation* at Carmignano, in an unreal leaping of lights and surfaces, are quite unforgettable. Ghirlandaio's meeting takes place in open hilly terrain that a wall divides from a city on the far horizon - Florence once again, with the lofty "campanile" of Santa Maria Novella and other towers. Large aquatic birds are streaking across the sky. The event portrayed is the measured and affectionate embrace between the two women, a demonstration of
56 mutual respect. Various women spectators are witness to it. Among them Vasari identifies "... Ginevra de' Benci, a most beautiful girl". The person he refers to is standing on the right, though it is much more probable that she is actually Giovanni degli Albizzi, who in those very years became the wife of Lorenzo Tornabuoni. This marriage, which united the Albizzi family (long-standing enemies of the Medici), with the Tornabuoni family (their relatives and good friends), seemed to be a symbol of peace. It was celebrated with solemn feasts at which famous artists were present. Sandro Botticelli portrayed the young Lorenzo being presented by Minerva to the liberal arts and Giovanna offering her marriage veil to Venus, with the Graces around them. This fresco, now at the Louvre, had been done for the Villa Tornabuoni at Chiasso Macerelli. But it was a marriage of short duration. Like her mother-in-law, Giovanna Tornabuoni died young

56. Stories of the Baptist: Visitation
right-hand detail showing Giovanna Tornabuoni (third figure from right)
Florence, Santa Maria Novella

in childbirth in 1488, and Lorenzo, like his father, remained a widower when he was a young man. Shortly after, the fortunes of the family were to take a very sad turn.

Giovanna degli Albizzi is sketched with firmness and decision, almost as if she were modelled in a rather cold material, like precious stone. The lavish dress, with its shining silk and golden embroidery, is typical of the refined Florentine elegance of the time. The lines of her face are clear and precise, as in a glossy cameo, and she has simply-plaited blond hair. Behind her, in much plainer clothes, are Dianora Tornabuoni, the young wife of Pier Soderini, and another no better identified woman wearing ordinary clothes but with rich jewels and a fashionable hair-style; another pair of
women are Elisabeth's companions. On the left is a 55
group of three more sprightly maidens dressed in gay colours, their soft veils providing a pleasing touch of movement. A gently sloping road rises up from the town. Coming along it is a man dressed in red and a woman with swaying hips and a basket on her head. Rather resembling a road near to Porta San Giorgio, it is certainly one of those half-real, half-imaginary slices of Florentine life which Ghirlandaio could not resist including.

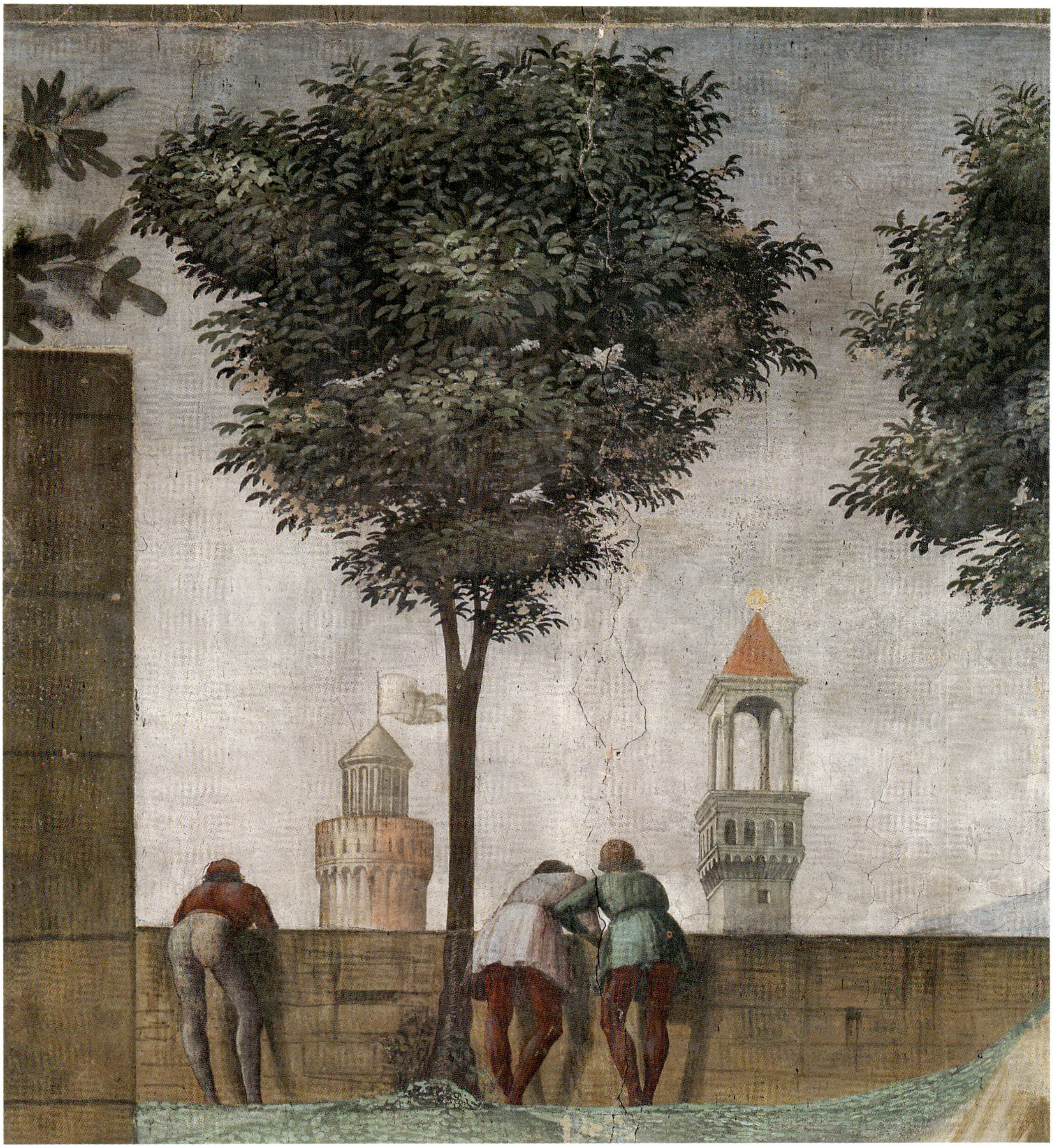

57

57. Stories of the Baptist: Visitation, detail
Florence, Santa Maria Novella

58 "In the fourth scene, next to this, Zacharias, still dumb... writes down the words "His name shall be John" (Vasari). The figures move around a seated priest, in easy and realistic poses, while a young woman, kneeling, presents him with the newborn baby. All are contained within a large portico paved in marble with geometrical decoration. Through the arches of the background is a tranquil, open landscape with trees, roads and, to the right, a city that appears once again to be a reminder of Florence. A boat seems to be rocking gently in a placid stretch of water, a motif already familiar in the works of Sandro Botticelli and, for that matter, in a large part of contemporary Florentine painting.

One of the most beautiful and most Florentine of the stories is certainly the *Birth of the Baptist*, which is fully 59
described and interpreted by Vasari. "... the birth of St John, with a beautiful idea that, while Elisabeth is in bed and being visited by her neighbours and a nurse is suckling the child, a woman is eagerly calling the at-

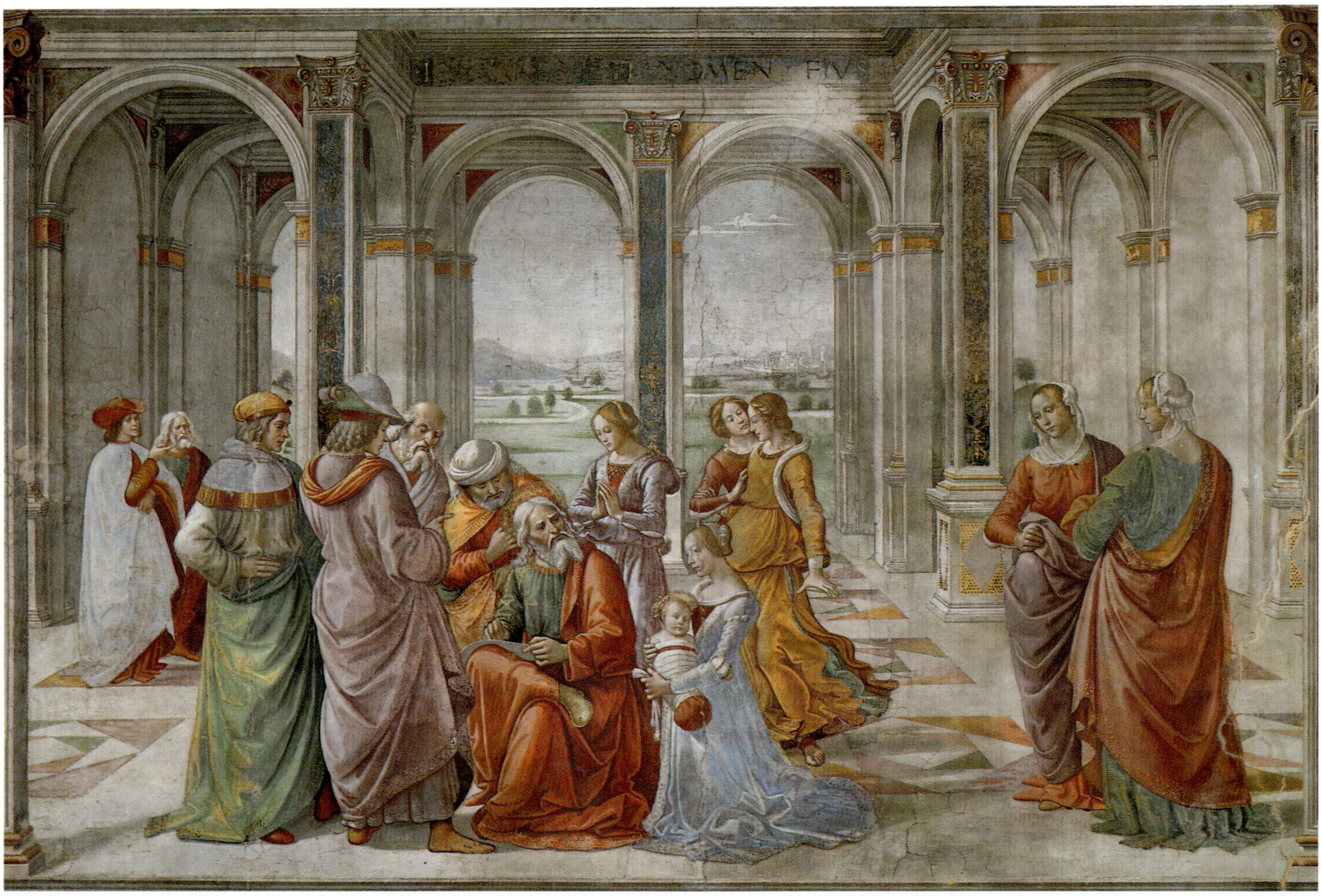

58

58. Stories of the Baptist: Zacharias writes down the Name of his Son
Florence, Santa Maria Novella

59. Stories of the Baptist: Birth of St John
Florence, Santa Maria Novella

tention of the visitors to the wonder that has come to her mistress in her old age; and lastly there is a woman bringing fruit and wine from the city, in conformity with the Florentine custom. This is very fine". In this scene there is a great harmony between the figures and their surroundings, between motion and movement. There is the weary, but contented abandon-
60 ment of Elisabeth receiving her visitors in a large bed, her tender face illumined by the bright light that enters from the small high window. The same light makes the sheets brighter and gives a sparkle to the bottles and glasses set on the large tray carried in by a young maid, who is clearly delineated against the dark flowered curtains. The room, the high bed on its raised platform, the linear architecture and the coffered ceiling, are all in a Florentine style. It must, for example, have resembled rooms in the house of the Tornabuoni family, who commissioned the work. Florentine too are the hairstyles of the wet-nurses and of the ladies who are making their entrance followed by abundant gifts of fruit and wine. One of the ladies, the eldest with her head wrapped in a white headcloth, is almost certainly Lucrezia Tornabuoni, the mother of Lorenzo il Magnifico and sister of Giovanni. Lucrezia Tornabuoni had been a woman of noble virtues; a friend of Agnolo Poliziano, she was also close to Luigi Pulci, who called her "the haven of all wretches". One might speak of her at some length; she was a poetess, was interested in political affairs, was received by the Papal court in Rome, but in Florence devoted herself to accumulating wealth, even though she was considered, especially by her mother-in-law Contessina, who loved her dearly, the intellectual of the family together with her husband Piero. It is no surprise to find her here, at this birth, for among her poetical works there was also a life of St John the Baptist. Lucrezia had died four years before Ghirlandaio executed this work, but no one in Florence had forgotten her. The memory of her was alive, so alive that her portrait has nothing adulatory about it; Ghirlandaio represented her as Florentines had seen her, going about her business in her palace, her villas and the streets of her city.

Lucrezia accompanies a beautiful, unidentified maiden who probably belonged to her family of origin, the Tornabuoni. She is very young and splendidly dressed up, her blond hair framing a tender face that reveals a slight frown, as if to demonstrate how preoccupied she is by the task she has been entrusted with - that of honouring the saint in childbirth. Her manner is intended to be uninhibited, though she is evidently embarrassed, as if this were really one of her first appearances in public.

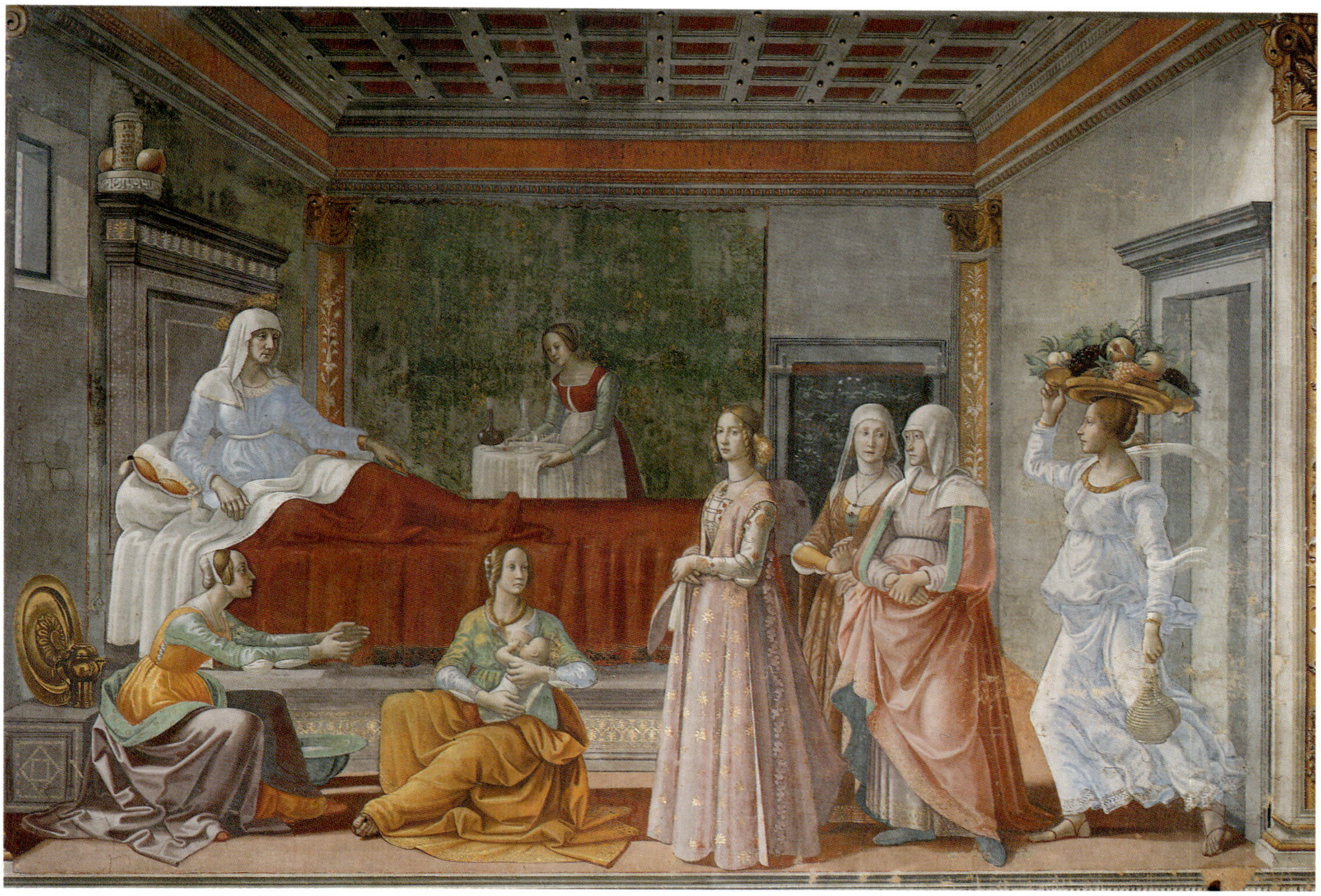

59

61 The last figure on the right, obviously a maid carrying gifts, is quite agitated, which contrasts with the play of folds and veils in the composed procession of the others. Hers is almost a dance step, and one might well ask why. It could be a deliberate reference to Ghirlandaio's immediate predecessor Filippo Lippi or even some more lively Botticellian inspiration, though it does seem rather forced and somewhat disharmonious in the midst of such calm.

Alongside the many Florentine references in this scene are some reminiscences of the Flemish world, which seem to have been almost forgotten or only
7-10 barely intimated since the "Stories of St Fina". Flemish attention to reality, for example, can be seen in the
60 cruets and glass which shine with myriad reflections, and in the delicate rendering of the tablecloth spread over the large round tray. In the shining glass one has a clear, tactile sensation of the slightly tinkling fineness of the material, which has become almost precious by virtue of its reflecting so much light. It may be seen in the tree-shaped vase with stylized flowers, and in the shelf that has the colour and warm softness of wood, so similar to the objects painted by Hugo van der Goes in the Portinari *Adoration of the Shepherds*. The same vivid reality is also evident in the two pomegranates, a symbol of fertility, placed by the side of the vase. This almost intentional reference to recent past experiences, now enjoying a new lease of life in Ghirlandaio's soul, has become almost poetry.

"The fifth contains the preaching to the multitudes, showing the attention of the people in hearing new things..." (Vasari). This story, and the following one
with the *Baptism of Christ* which shows, "... his 62
reverential attitude displaying the belief which he had in that sacrament, and... he represented a crowd of naked and bare-footed figures waiting to be baptised, their faces displaying faith and desire, one especially who is taking off his shoe being energy itself", are perhaps the scenes most faithful to traditional iconographical models. The *Baptism* in particular reminds us of similar representations with a quite different mood: that of Masaccio in the Cappella Brancacci, in which the protagonist is St Peter and the famous "... naked man who shivers", and Verrocchio's *Baptism*, now in the Uffizi, where the poses of the admittedly more plastic and dynamically tense figures are accompanied by Leonardo's first pictorial accomplishment in the angel on the left and the softened landscape in the background.

Here the two landscapes are similar, inspired as they are by the same Tuscan countryside which at that time really was at the gates of Florence. A certain fanciful elaboration of buildings and towers on the right in the background of the *Baptism* might also be Florence. There are no portraits in either story, but a great biblical crowd of priests and believers struck by a blinding light that emphasizes the nudity of the neophyte on the far left, the rapt face of the one who is taking off his shoe and, in the *Preaching*, the animated group of four women in a corner with intense faces and rather

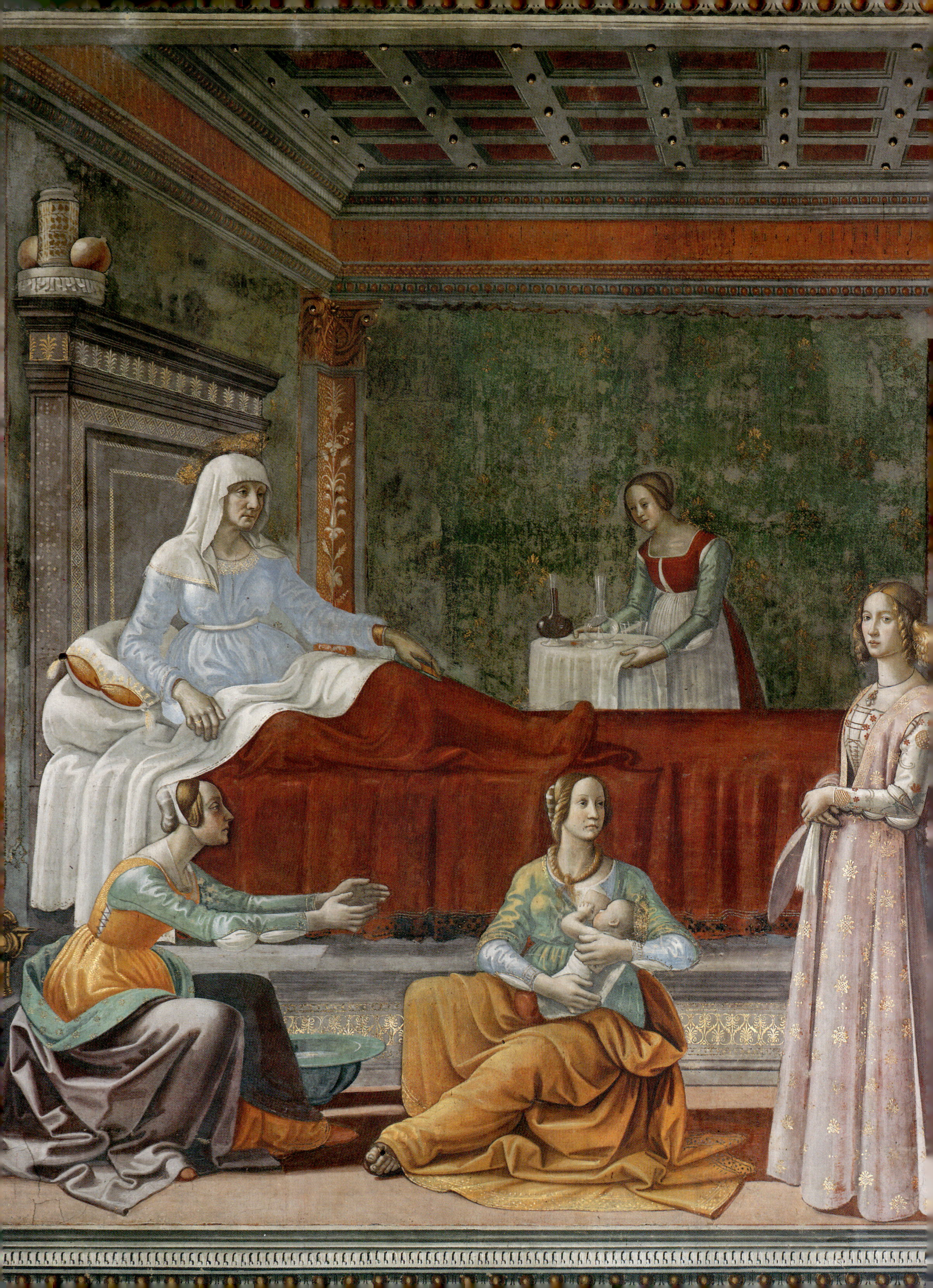

elaborate hairstyles. There is a beauty in the majestic figure of Jesus as he emerges into the light among the rocks, holding back slightly, with his handsome face bowed, absorbed in a silent and intent contemplation as he is heralded by the Baptist. There is beauty too in the plastic and yet tender female figure, seen from behind, who although not emphasized has all the appearance of a lady attentive to the words of John, her head a little foreshortened, and her noble pose underlined by an elegant neckline.

In the last story, above, possibly assigning much of
63 the work to assistants, Ghirlandaio painted the *Dance of Salome and the presentation of the Baptist's head to Herod*. "The last scene, in the arch next to the vaulting, is the sumptuous banquet of Herod, with the dancing of Herodias, and a troop of servants... It contains a large building shown in perspective, and in conjunction with the paintings displays Domenico's skill" (Vasari). In this scene the architecture is more elaborate than elsewhere, the grandiose coffered vault of the large central arch being a complex interplay of criss-cross lines. In the background is the mere suggestion of an anonymous landscape. The scenic composition is a little theatrical: the sumptuously laid banquet table; the king in the centre with his dignitaries arranged in somewhat conventional poses; at the sides the court, with the men on the right and the elegant and charming ladies dressed up in the latest fashions on the left. Standing behind them an orchestra of wind
64 instruments accompanies Salome's dance, whose lively rhythm sends the hem of her dress swirling in motion, but which apart from this is a little too static. The court scene is complete, and even contains a dwarf jester, a figure characteristic of fifteenth and sixteenth-century Europe (the most famous being the dwarves of the House of Gonzaga at Mantova). Herod's jester turns his back on us and looks toward the slim, elegant figure of the servant on the left, who is presenting the king with the head of St John the Baptist on a large silver tray. Once again we must emphasize the total absence of any drama; that Ghirlandaio's spirit is as free as ever from disturbing sentiments. There are no expressions of horror or fear, nor is there any excessive curiosity; I would suggest that there is mild disappointment at the most. The light falling on the white tablecloths once more gives emphasis to the procession of shining bottles and glasses, some precious dish, a cool splash of glossy cherries.

Domenico was also responsible for the central altarpiece in this chapel, described by Vasari as "Our Lady who appears with the Child in celestial glory together with the archangel Michael and St John the Baptist, and at the sides St Catherine of Siena and St Laurence dressed as Deacon". This work was lost in the careless restoration of 1804, but the frescoes which framed it with the "Stories of St Peter Martyr", probably executed by David and Benedetto Ghirlandaio,
65 have survived. So too has the *St John in the desert*, one of the most famous frescoes, which was by tradition attributed to the young Michelangelo. Certainly, when compared with the solemn and serenely elegant

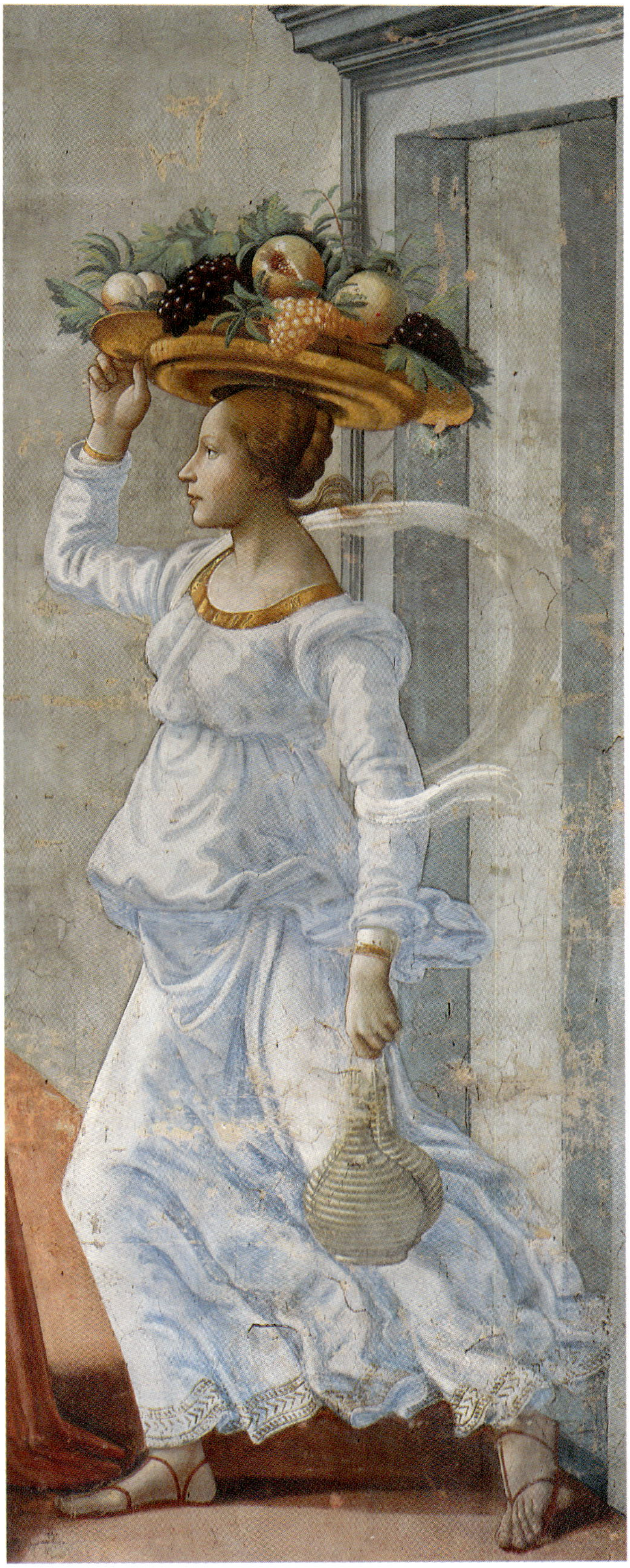
61

60, 61. Stories of the Baptist: Birth of St John, details
Florence, Santa Maria Novella

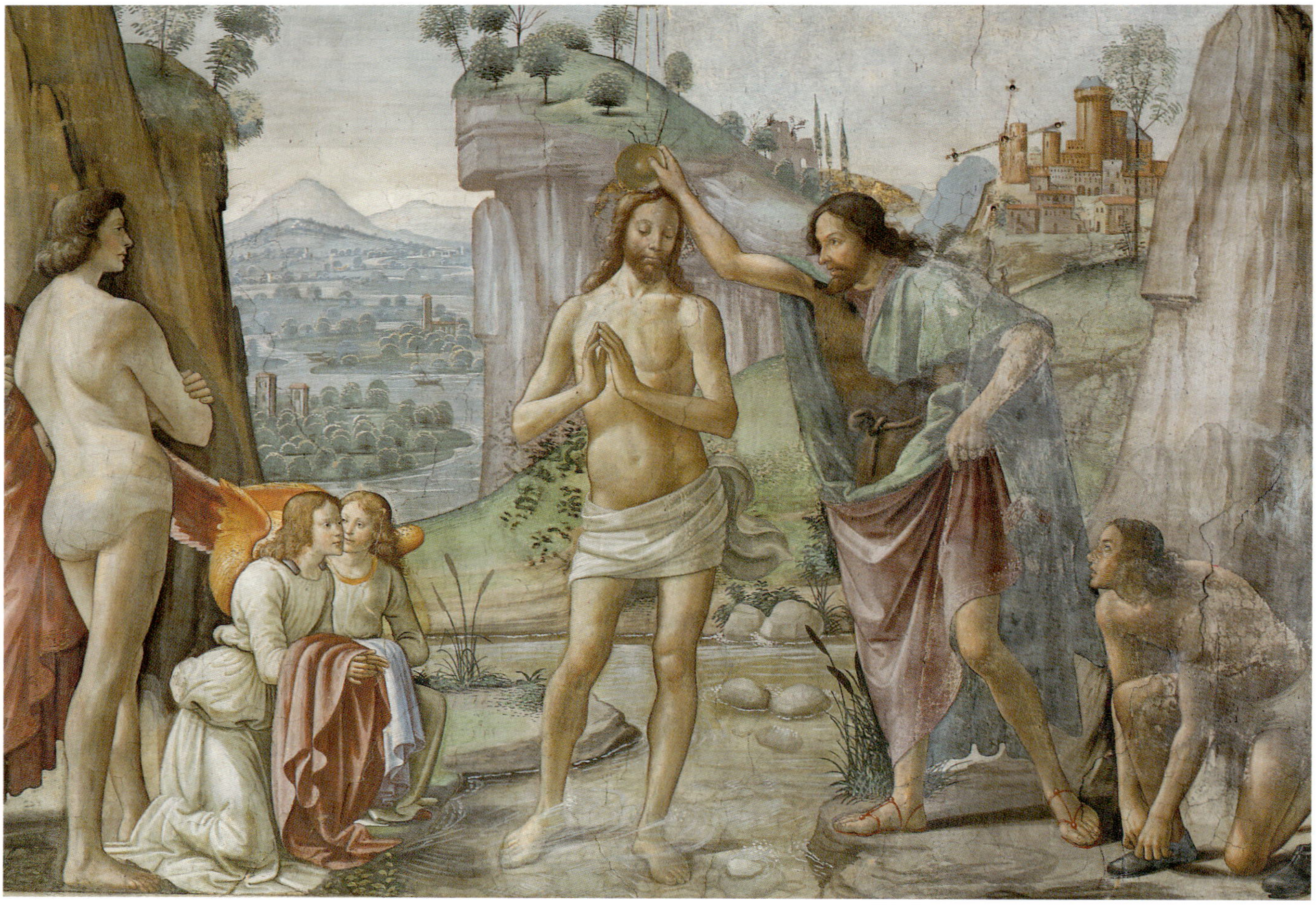

62

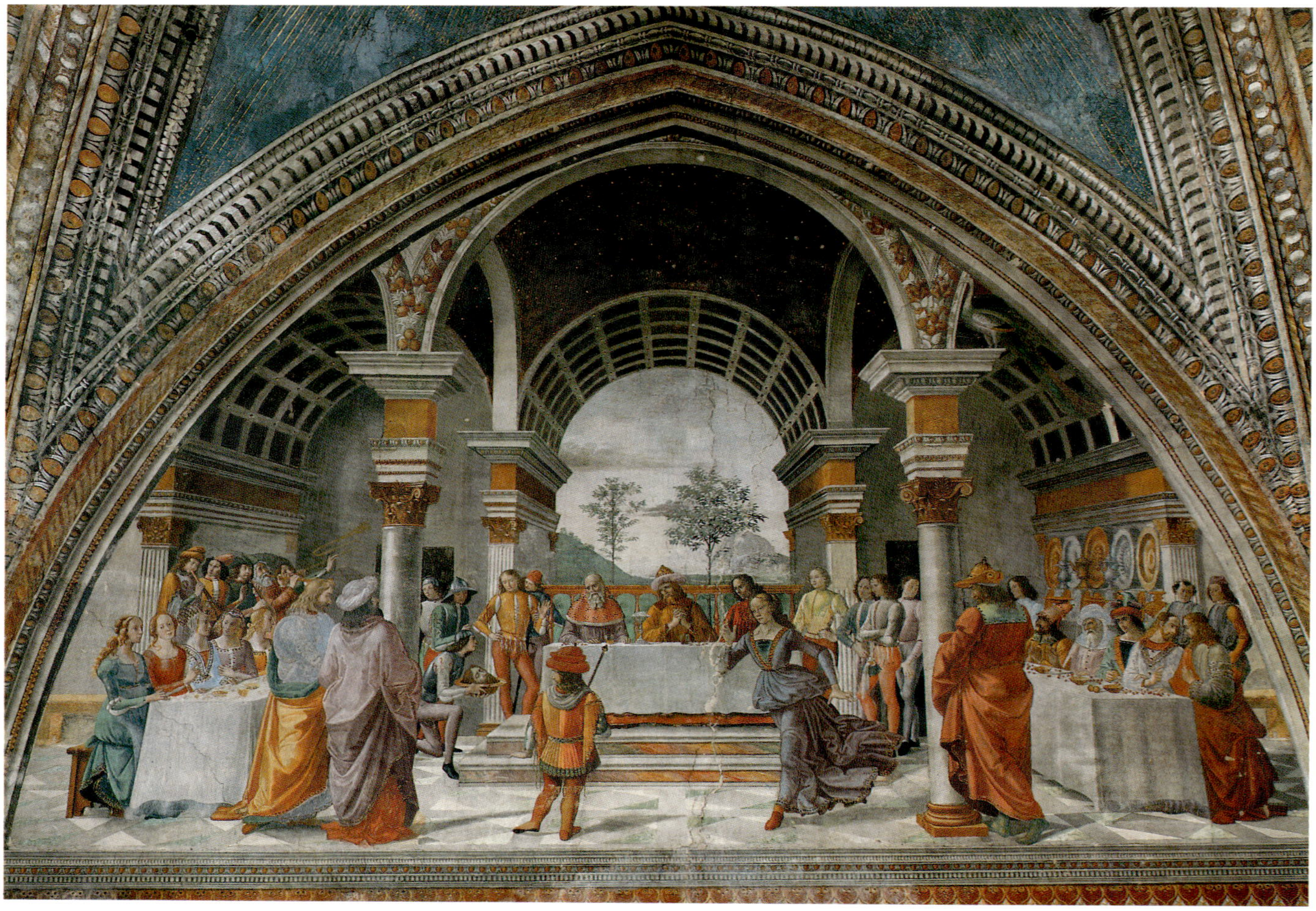

63

62. *Stories of the Baptist: Baptism of Christ, detail*
Florence, Santa Maria Novella

63. *Stories of the Baptist: Herod's Banquet*
Florence, Santa Maria Novella

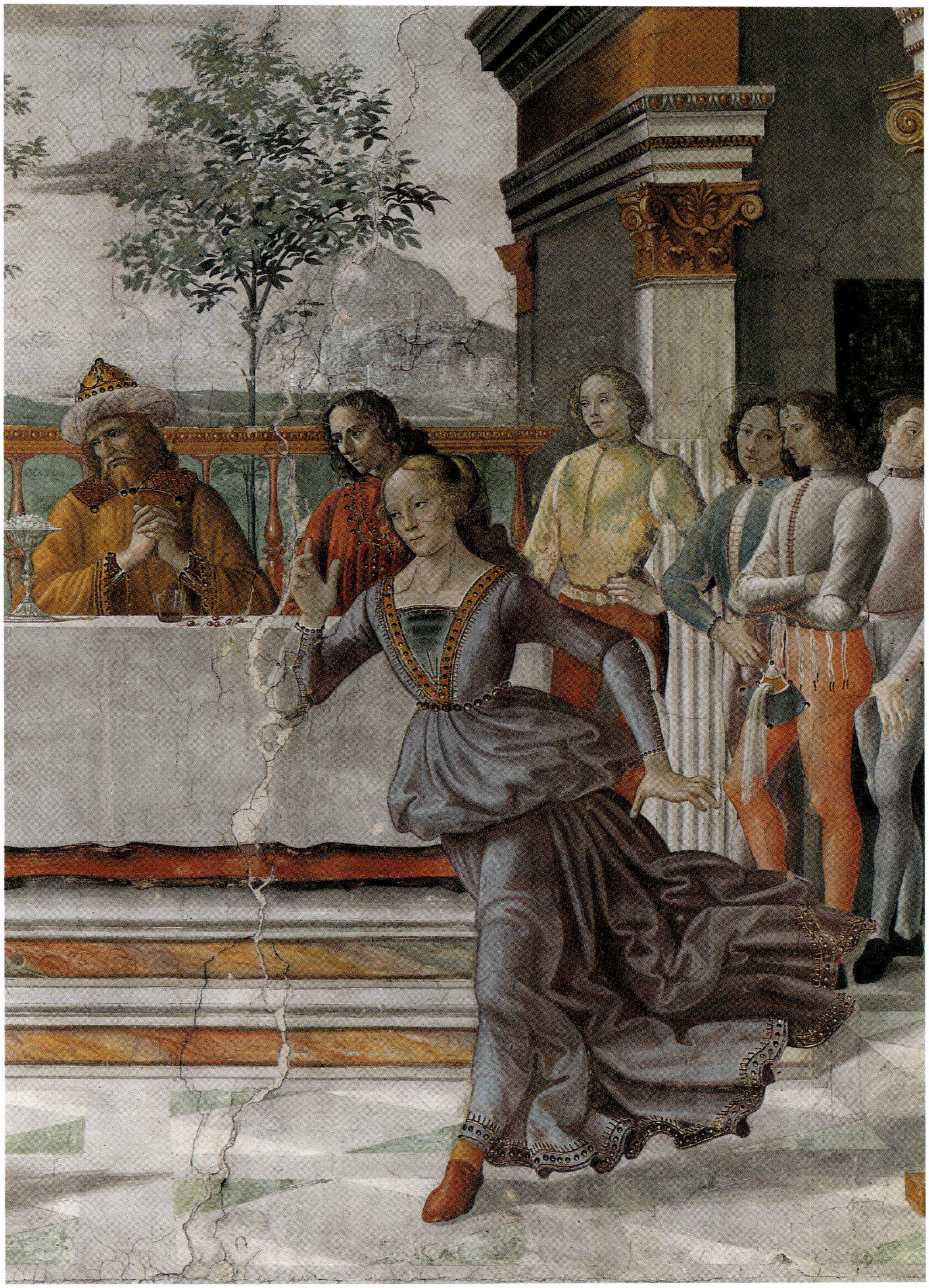

64. *Stories of the Baptist: Herod's Banquet, detail*
Florence, Santa Maria Novella

64

figures that populate Ghirlandaio's world, the robust and half-smiling young "prophet" who sets out with such determination toward an invisible desert, leaving turreted castles and still waters behind him, is of a quite different substance. There is something quite different here, especially in the chubby face with its soft, almost sculpted flesh and the steadiness of the slender young legs, however far removed it still is even from Michelangelo's first documented works.

On the other hand Vasari, Michelangelo's friend and worthy biographer, speaks of the young Buonarroti at Ghirlandaio's workshop, which by now had many followers. Thus, the biographer narrates in the life of Michelangelo: "It was about this time that Michelangelo became friendly with the young Francesco Granacci, who had been sent as a boy to learn the art of painting from Domenico Ghirlandaio. Francesco saw that Michelangelo had a great aptitude for drawing, and as he was very fond of him he used to supply him every day with drawings by Ghirlandaio, who was then regarded, throughout all Italy let alone in Florence, as one of the finest living masters. As a result Michelangelo grew more ambitious with every day that passed, and when Lodovico realized that there was no hope of forcing him to give up drawing he resolved to put his son's aspirations to some use and make it possible for him to learn the art properly. So on the advice of friends he apprenticed him to Domenico Ghirlandaio". In the years of the execution of the frescoes in the Cappella Maggiore of Santa Mar-

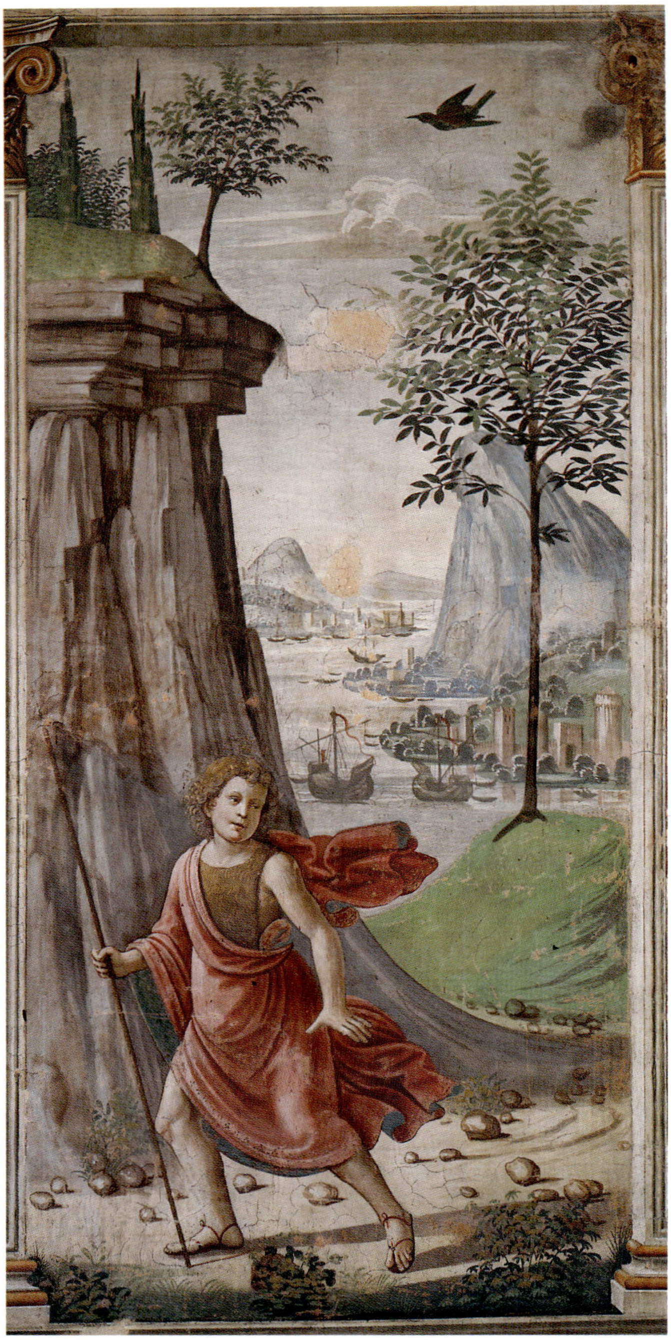

65

65. St John in the Desert
Florence, Santa Maria Novella

66. Giovanni Tornabuoni
Florence, Santa Maria Novella

67. Francesca Pitti
Florence, Santa Maria Novella

ia Novella Michelangelo was fourteen years old, and despite the fact that "the development of Michelangelo's talents and character was quite out of the ordinary...", and amazed his master, perhaps it is too much to expect that Ghirlandaio had him execute the St John in the desert all on his own. Certainly the hand that drew the landscape below and the rocks is different from the one that painted the sturdy child which with some imagination we might liken to Michelangelo's Child of the *Doni Tondo*. It may be that the impatient hand of the great painter, still but a youth, sketched something in the face and determined gait of the child Predecessor. It may be anti-scientific and anti-historical, but now and then it is nice to let the imagination have free rein for a moment.

The two portraits of the patrons, Giovanni Tor- 66
nabuoni and Francesca Pitti, praying at the sides of the 67
main altar, bring us abruptly back to reality. Their
poses are similar to those of Francesco Sassetti and 38
Nera Corsi, but their appearance and the setting are 37
quite different. Giovanni Tornabuoni, on the left, is austerely dressed in an almost monastic purple-red robe, his arms clasped over his breast in profound contemplation. His figure is enclosed within an arch, or rather in a series of arches that give movement to a perspective effect that by now is no longer affected, but natural and free. Beyond is a radiant landscape and a classical colonnade that serves to give depth to the scene, an intentional touch of solemnity that offers many possibilities for the play of light on surfaces. On the right, also kneeling, is Francesca Pitti with her hands held together. Her face, almost monastically framed by the white headcloth, has less vitality. It is a posthumous portrait, wanted by Giovanni, of the wife who had died some years before and had not accompanied him into old age. A mock tombstone on the right bears the date and epigraph of the work's completion: *An MCCCCLXXXX quo pulcherrima civitas opibus victoriis artibus aedificisque nobilis copie salubritate pace perfruebatur* [Year 1490 in which the wonderful city, renowned for its treasures, victories, activities and buildings, enjoyed salubrity and peace]. In these words there is the satisfaction and complaisance of the great Florentine bourgeoisie, which in the years between 1480 and 1490 enjoyed glory and riches. Their wealth was also used to make the city splendid. This had already happened some years earlier with the Brancacci family, friends of the Strozzi, who between 1424 and 1426 had commissioned the innovative young Masaccio to execute the "Stories of St Peter" in their chapel at the Carmine.

It must be stated again that over and above any assertion about the ease and absolute mastery of his art, or otherwise, Domenico Ghirlandaio is the most complete, pleasing and faithful illustrator of this society in perhaps the most splendid period of the city, which he brings back to life almost day by day in its characters, its streets and palaces, in the very atmosphere which surrounds them and which at times reaches us in the most vital way. A hundred years later the Medici, especially with Agnolo Bronzino, would have their court portraitist. His portraits are numerous and unforgettable, from Cosimo I in armour to that splendid painting of his beautiful Spanish wife, Eleonora di Toledo, and his children: Bia, Maria, Giovanni with his goldfinch and chubby smiling face, and the already serious and rather introverted Francesco.

In the last twenty years of the 15th century the figure

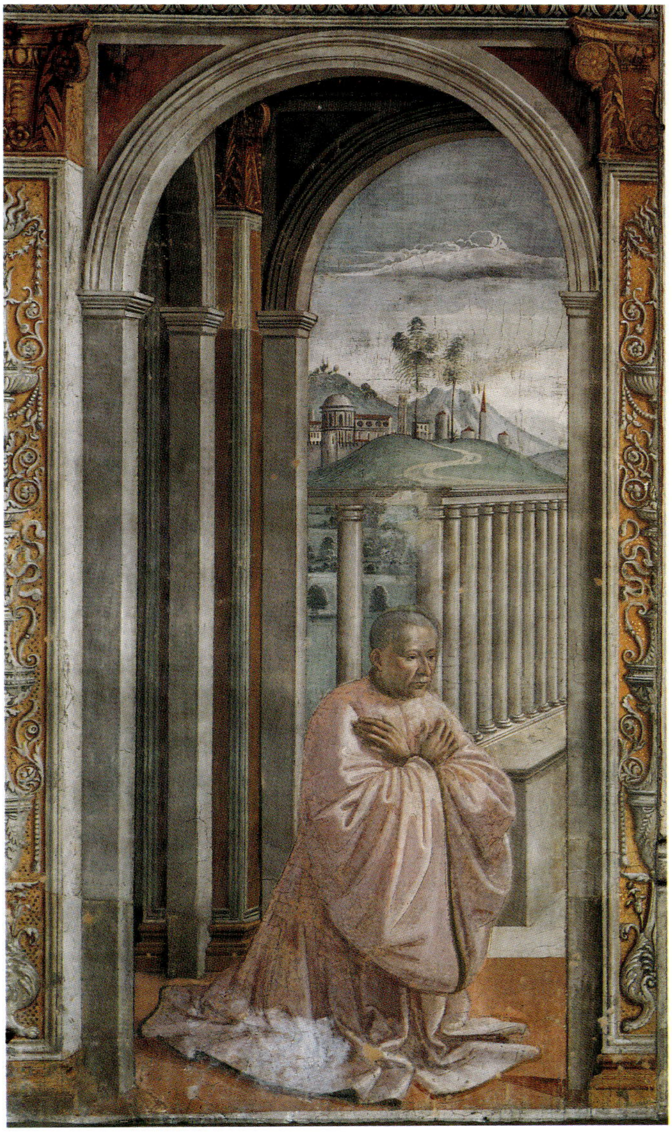

66

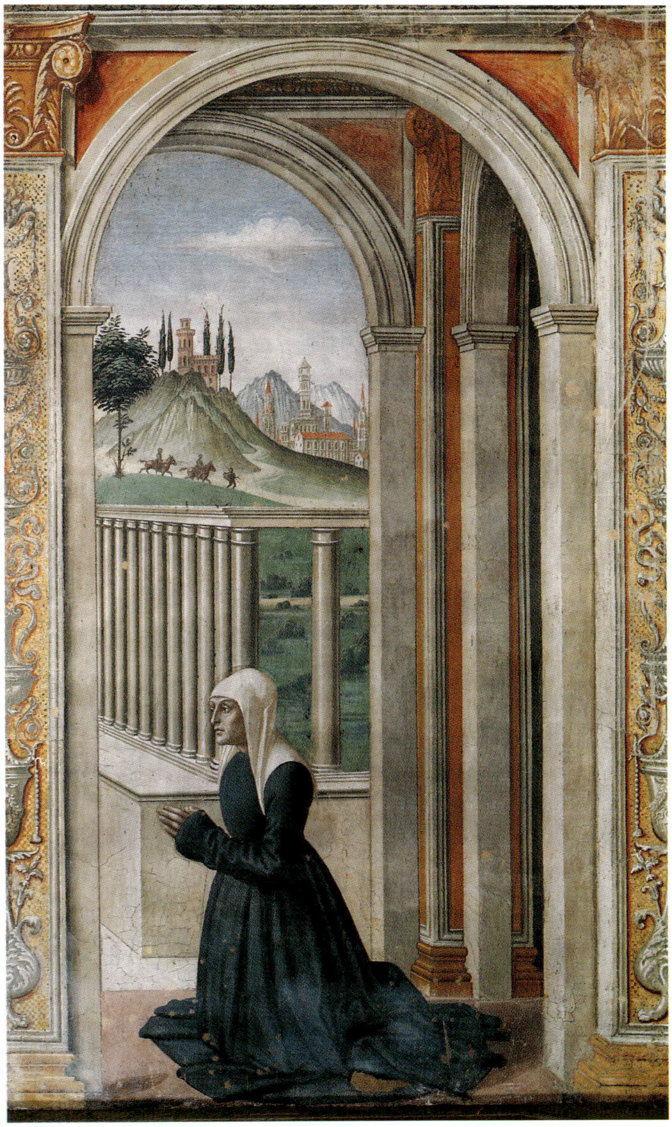

67

of the portraitist working for the great families, almost all of them enjoying a similar degree of economic power, did not yet exist. Only Mantegna, in the Camera degli Sposi at Mantova, had portrayed the Gonzaga family. Ghirlandaio, however, could already be considered if not the official portraitist of the highest Florentine bourgeoisie, the most important and sought-after artist of the ruling class. In our brief survey of his paintings we have seen almost all the most important figures in the public eye at that time, from Cosimo il Vecchio, *pater patriae*, to Lorenzo, his young children and the most important people in the Medicean circle with them, as well as many of the artists working for them and for others in a city that was becoming more and more beautiful. Leaving aside any other consideration, I really do believe that Ghirlandaio deserves recognition for providing us with the opportunity to relive a probably happier time so remote from our own. Every so often, when looking at his painting, one can almost hear the sounds and voices that filled it.

Nor must we forget the enchanted and enchanting world of his colours that range from the most intense tones to others that are almost transparent, like blown glass, which fill the richly embroidered clothes, the robes and cloaks, becoming perhaps most delicate in the soft flesh tones of the women. The female portrait, indeed, seems to be one of Ghirlandaio's ideals. His colours are charged with intensity in the furnishings, they play in a quivering and in a spreading out of surfaces in the architecture, both external and internal, and assume an airy lightness in the great skies of the background, at times limpid, at times just shadowed by wispy clouds. From out of the air the light changes colour as it enters into houses, falls on the castles in the background, on the trees, on the lustrous stretches of water, and on the dense woods that are often warmed by the setting sun.

One might argue that Domenico is superficial, that his art is without problematic or sentimental cultural implications; but like no one else, either before or after, he is the faithful illustrator of an environment and its many characters, observed with a careful, subtle, admiring eye.

68 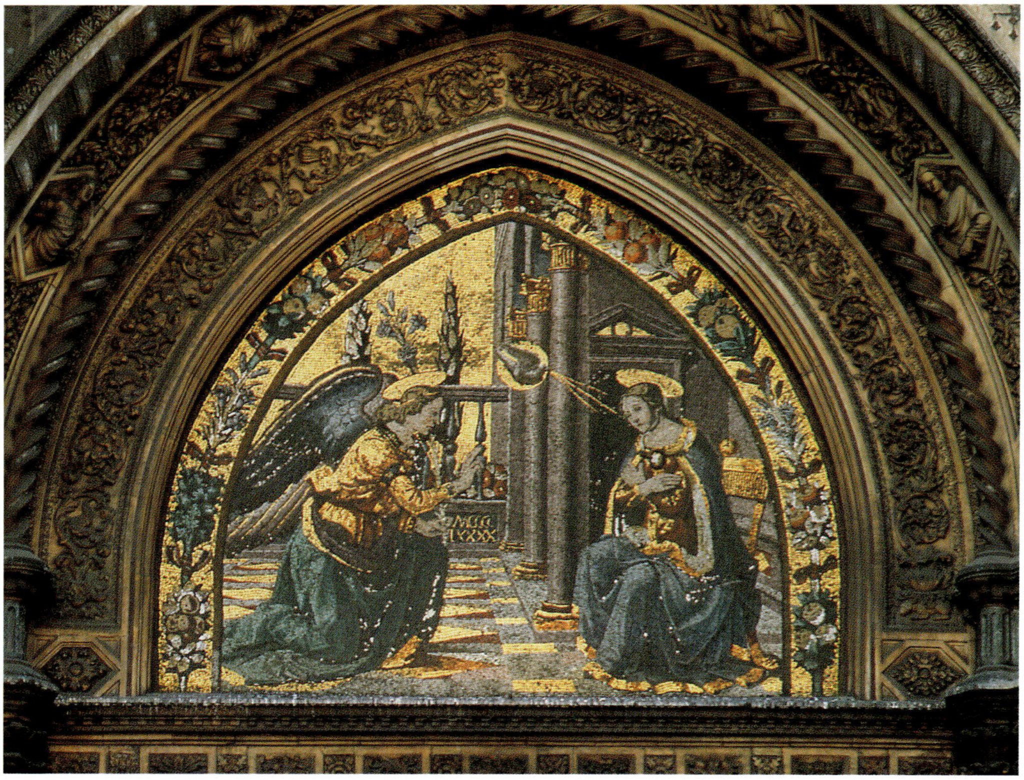

68. Domenico and David Ghirlandaio Mosaic representing the Annunciation Florence, Duomo (Door of the Mandorla)

The Paintings on Wood

We have already spoken of some works by Ghirlan-
12 daio on wood: the *Madonna and Saints*, painted for
the church of San Giusto and now at the Uffizi, data-
39 ble to around 1480; and the altarpiece with the *Ado-
ration of the Shepherds* from above the altar in the Sassetti Chapel in Santa Trinita, which although from about the same period reveals quite different interests and intentions on the part of the painter.

Other numerous works on wood complete the career of Ghirlandaio, who was known above all as a fresco painter. They are works which again emphasize his abilities as a colourist, the harmonious pleasantness of his composition, and his faithfulness to certain models of his time and his school. Certainly, when compared with the great artistic talents who were either then asserting themselves in Florence, or who were shortly to appear on the scene, Domenico, in his unruffled and somewhat muted way of expressing himself, lacked creative genius.

Vasari is so attentive, precise and admiring a narrator of Ghirlandaio, the painter of frescoes, that he gives little attention to Domenico's work on wood, and instead refers to his skill as a mosaicist, a pupil of Alesso Baldovinetti in this art. "Domenico enriched the modern art of working in mosaic infinitely more than any other Tuscan, as his works, though few, amply demonstrate...". Thus writes Vasari, who had previ-
68 ously recorded an Annunciation in mosaic in the Duomo of Florence. "Over the side door of Santa Maria del Fiore leading to the Servites there is a very fine Annunciation in mosaic by Domenico, and nothing better has been produced by modern masters. Domenico used to say that painting was design, but that the true painting for eternity was mosaic". Of this mosaic destined for the door of the Mandorla he only executed the cartoon, which was probably translated into mosaic by his brother David.

It would be opportune, however, to dwell for a moment on Domenico's painting on wood. We have already said that in these paintings Ghirlandaio desired to remain, albeit in reduced format, an observer and narrator of pleasingly decorative stories and customs, in a Renaissance context fashionable in the cultured and opulent environment of mercantile and bourgeois Florence that revolved around the Medici House, which by this time had long asserted its supremacy.

A youthful work attributable to the period in which he was associated with Verrocchio is undoubtedly the *Madonna and Child* in the Kress Collection in Washington, in which in a tension of lines a vibrant plasticity fades into extreme serenity. The glassy quality of the jewels - an opal, four pearls and the corals - like the fineness of the veil which in its twisting becomes almost a diadem, already reveals Domenico's attention to Flemish art. The Virgin has a certain sharpness about her face that will later vanish, as will

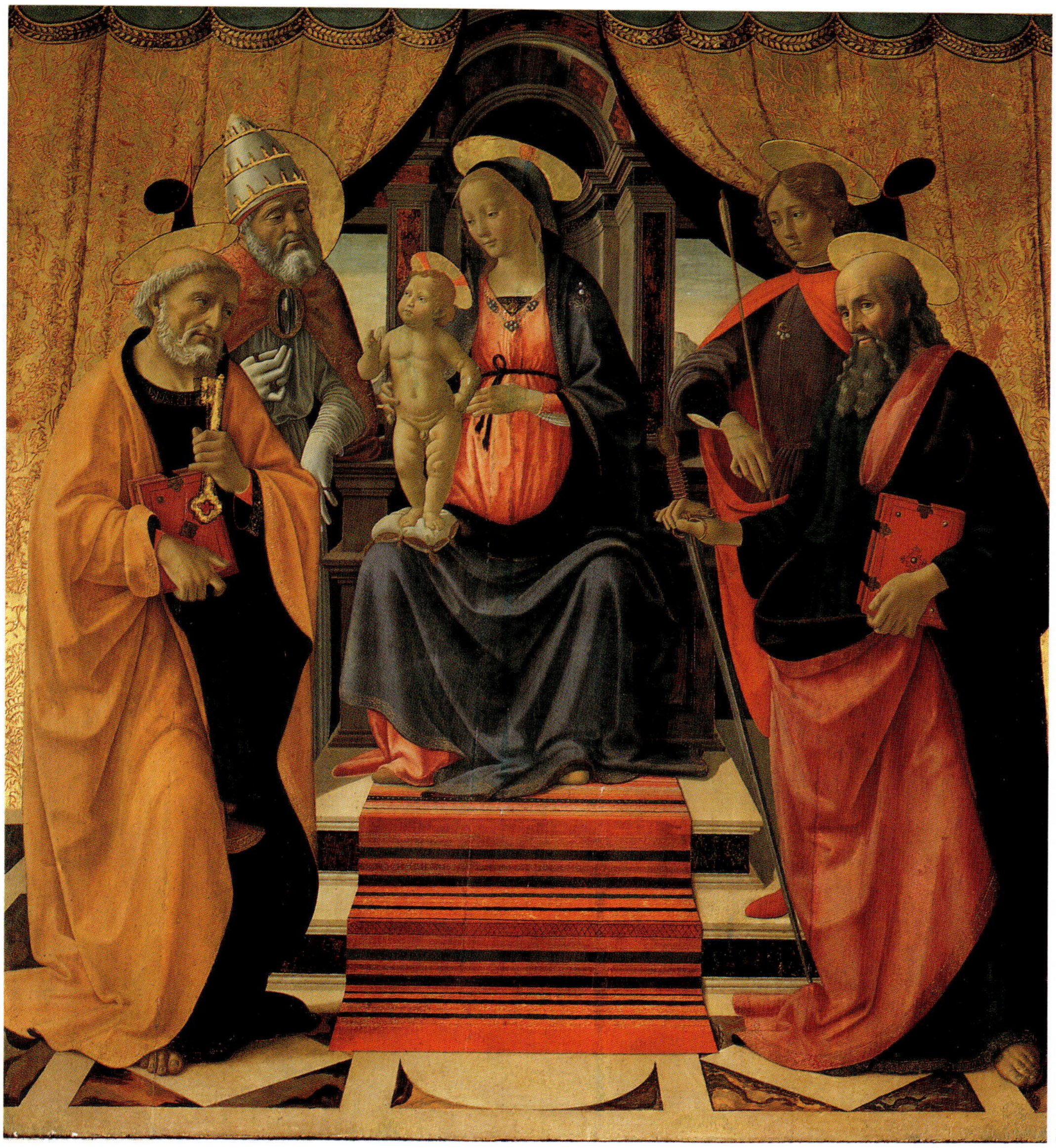

69

the plastic rotundity of the Child. In this youthful work Ghirlandaio reaches a height of expression and poses certain problems that seem to prelude a different kind of art, an art that would have derived from certain studies and arrangements of style and form which were not pursued or resolved. His art unfolds in an even style of serene simplicity, according to a measured structure and on the basis of well-established
7-10 precepts. In the now imminent "Stories of St Fina" he was already quite different; he had conquered the figurative and poetic world that he would not abandon until his premature death.

Although few were completely his own, Ghirlandaio's works on wood were numerous, punctuating and filling out his untiring activity as a fresco painter.

Domenico had become so famous, both in Florence and elsewhere, that the numerous commissions he received forced him increasingly to resort to the aid of friends and assistants. He was even unable to reserve his easel painting completely to himself. Since so many young artists were active at that time, evidently the wealthy Florentine bourgeoisie preferred turning to Ghirlandaio. In his work they presumably recognized themselves and revelled when they observed themselves in that faithful and rather flattering mirror. In his famous fresco cycles the artist had already shown himself to be a careful and accurate portraitist, capable of representing not only the exterior side of the person portrayed, but also some of his feelings and aspects of his character, with that sensitivity to reality that was typical of great Florentine portraiture and sculpture of the second half of the 15th century.

The portrait of an *Old Man with a Child*, now in the 70
Louvre, forms part of this Florentine tradition that aimed so directly at the realistic rendition of the subject. The work has no precise date, nor has it been possible to establish, nor even deduce, the identity of the person. However, we can place it close to the fres-

69. Madonna and Child Enthroned between Angels and Saints
Lucca, Duomo

coes of the Sassetti Chapel by virtue of certain stylistic affinities, particularly the background landscape which
39 is similar to that of the *Nativity*, with its purplish sky that turns into gold. The serpentine road climbs up to a small church and a group of towering cypress trees. The old man, certainly a grandfather, with his pimply nose, has the intense expression of an old Florentine, all shrewdness and wisdom. His grey hair is so real as to closely resemble certain Flemish images. His tender, smiling gaze is directed at the boy, who has a delicate profile and curly blond hair, and who in an expression of affection presses against his grandfather. By their clothes, both the old man and the boy reveal that they belonged to a well-to-do family; the red cloth of the man's garments with its fox-fur border, and the harmonious alternating of red and black with a faint touch of whiteness in the boy's clothes, are enough to tell us that the scene takes place inside a wealthy middle-class home in Florence.

71 The *Coronation of the Virgin* for the Duomo of Narni was probably painted in 1486. In the same period Ghirlandaio was beginning his frescoes for the Tornabuoni family at Santa Maria Novella. The *Coronation* is certainly a work of collaboration with others, even if, as often happens, it is difficult to identify the hands of the assistants. It is on the whole a little too crowded, removed from Ghirlandaio's measured structure; the gamut of colours however - soft, yet intense reds, blues and yellows - correspond with his taste. Despite certain touches that reveal a by now established style, the composition, whose perspective is achieved only by reason of the figures that slope from the lower to the upper levels, is closely reminiscent of Angelico's *Coronation of the Virgin*, originally from Sant'Egidio and now in the Uffizi. It was a vivid memory for Ghirlandaio who in the first years of his apprenticeship had followed his master Alesso Baldovinetti, busy working on his frescoes in that church, beside Domenico Veneziano and Piero della Francesca.

A year later Ghirlandaio painted the large tondo with
72 the *Adoration of the Magi*, now at the Uffizi, for his great patrons, the Tornabuoni family. It is confirmed by the date in Roman numerals: MCCCCLXXXVII. In a serene and pleasingly illustrative way this very famous work, perhaps more famous than its actual worth, condenses some of the fundamental precepts of the Florentine Renaissance of the second generation. I would say that the recent influence of Sandro Botticelli, who painted the *Adoration of the Magi* for the Cappella Lami in Santa Maria Novella in 1475, predominates here: a vast lighted sky, with classical ruins of great luminous nobility in the background. Within them, and containing the manger, is a shed with sloping roofs, which in the moment of the Adoration of the Child shelters only the ox and the ass. The Virgin, the baby Jesus and a contemplative St Joseph, are out in the open; Mary, as if on a throne formed by a piece of classical architecture, offers up her newborn child to the homage of the Kings who have come from the east. Even the arrangement of some figures is reminiscent of Botticelli, although the style is more mannered.

Although Domenico's warm, vivid colours become rather muted here, there are instances of great brightness, as in the striped clothes of the foreshortened black servant who bows his shaven head and places the crown on the blond-haired head of the young king, whose delicate profile is somewhat reminiscent of Filippino Lippi. Domenico cannot, and presumably does not want to, renounce his role as narrator and chronicler of surroundings and costumes. Here we find his careful and rather curious description in the figure standing on the left with a large red hat and in the person next to him wearing an ample yellow hood. In the background, resting after their long journey, the ranks of the bodyguard in helmets and armour stand by their restless and still pawing horses. And again there is that attention to Flemish tradition in the precise and yet poetic representation of the grass dotted with flowers, a large water-bottle and a rough cloth sack. A replica of this tondo, in smaller dimensions and entirely the work of Domenico's shop, is to be found in the Galleria Palatina at Palazzo Pitti in Florence.

In 1485 Ghirlandaio received the commission for the
great *Adoration of the Magi* for the main altar in the 76
church of the Spedale degli Innocenti. The man behind this assignment was Francesco di Giovanni Tesori, who was interested in artistic things for the Hospital certainly more than any other person of the Quattrocento. The great altarpiece was installed in 1488, just after its completion. Its belonging to Ghirlandaio, with the clear collaboration of assistants, has never been doubted. Besides, Vasari speaks about it at some length: "In the church of the Innocenti he painted in tempera a much-admired picture of the Magi, containing some fine heads and varied physiognomies of people both young and old, notably a head of the Virgin, displaying all the modesty, beauty and grace which art can impart to the Mother of God". The work is dated, but, even leaving aside this irrefutable proof, the painting belongs to the years in which Ghirlandaio and his assistants worked on the frescoes of the Cappella Maggiore of Santa Maria Novella.

There is the same breadth, the same brightness in the 77
landscape, closed in by that background wall which helps, rather than inhibits, the perspective and spatial effect. The work, as we have said, is dated 1488, this being inscribed on the decorated architrave high up on the right. The same prior of the church, Tesori, had commissioned the predella with stories of the Virgin and the great cornice of the altarpiece had been executed by the carpenter Francesco Bartolo on designs by Giuliano da Sangallo.

70. Portrait of an Old Man with a Child
62 x 46 cm
Paris, Louvre

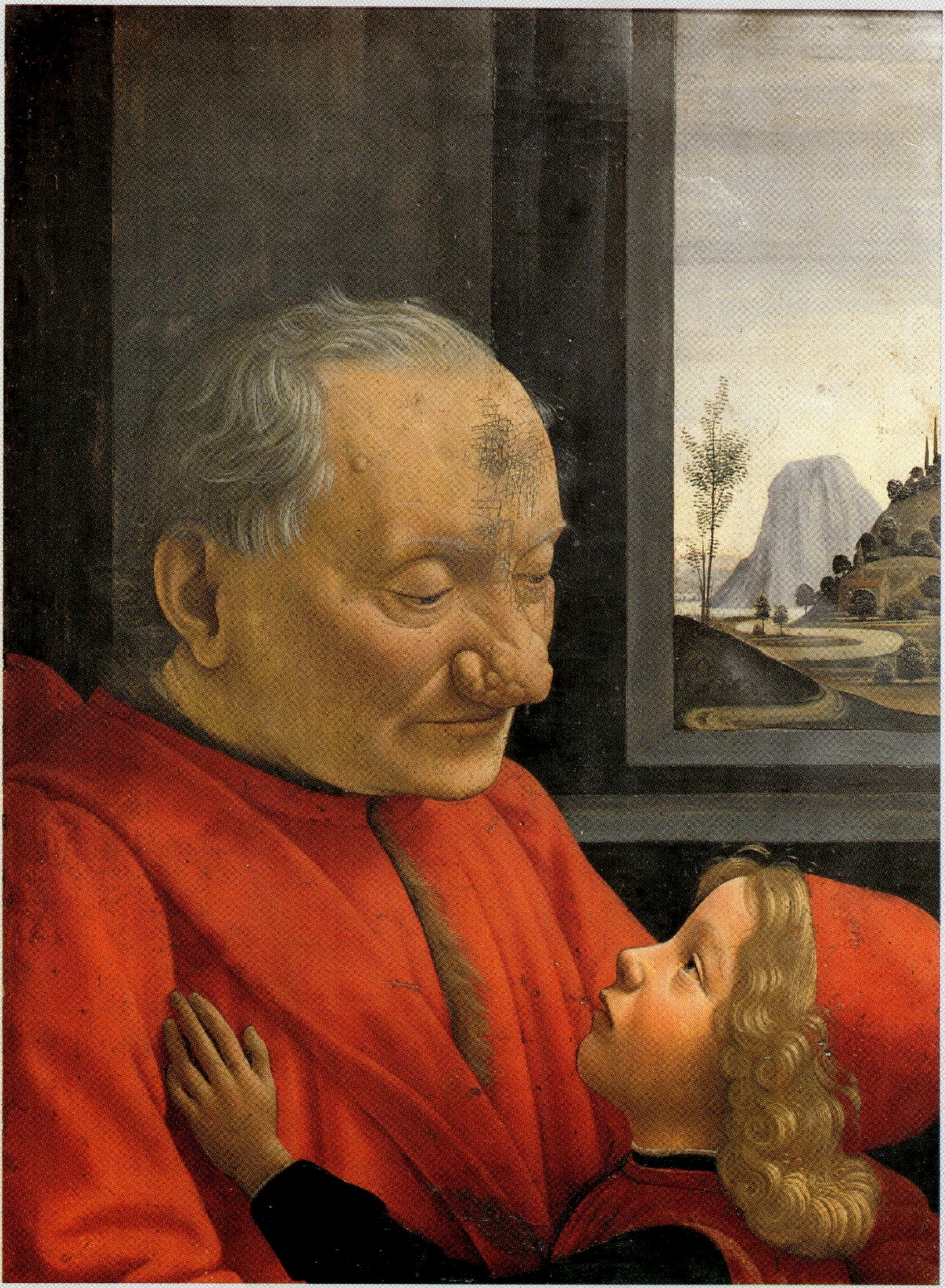

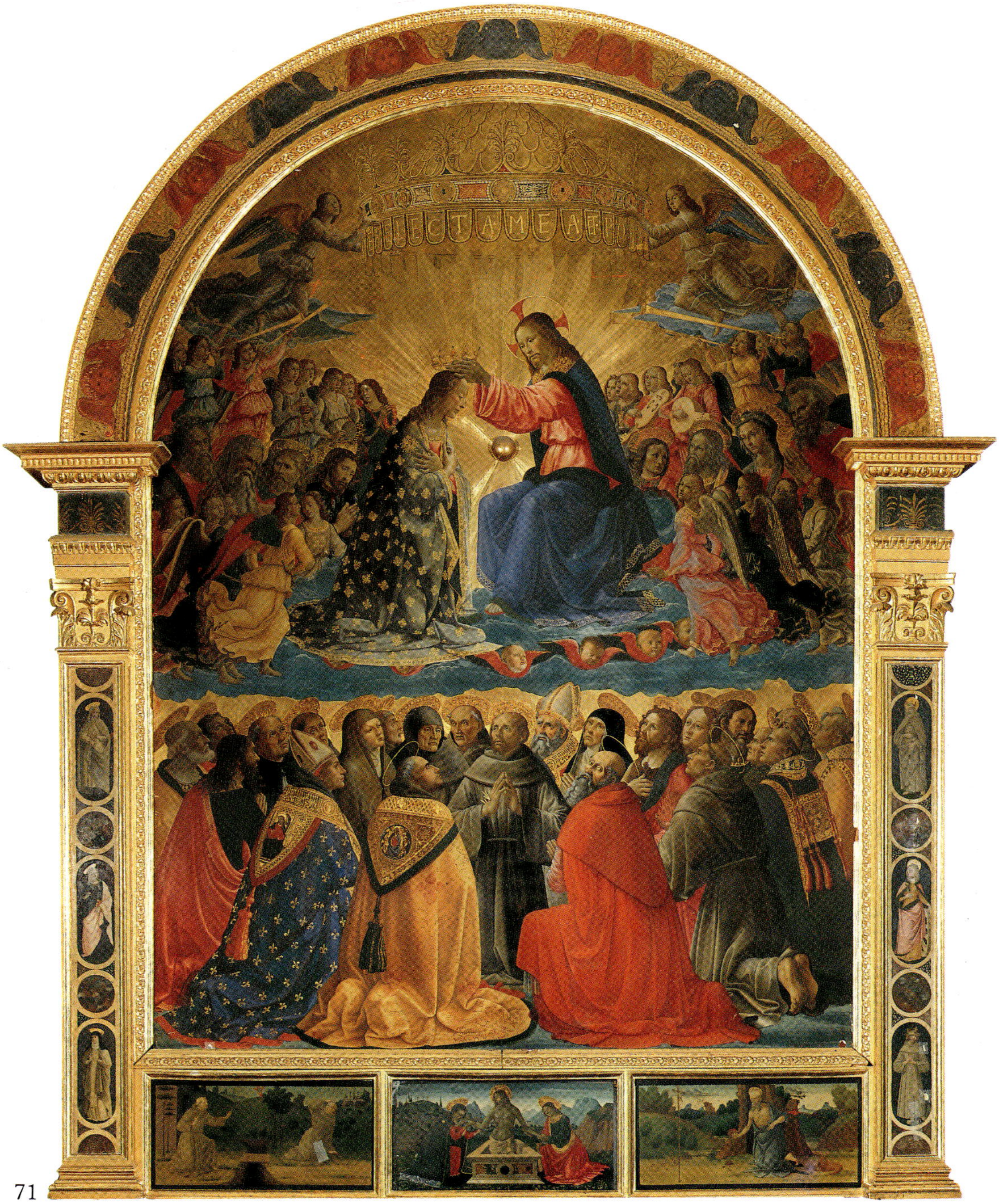

71

79-85 The scenes of the predella are the work of one of Ghirlandaio's pupils, Bartolommeo di Giovanni; this is confirmed by the records and the workmanship of the fine, slender figures which are characteristic of him. The painting remained over the altar until 1786, when the inside of the church was restored and the altarpiece placed in the wall behind the altar. In 1917 it was transferred to the Hospital's museum. The predella, with the Martyrdom of St John the Evangelist, the Annunciation, the Marriage of the Virgin, the Deposition, the Presentation in the Temple, the Baptism of Christ, the Consecration of the Church of the Innocenti, had been dismembered at the time of the restoration of the great altar (1615). In the 19th century the seven panels were in the Sala delle Adunanze. Later they were reunited with the painting, which was

71. Coronation of the Virgin
330 x 230 cm
Narni, Civic Picture Gallery

72. Adoration of the Magi
diam. 171 cm
Florence, Uffizi

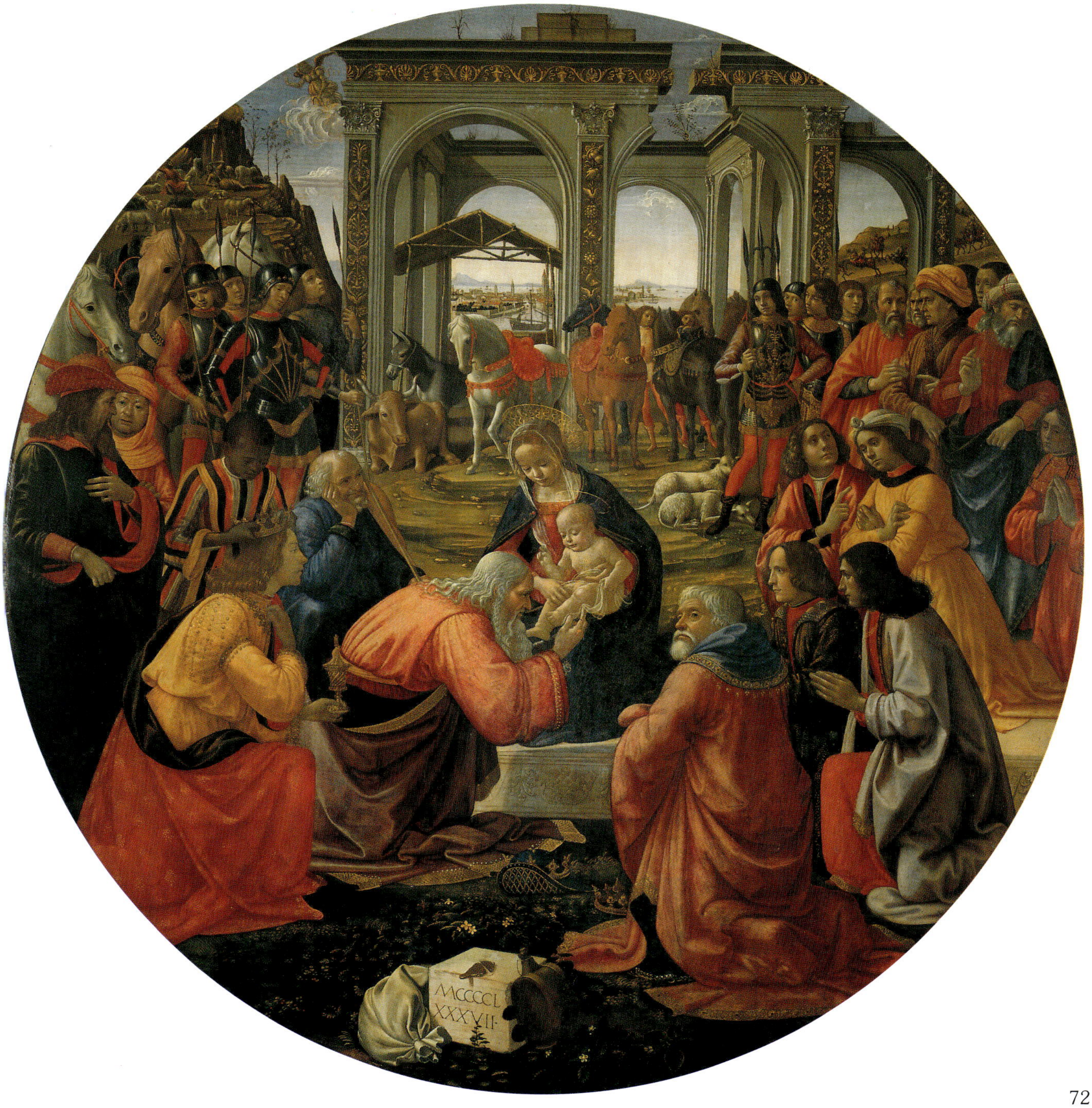

72

now devoid of Sangallo's fine cornice that was destroyed in the restoration of 1786.

75 The self-portrait of the artist behind the young king is very similar to that of the Santa Maria Novella painting with the *Expulsion of Joachim from the Temple*
42
1 and the other in the *Adoration of the Shepherds* at Santa Trinita. The priest nearby is almost certainly the man who commissioned the work, Francesco di Giovanni Tesori, the prior who embellished the Spedale degli Innocenti with many important works of art. Ghirlandaio's portrait shows him to be a keen, sharp and intelligent man.

The work is polished and complete in all its parts, and taken as a whole represents one of Ghirlandaio's most important "easel" works, possibly because it was also the most official of them all. Here too the assistants were at work. Indeed, in the harrowing scene of the Slaughter of the Innocents in the background, 75
Berenson recognized the hand of Bartolommeo di Giovanni whom he poetically called "Domenico's friend".

The tender Virgin, again outside the shed, which is reconstructed on highly ornate classical pilasters, offers up her Child to the homage of the kings and devotees who are grouped around, in a profusion of vivid expressions, gestures and costumes and a blending and alternation of the most splendid colours.

Once again a peculiarly Flemish attention to detail emerges in Ghirlandaio's art - and particularly in the lavish oriental costumes, which were in fact probably inspired by the grandeur of those great occasions frequented by the richest citizens of Florence. Note the

73
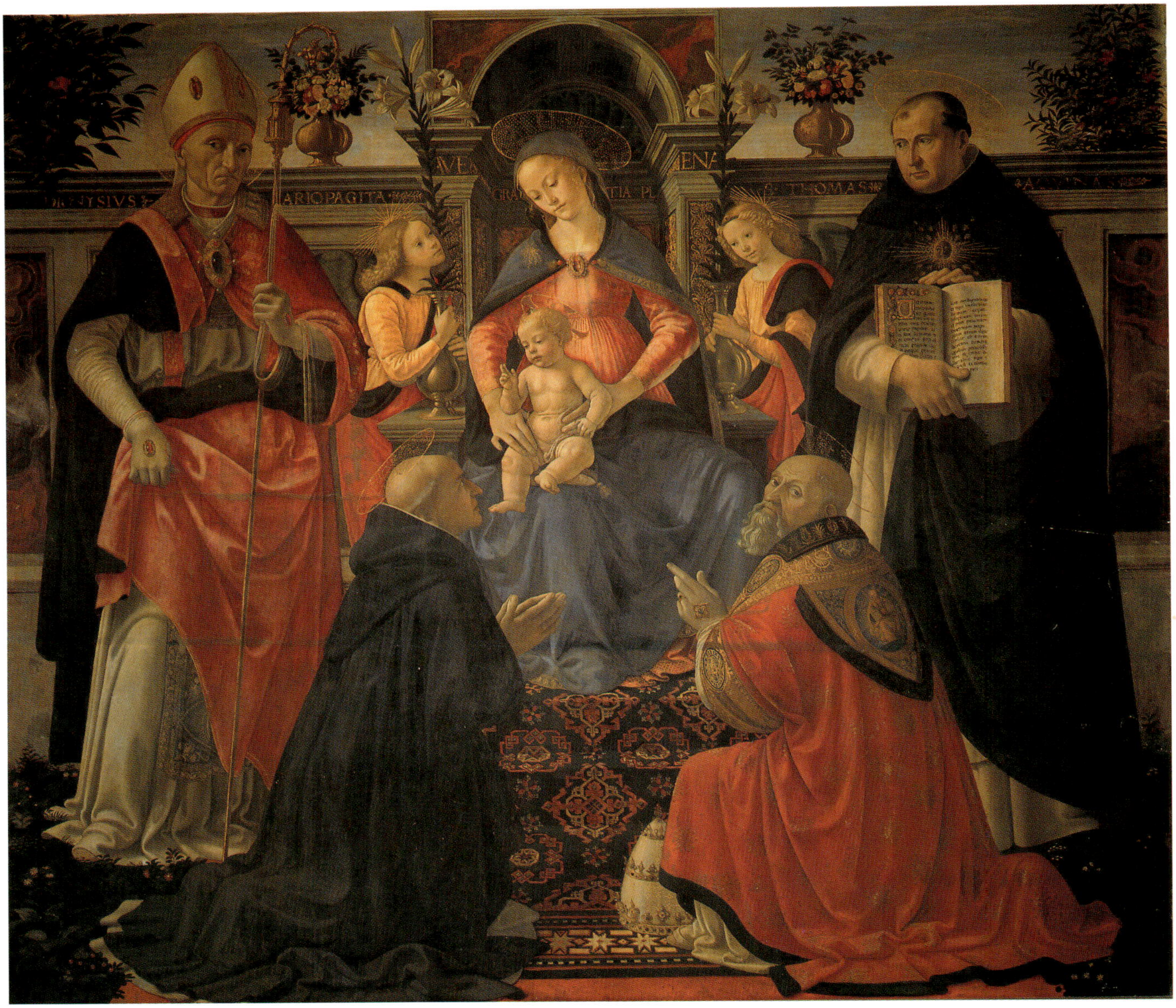

73. Madonna and Child Enthroned between Angels and Saints
168 x 197 cm
Florence, Uffizi

great turban of the fat man on the right, studded with pearls and rubies, or the hat of the person next to him, with its raised side edged with precious jewels and with the gold chain around his neck and the huge precious pendent; or the border of pearls and other gold-work ornaments of the dark young man standing slightly back from the others. In contrast is the simple figure of the Baptist in the act of pointing to the Child. Here too, however, Ghirlandaio cannot resist a rich red and black cloak with a golden border. Innocent young saints in their small transparent white tunics, haloed with gold, pay their homage to the Child Saint. Beyond the wall is an imaginary city, a kind of Florence-Jerusalem, and an open landscape of limpid radiance, shining waters and mountains. Boats, ships and figures move about in it in a calm, peaceful atmosphere. A small tree is silhouetted against the clearness of the sky. In the background scene depicting the Slaughter of the Innocents, as already mentioned, one may discern the hand of Bartolommeo di Giovanni, the author of the stories from the predella. In these, the artist who painted nine of the ten lunettes frescoed in San Martino brought out the best in himself and his kind nature that must have complemented well the character of his master, Domenico Ghirlandaio.

Another fine work by Ghirlandaio is the *Visitation*, 86
now at the Louvre, which probably dates to around 1491. The meeting takes place in a broad landscape of rarefied atmosphere, with a series of large buildings bathed in sunlight. It is an affectionate, yet measured, encounter. The gentle submissiveness of Elisabeth is emphasized, as is the humble, modest attention of Mary with her face sweet and full of trepidation. The light veil, with its soft folds of fine, gossamer material, is full of delicate highlights. A large clasp of pearls and gold closes the cloak over her breast, a jewel of hard glassy material that contrasts somewhat with the softness of the colours and contours which give a not easi-

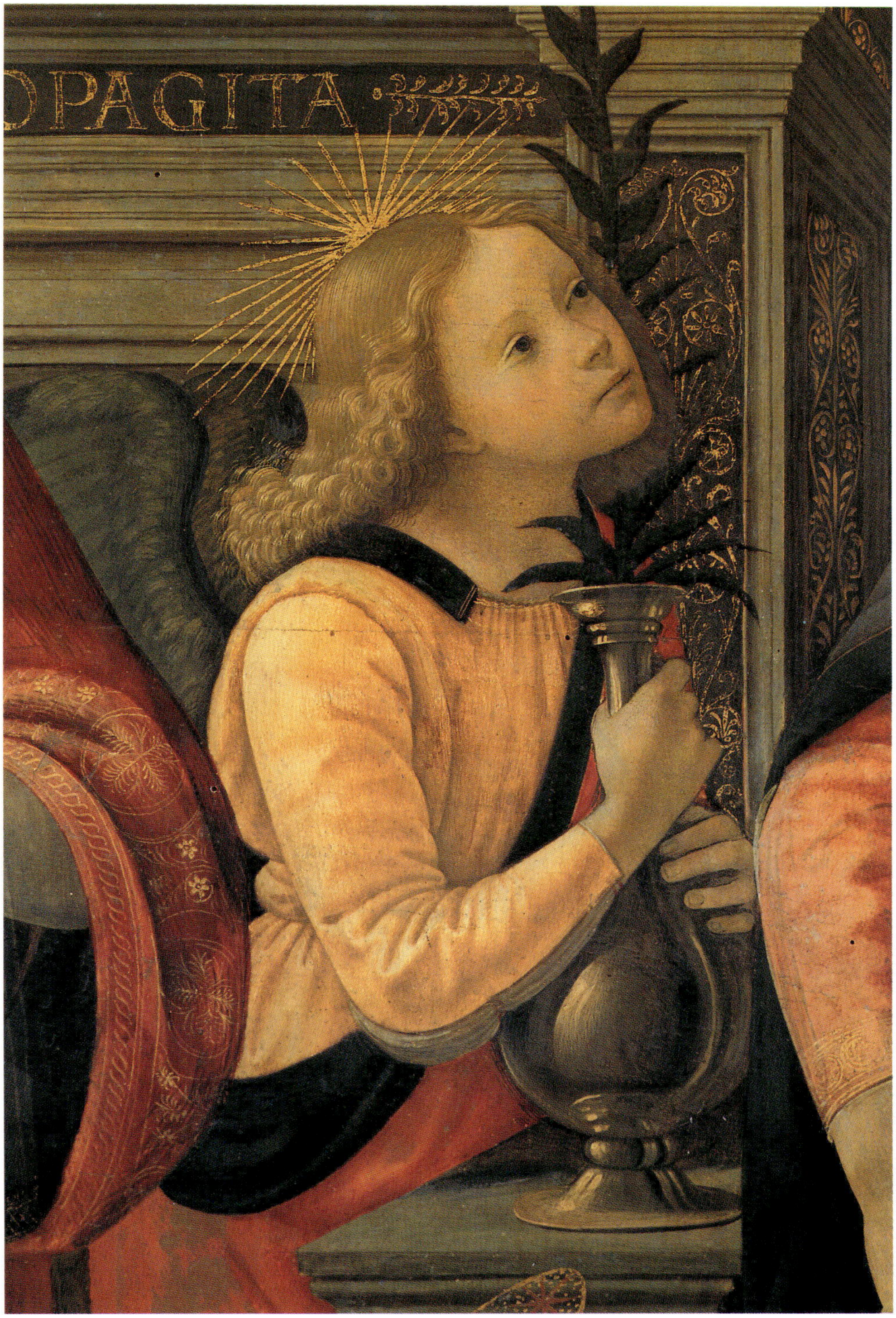

74

74. *Madonna and Child Enthroned between Angels and Saints*
detail of the angel on the left
Florence, Uffizi

ly achieved mellowness to the whole, and which is once again reminiscent of the Flemish style. This work is also the product of collaborators, as the difference in the rendition of the two female figures reveals. Sebastiano Mainardi may have been responsible for the slightly harder and more static St Elisabeth, while the Virgin, all veils and chiaroscuro, is by Ghirlandaio. Other works on wood by Domenico Ghirlandaio are:
the *Christ in Heaven with four Saints and a Donor* 89
painted for the Camaldolite abbot Buonvicini of the Badia di San Giusto, outside Volterra, and now in the Civic Picture Gallery of that town; the lovely
Madonna and Child with Angels and Saints in the 69

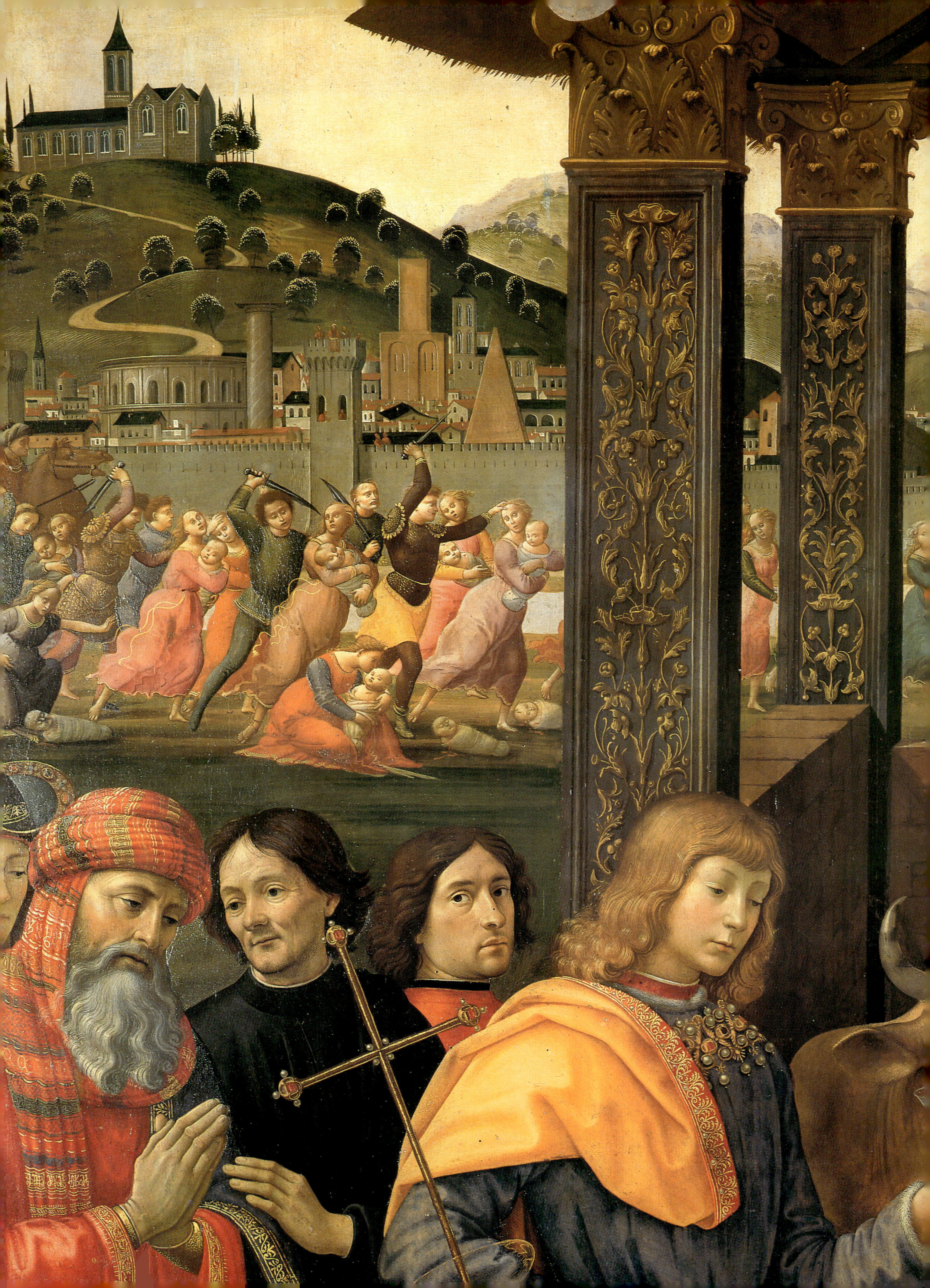

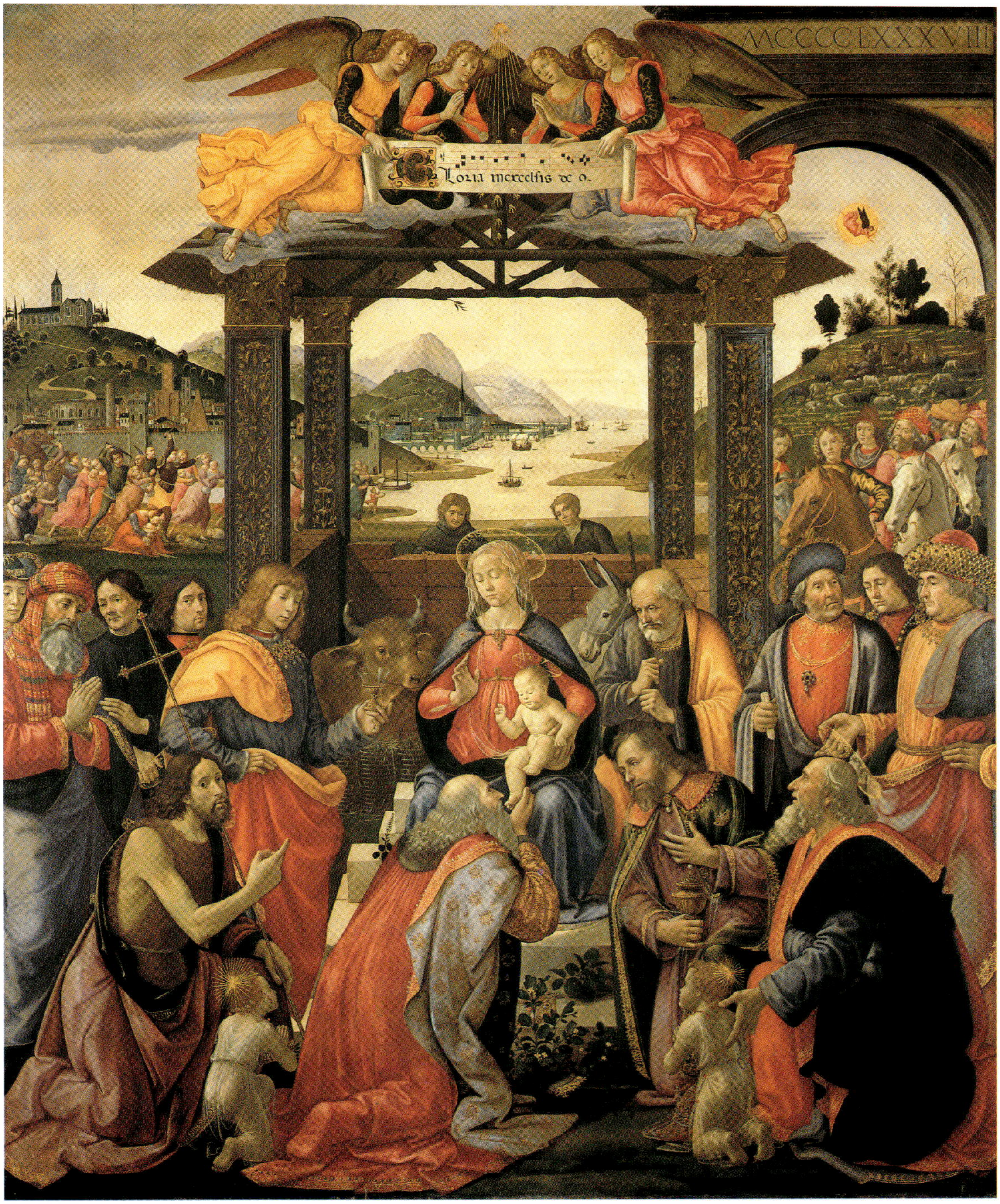

76

75, 76. Adoration of the Magi and detail of the Slaughter of the Innocents
285 x 240 cm
Florence, Spedale degli Innocenti

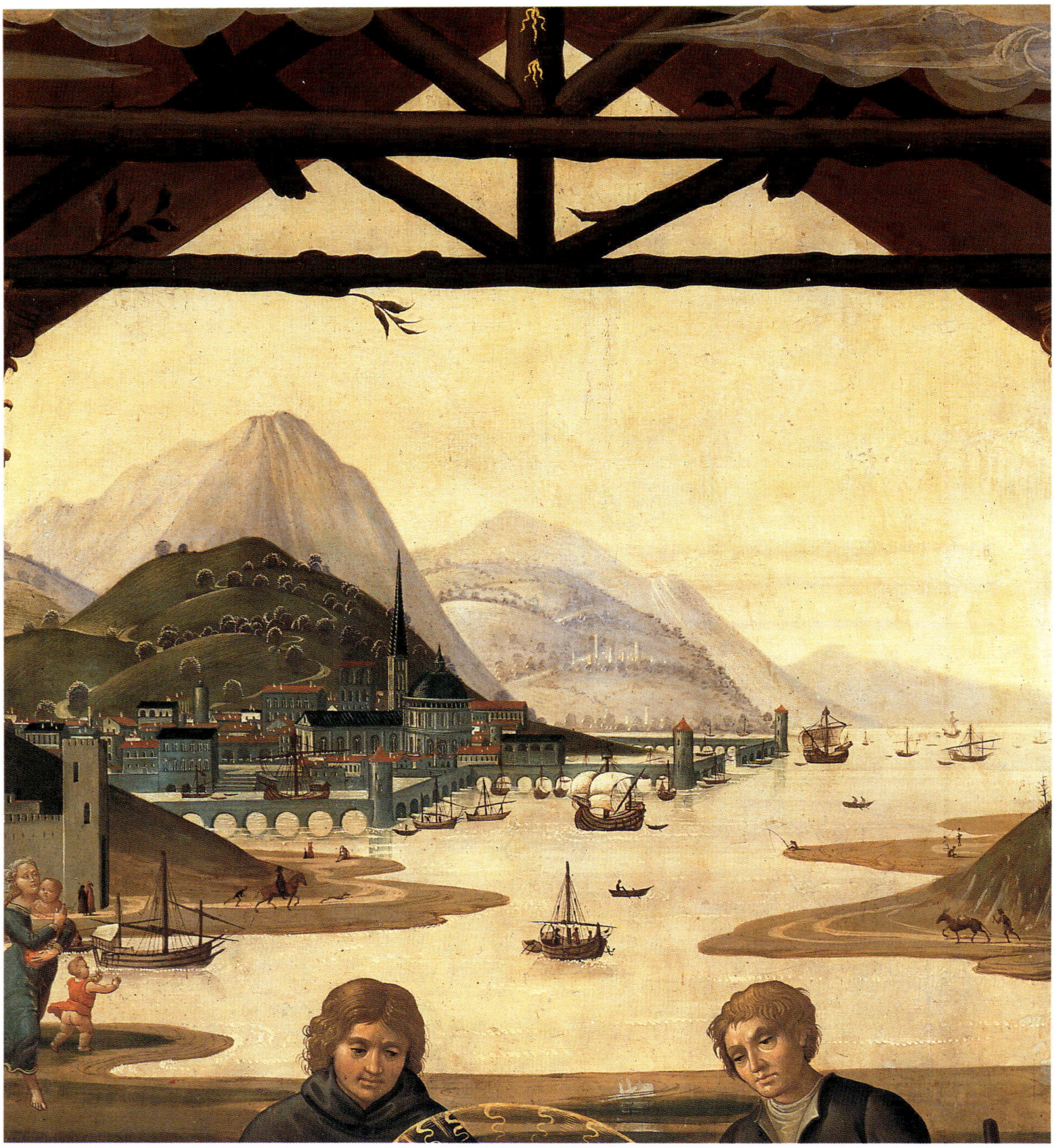

77

Duomo of Lucca, datable to 1486; the altarpiece with
87 the *Coronation of the Virgin* from Città di Castello, which is, however, not an autographed work.

88 The portrait of *Giovanna Tornabuoni*, now in the Thyssen Collection in Lugano, is undoubtedly the loveliest work on wood executed by Ghirlandaio. On a scroll ornament in the background, with the date "MCCCCLXXXVIII", is a Latin inscription which reads *Ars utinam mores animumque effigere posses pulchrior in terris nulla tabella foret*. [Art, if only you could portray mores and spirit, there would be no more beautiful picture on earth].

It is generally considered to be the portrait of Giovanna degli Albizzi, wife of Lorenzo Tornabuoni, the same
56 figure who appears in the scene of the *Visitation* in the choir of Santa Maria Novella. It may be regarded as one of the finest portraits of the Florentine school of the Quattrocento, revealing an extremely skilled and refined workmanship. The perfect profile of the young

77, 78. Adoration of the Magi, details Florence, Spedale degli Innocenti

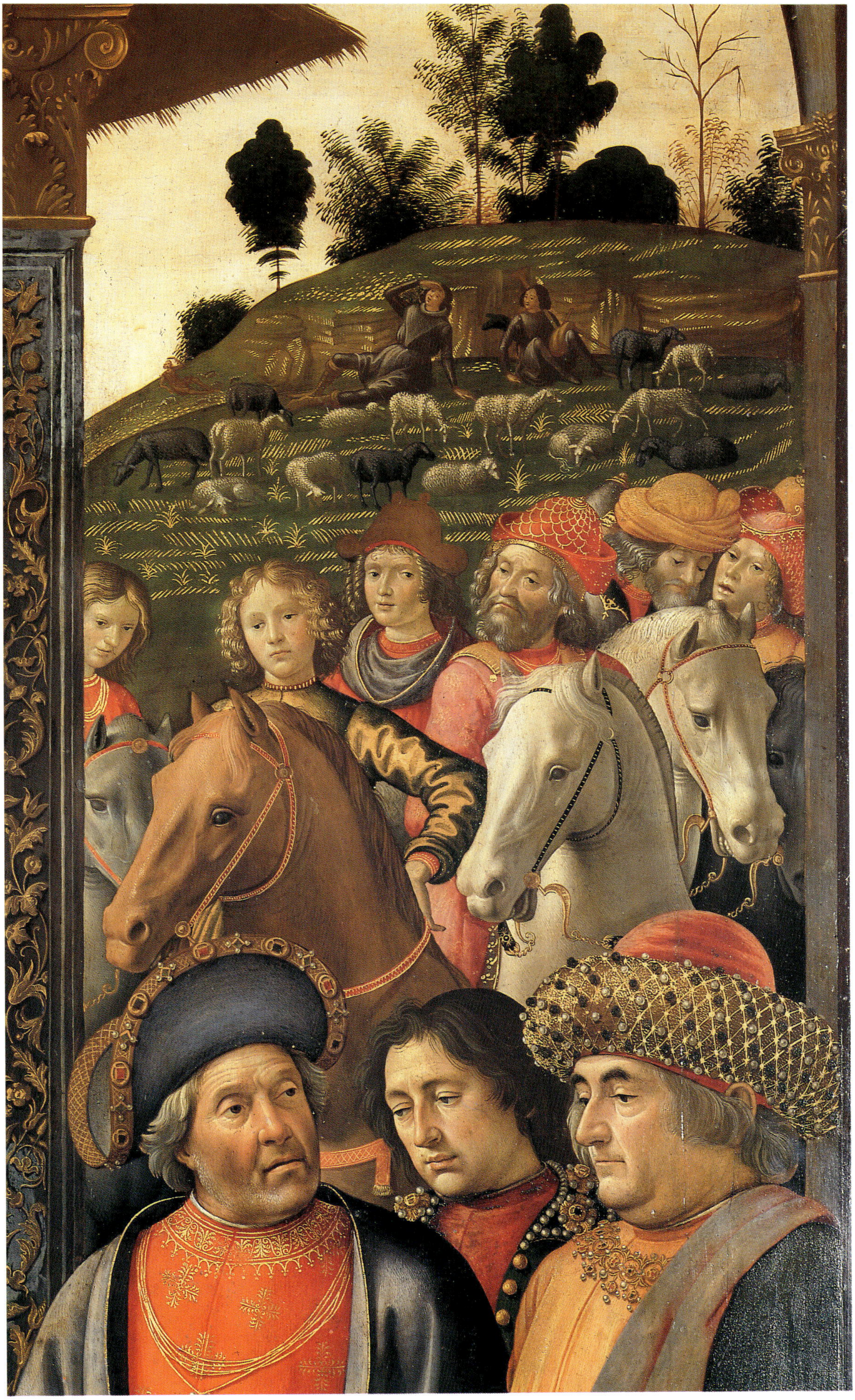

78

79 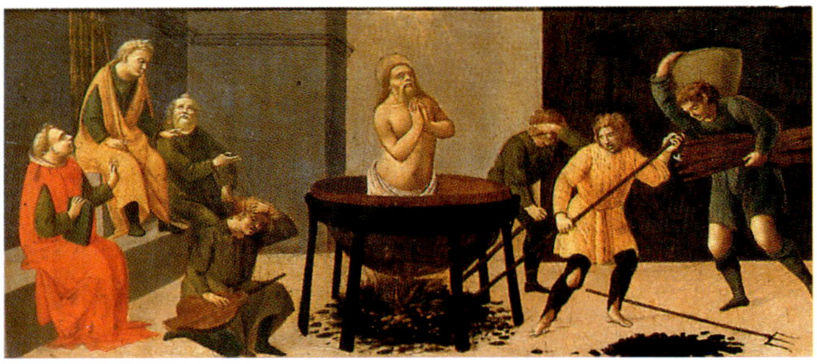

79. Adoration of the Magi, predella
Martyrdom of St John
Florence, Museum of the Spedale degli Innocenti

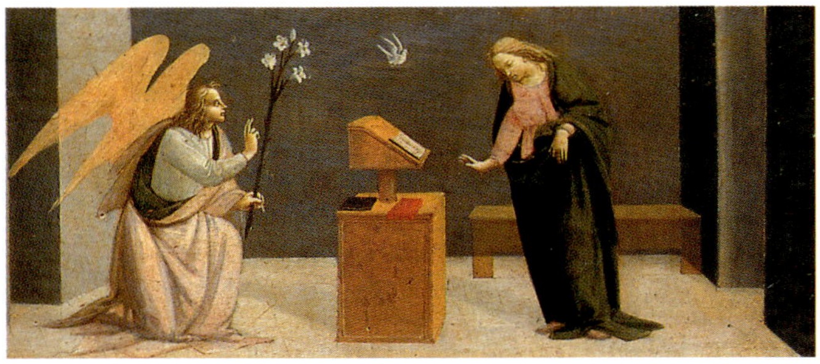 80

80. Adoration of the Magi, predella
Annunciation
Florence, Museum of the Spedale degli Innocenti

81 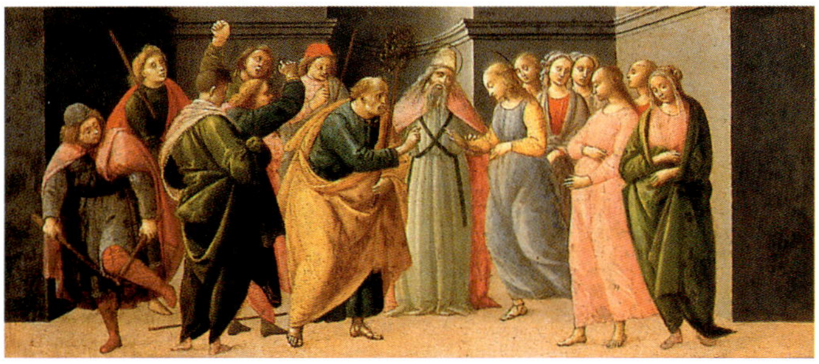

81. Adoration of the Magi, predella
Marriage of Mary
Florence, Museum of the Spedale degli Innocenti

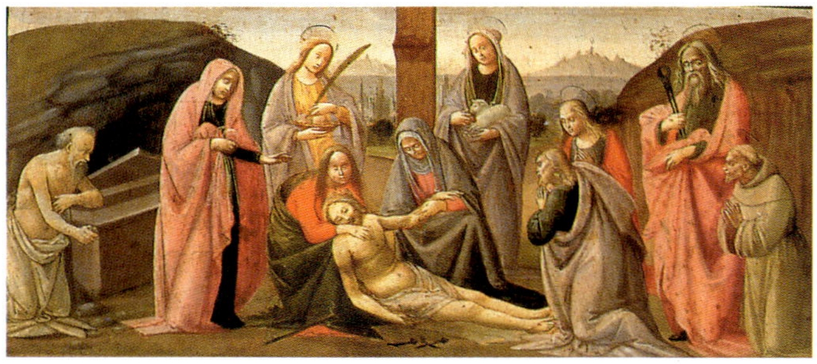 82

82. Adoration of the Magi, predella
Deposition
Florence, Museum of the Spedale degli Innocenti

83 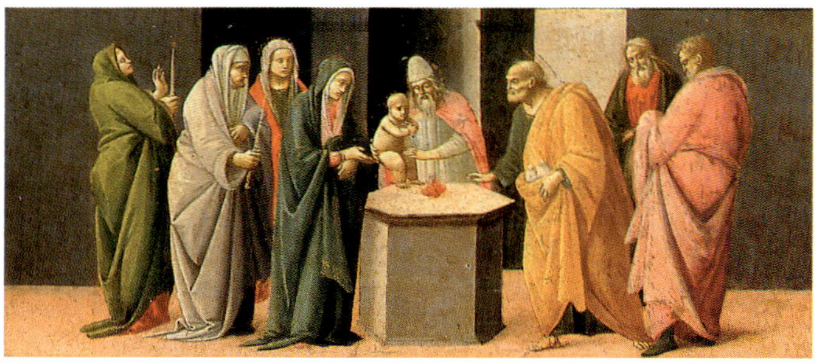

83. Adoration of the Magi, predella
Presentation at the Temple
Florence, Museum of the Spedale degli Innocenti

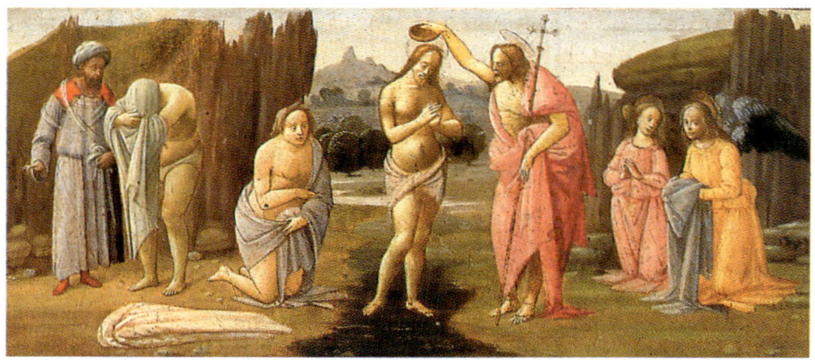 84

84. Adoration of the Magi, predella
Baptism of Christ
Florence, Museum of the Spedale degli Innocenti

85 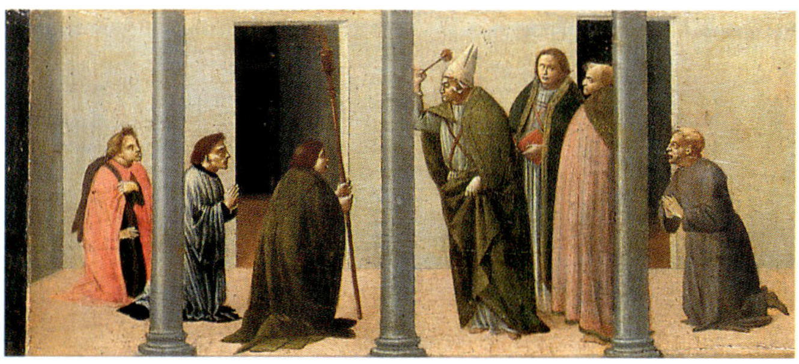

85. Adoration of the Magi, predella
Consecration of the Church of the Innocents
Florence, Museum of the Spedale degli Innocenti

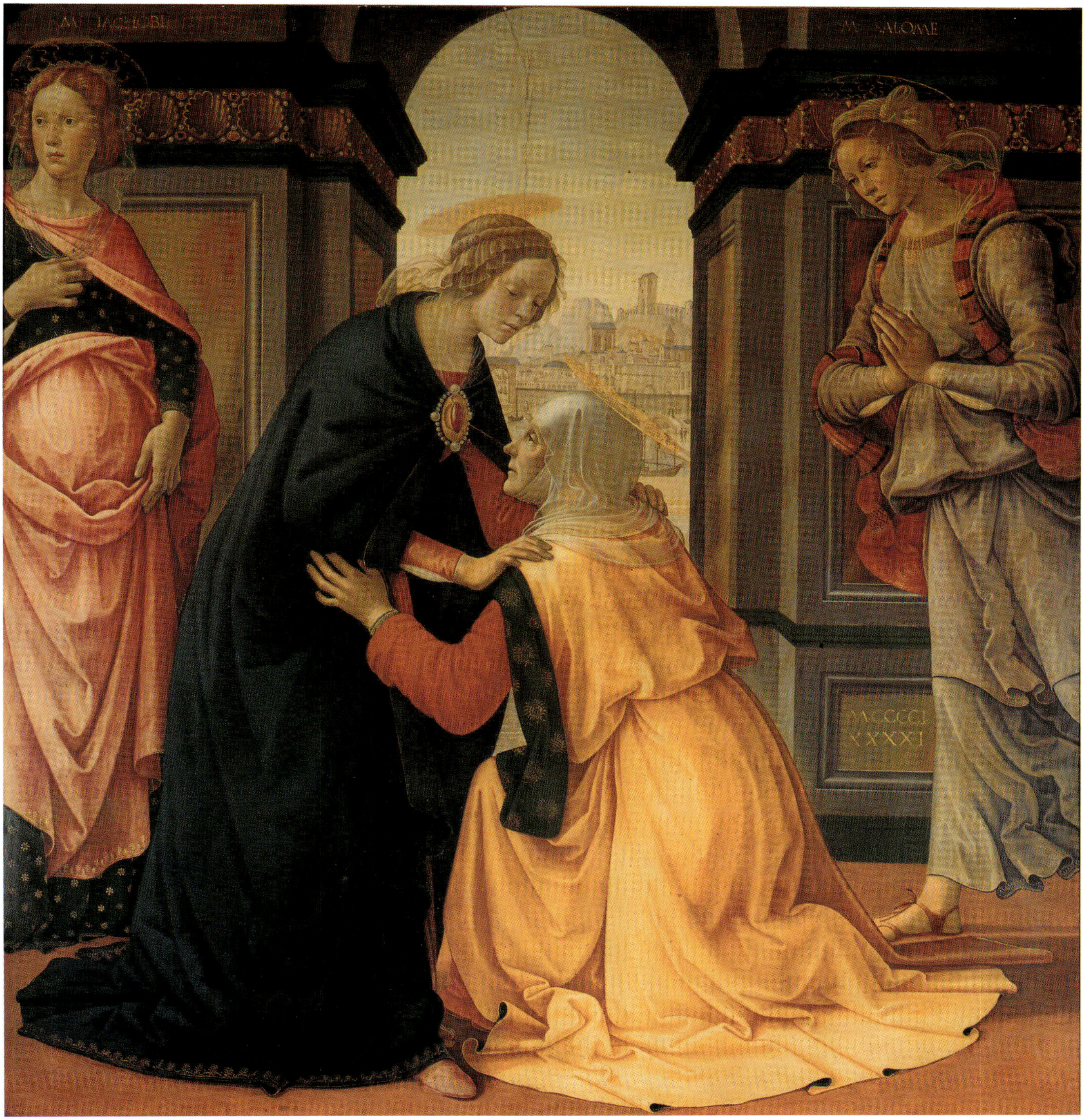

86

86. Visitation
172 x 165 cm
Paris, Louvre

woman stands out clearly against the dark, shiny background. The erect posture, almost like a shapely column, does not hide the gentle curves in her soft back and in her magnificent, brightly-coloured costume of silk and brocade. The jewels, at once splendid and sparing, shine resplendently in a play of brilliant colours: the large pearls and a ruby, a gold ornament around her neck and another resting on a shelf opposite a half-closed prayer-book with gilt-edged pages, a necklace of red corals suspended from a board. In her clasped hands she holds a silk handkerchief. There is here a return to a certain metaphysical quality that is reminiscent of Paolo Uccello's profiles. It is evident in his masterly use of a material that becomes precious in the harmonious interaction of the

87 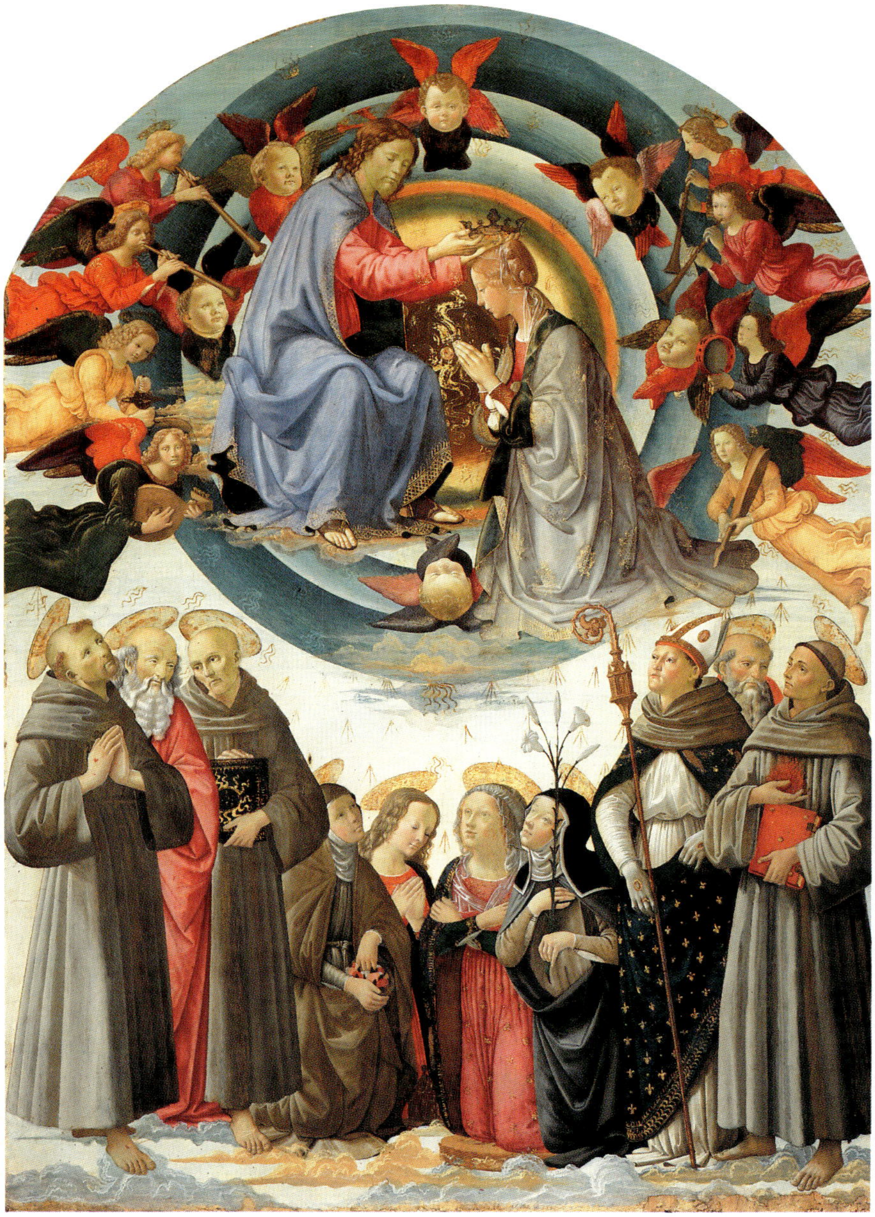

space and the figure, which renders even the young woman's deliberately static pose agreeable and moving. With this work I wish to conclude these brief notes of mine on Domenico Ghirlandaio, because the portrait is often congenial to the painter, and I would suggest that in the female portraits the artist expressed the best part of himself. It seems almost that he infused in them something of his own melancholy... perhaps a note of his aspiration to a certain complete and fully expressed ease which his art never reached.

87. Coronation of the Virgin
Città di Castello, Civic Picture Gallery

88. Giovanna Tornabuoni
76 x 50 cm
Lugano, Thyssen-Bornemisza Collection

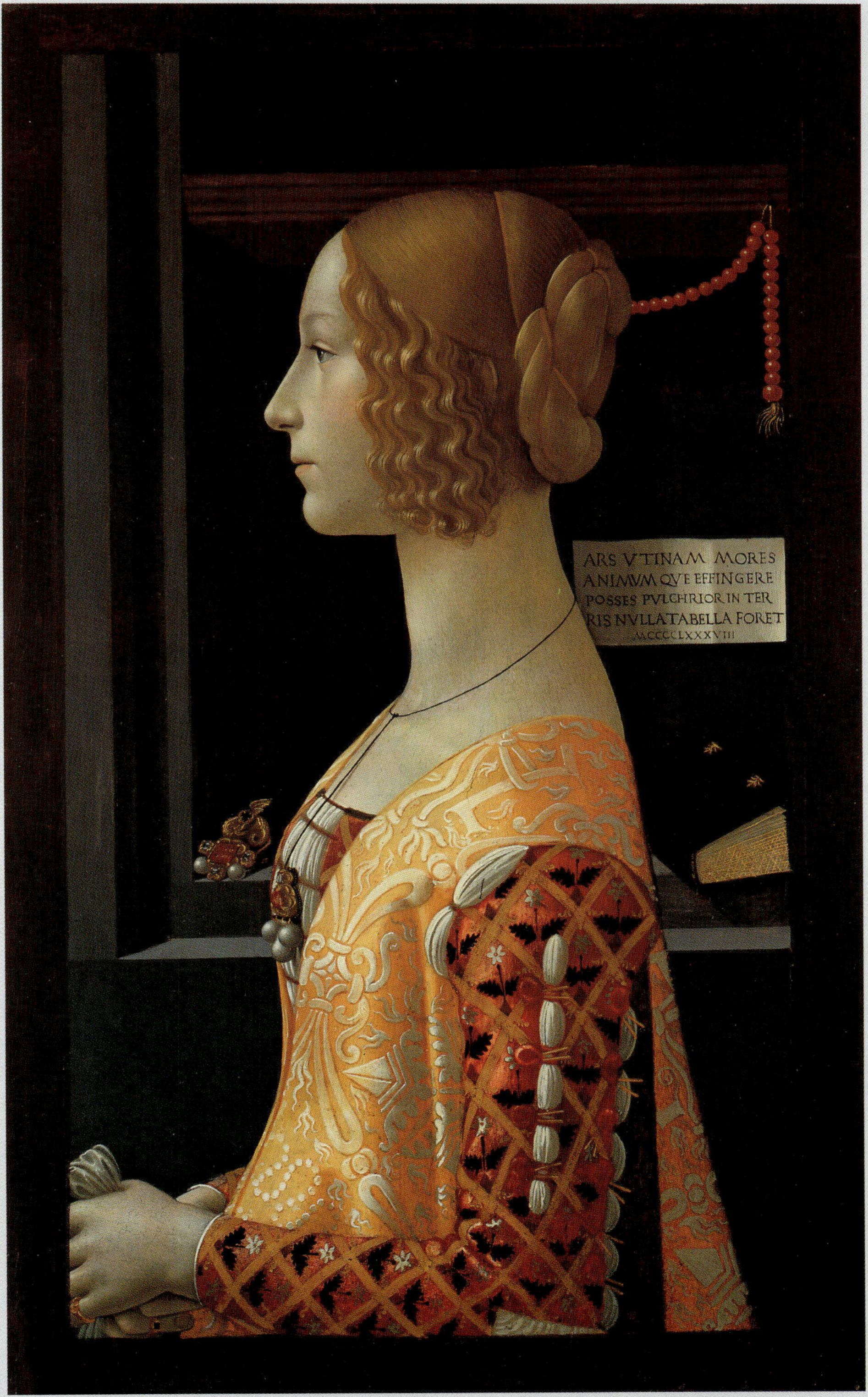
ARS VTINAM MORES
ANIMVM QVE EFFINGERE
POSSES PVLCHRIOR IN TER
RIS NVLLATABELLA FORET
MCCCCLXXXVIII

89

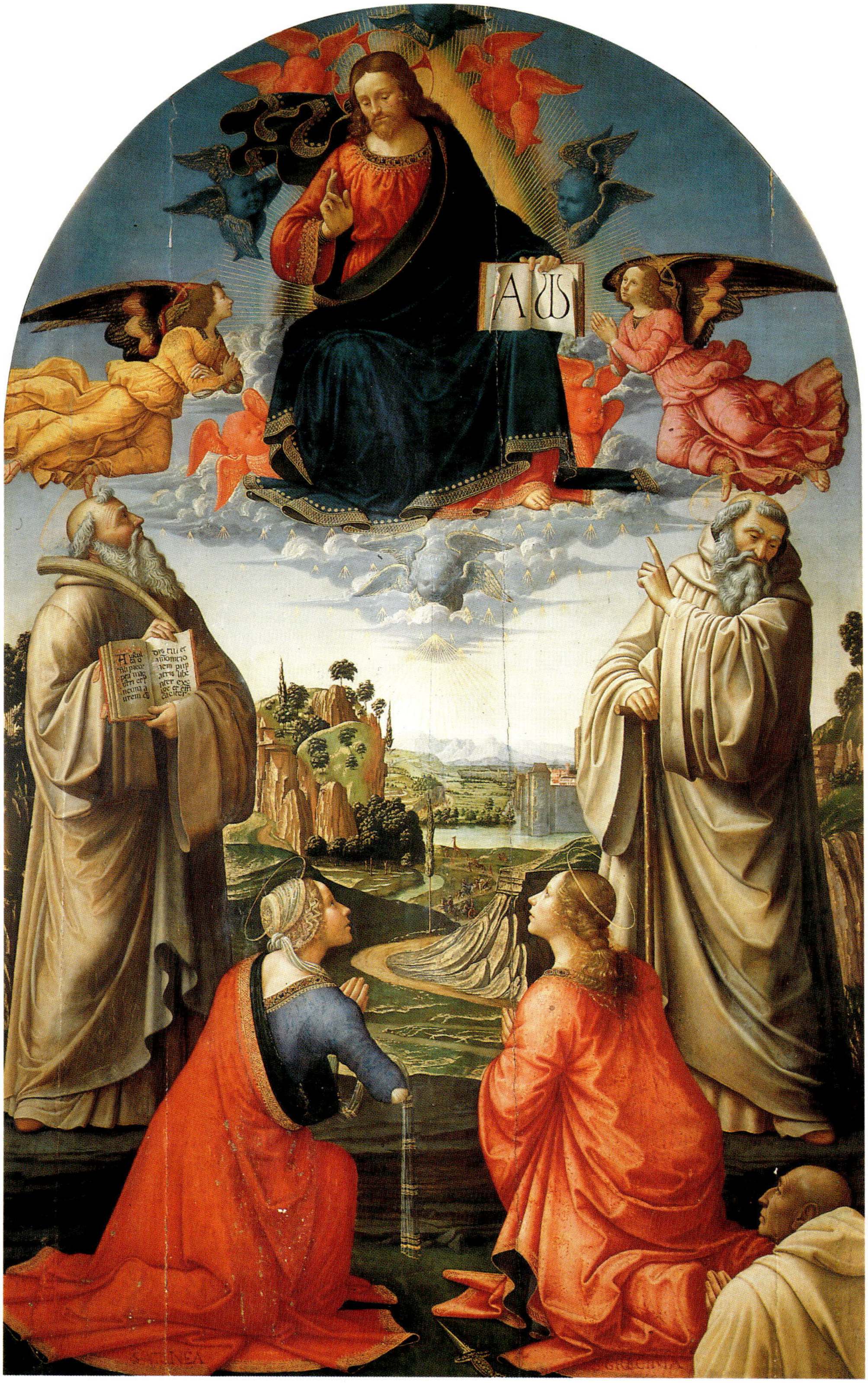

89. Christ in Heaven with four Saints and a Donor
Volterra, Civic Picture Gallery and Museum

Short bibliography

G. VASARI, *Le vite dei più eccellenti pittori, scultori e architettori*, VI (ed. Milanesi), 1568

H. HAUVETTE, *Ghirlandaio*, Paris

G. S. DAVIES, *Ghirlandaio*, London, 1908

A. VENTURI, *Storia dell'arte italiana*, Milan 1911, VII, I

P. H. KÜPPER, *Die Tafelbilder des Domenico Ghirlandaio*, Strasburg 1916

J. LAUTS, *Domenico Ghirlandaio*, Vienna, 1943

A. SABBATINI, *Domenico Ghirlandaio*, Florence

P. BARGELLINI, *Il Ghirlandaio*, Florence, 1945

G. MARCHINI, *Enciclopedia Universale dell'Arte*, VI (ad vocem), 1958

Index of illustrations

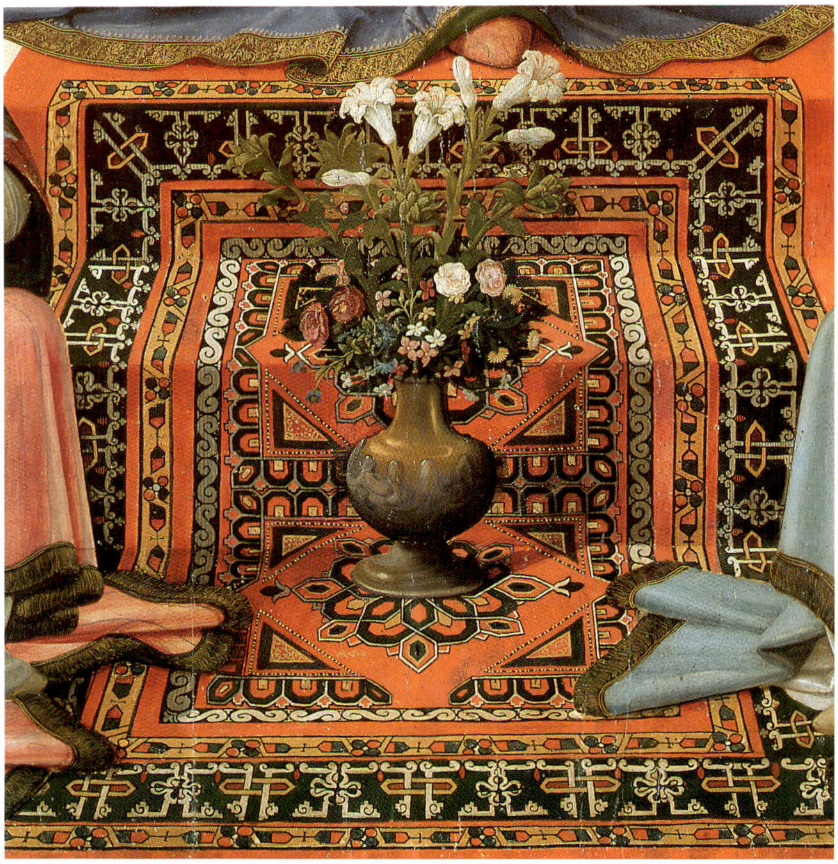